MW01087717

"In addition to English translations of Bavinck's *Dogmatics* and *Ethics* for academics and pastors and Bavinck's *Wonderful Works of God* for the college-educated, we now have this competently translated and richly annotated *Guidebook* prepared for high school students. Arguably, as an entry-level introduction to the riches of the Reformed Christian faith, it may be the most important of the three. It is also a wonderful introduction to a great modern-era Reformed theologian; a tribute to the longing of a learned professor to pass on the riches of the faith to the next generation at an early stage in their religious development—and it is timely! In his preface, Bavinck describes conditions in the educational world of his day that bear eerie resemblance to ours. The publication of this volume deserves three cheers."

—John Bolt, Jean and Kenneth Baker Professor of Systematic Theology Emeritus, Calvin Theological Seminary

"More and more, academic theologians are trying to write books that are welcoming and readable for regular Christians who want to grow in their knowledge of God. Over a century ago, Herman Bavinck resolved to do this as well, offering an accessible, ecumenical, and condensed version of his greater work *Reformed Dogmatics*. Particularly, Bavinck had curious young adults in mind for his audience. *Guidebook for the Instruction in the Christian Religion* is a great introduction into Bavinck's theology for the whole church. Rich theology is not just for academics; it's for all God's people! I'm thankful for Cameron Clausing and Greg Parker's work on this translation into the English language to offer to a new generation."

—Aimee Byrd, author of *The Sexual Reformation* and *Recovering from Biblical Manhood and Womanhood*

"A formidable scholar and prolific writer, Herman Bavinck was also an accomplished popular communicator. Originally offered as an introduction to Christian doctrine for senior high school and undergraduate students, the *Guidebook* provides a convenient point of entry to his theology. It is a welcome addition to the body of Bavinck's work now available in English translation."

—David Fergusson, Regius Professor of Divinity University of Cambridge

"Continuing the Bavinck renaissance, this new English translation of his *Guidebook* is a welcome treasure. Geared toward a broader audience than his *Reformed Dogmatics*, this work is just as faithful to God's word but more accessible. The opening sentence tells all: 'The highest good of man is God and God alone.' The introduction is a great overview, and the clarity of the translation conveys the beauty as well as truth of Bavinck's prose. This book is ideal for personal and group study."

—Michael Horton, J. Gresham Machen Professor of Systematic Theology and Apologetics Westminster Seminary California

"In this translation, Parker and Clausing have unearthed for anglophones yet another treasure from Bavinck's corpus. Rightly known as a theologian par excellence, in his *Guidebook* we see not only Bavinck's academic rigor but also his commitment to catechesis and robust theological education for young Christians and lay readers alike. Bavinck offers his readers a theologically deep yet wonderfully accessible guide to the riches of the Christian faith. This book is a gift to the church and the world."

—Jessica Joustra, Assistant Professor of Religion and Theology, Redeemer University

"I'm so grateful for the renaissance of interest in Herman Bavinck's theology that has been taking place in recent years. He is one of those rare theologians who was soaked in classic orthodoxy and yet could speak in creative, deeply learned, and rich ways as he took both Scripture and his present day seriously. But what we have in this volume is a distinct gift: writing for a broader audience, including younger adults, he distills his theological prowess in a way that is brief and accessible yet not simplistic or naive. Using paragraphs and pages rather than chapters and books, he quickly covers vast terrain with ease and speed. Along the way, he seems to follow Augustine's model of keeping a focus on the heart rather than merely the head as he unpacks theological truths. Thanks to the wonderful work of Clausing and Parker, it is a joy to commend this book to all, especially those who have heard about Bavinck but have found the size of his larger dogmatics volumes overwhelming. Here is a first step, but hopefully not a last one."

—Kelly M. Kapic, Professor of Theological Studies, Covenant College

"The renewed interest in Bavinck's theology is an encouraging movement—a movement bolstered by Parker and Clausing's fresh translation of his catechetical guide."

—Brandon D. Smith, Assistant Professor of Theology and New Testament, Cedarville University

"Herman Bavinck's *Guidebook for Instruction in the Christian Religion* is by far his shortest articulation of Christian theology, but in no way should it be regarded as less rich than his longer works. Indeed, since this was written later than either his full dogmatics (for the academic) or his *Magnalia Dei* (for college-educated professionals), in some ways the *Guidebook* represents his mature thought. It is also his presentation of the Christian faith to the widest audience, since it was written for, what we would today in the United States call, the high school student. I've been working through it, and it is a delight to see so much profound learning made so accessible. I can't recommend his work highly enough."

—Tim Keller, Redeemer City to City

"This translation of Bavinck's book is a treasure. It still serves its original purpose of giving clear theological instruction at a level accessible to high schoolers. But alongside that, it provides an accessible introduction to the rich and textured theology of Herman Bavinck, whose standing and reputation have risen dramatically within the English-speaking world in recent years. For those familiar with Bavinck's theology, Clausing and Parker's editorial work provides judicious guidance into some of the nuances of his phrasing and terminology. In short, here is a book well worth reading, rereading, and keeping close at hand."

—Jonathan Master, President
Greenville Presbyterian Theological Seminary

"While reading, I repeatedly thanked God that Gregory Parker, Jr. and Cameron Clausing know Dutch and that they channeled that knowledge into making this volume available to those of us who don't. This outstanding work informs, clarifies, edifies, and above all, captivates the reader's heart with the glory, grandeur, and grace of the Triune God. Christians without formal theological training should not think it beyond their reach, and those possessing it will likewise profit."

—Keith Plummer, Dean School of Divinity
Professor of Theology Cairn University

"Gregory Parker Jr. and Cameron Clausing are to be sincerely commended for bringing Bavinck's *Guidebook* to us in clear, modern English. In many ways, this book shows Bavinck at his best: lofty yet approachable, profound yet clear. As you read this new translation from one of the more formidable orthodox theologians in the Reformed tradition, you will no doubt find that Bavinck taught theology out of an academic context, but he did so always for the church—and for every church member too."

—Zachary Purvis, Lecturer of Church History
Edinburgh Theological Seminary

"Herman Bavinck's reputation as one of the twentieth century's leading Reformed academic theologians is now well established. In the English-speaking world, he is beginning to receive the recognition he deserves as a gifted catechist thanks to the translation of volumes such as the present one. Bavinck's *Guidebook for Instruction in the Christian Religion* is a profoundly simple and simply profound introduction to the catholic faith of the Reformed churches. Parker and Clausing's translation is elegant and easy to read, assuring its usefulness to Bavinck's intended audience (high school students). At the same time, the book's scholarly apparatus guarantees its usefulness to the growing field of Bavinck studies. My sincere hope is that this edition will be widely purchased, widely read, and widely taught in Christian churches, schools, and homes."

—Scott Swain, President
James Woodrow Hassell Professor of Systematic Theology
Reformed Theological Seminary, Orlando

"Bavinck shows us how the most profound theology can also be eminently clear. Avoiding both an experiential triviality and a musty dogmatism, he gives the reader a representative taste of the mystery of the Christian faith. The editors are to be commended for providing an inestimably helpful resource for today's catechists. This should be a must-read for church youth groups, college Christian unions, and anyone looking to mine the theological depths of the gospel."

—Adonis Vidu, Professor of Theology
Gordon-Conwell Theological Seminary

Guidebook for Instruction in the Christian Religion

HERMAN

BAVINCK

Guidebook for Instruction in the Christian Religion

TRANSLATED AND EDITED BY

GREGORY PARKER JR. & CAMERON CLAUSING

an imprint of Hendrickson Publishing Group

Guidebook for Instruction in the Christian Religion

Published by Hendrickson Publishers
an imprint of Hendrickson Publishing Group
Hendrickson Publishers, LLC
P. O. Box 3473
Peabody, Massachusetts 01961-3473
www.hendricksonpublishinggroup.com

ISBN 978-1-68307-299-7

Printed in the United States of America

First Printing — March 2022

Cover background by belterz / iStock / Getty Images Plus via Getty Images.

Cover design by Karol Bailey.

To Mpho Grace, Calvin Jack, Madelyn Joy, Calvin Joseph, Oscar James, Judah Gracen, Everett Benjamin, Rosie James, Charles Michael, Augustine Joseph, Maximillian Gustav, and Magnolia Jean

May you know and love the One who first loved you (1 John 4:19)

Contents

Acknowledgments

Any book that is worth the effort of writing, or in this case translating, is never accomplished alone. We would like to express great appreciation to Dr. James Eglinton for his aid in various areas of the translation. His generosity of spirit nurtured our enthusiasm for the project, and we especially want to thank him for writing the foreword. Dr. Dolf te Velde deserves special mention. In the midst of a busy stretch, he took the time to read portions of this in manuscript form for any issues with the translation. His help was generous and helpful.

We are also grateful for the Edinburgh School of Bavinck of which James is the progenitor. These scholars have made fertile ground for the translation of the Dutch neo-Calvinist. Thank you, Dr. Cory Brock, Dr. Bruce Pass, Dr. Nathaniel Gray Sutanto, Dr. Ximian Xu, Terrence Chu, Israel José Guerrero Leiva, and Sebastian Bjernegård. This book likely would not have reached the Anglophone world without your academic and ecclesial activity. Moreover, your encouragement in the project should not go unheralded.

We'd like to also thank our publishing friends, the staff at Hendrickson Publishers, who have been a delight to work with and have played no small role in the renaissance of Bavinck. Added to this, we would like to thank Henry J. Hoekstra for his work on the Scripture and Subject Indexes.

Most of all, we desire to express gratitude to our families for their unyielding support. Their love, patience, and championing of our scholarship furnished the necessary time to complete the translation and editorial work. Translation projects, though enjoyable, are often arduous; thus, in addition to the above, we are thankful for friends who have supported the project in sundry ways. I, Greg, would like to especially thank Dr. Albert Cheng, Dr. Ty Kieser, Dr. Gayle Doornbos, Dan Hoffstetter, Mark Horn, Andrew and Caitlin Keenan, Trevor and Susy Smith, Mark Evans, Alec Simpson, Camille Simpson, Jeff Mindler, and David Smiley. To the little ones in my life: Madelyn Joy, Calvin Joseph, Judah Gracen, Everett Benjamin, Rosie James, Charles Michael, Augustine Joseph, Maximillian Gustav, and Magnolia Jean, it was truly a joy to undertake this project with you in mind. I, Cam, would like to make special mention of my colleagues at the two institutions where I taught while I worked on this translation: Covenant College and Christ College. Of particular mention, the Bible and Theology department at Covenant College with Dr. Herb Ward, Dr. Hans Madueme, Dr. Scott Jones, Dr. Kelly Kapic, Dr. Dan. MacDougall, Dr. Ken Stewart, and Dr. Jeff Dryden. Christ College's faculty have encouraged me at the tail end of this project particularly: Murray Smith, Dr. Greg Goswell, Dr. John McClean, Dr. Jon Pratt, and Dr. Ian Smith. Finally, I don't think I could have finished the work on this without the constant encouragement from my family. My wife, Taryn, has been a constant prod to finish this project. She is my rock, the one who keeps me sane, and connected to reality. My children, Mpho Grace and Calvin Jack, have been the inspiration behind this project. I look forward to the day when I can use it to encourage them in their faith and point them to Jesus.

Soli Deo Gloria

Gregory Parker Jr.
Barto, Pennsylvania

Cameron Clausing
Sydney, Australia

Foreword

When Herman Bavinck published the second edition of his *magnum opus*, the four-volume *Reformed Dogmatics*, readers praised its clarity, erudition, depth, and breadth. Across thousands of pages, he led readers through careful interaction with Scripture, the development of Christian theology across its history, and its path forward in the modern age. In the circles for which it was intended—academics, pastors, and theology students—it was an instant classic. Despite its brilliance, though, Bavinck's efforts were not without their critics: one newspaper review warned readers that the *Reformed Dogmatics* was "not a devotional book, but rather a study book that has only been written for the scientifically educated," also noting that "the price of such a work means that it is certainly not within reach of everyone's budget."

To many professors, of course, such criticism is easy to ignore: a heavyweight multivolume *Dogmatics* might be necessary and acclaimed, but it is not likely to be accessible to a general audience. There is only so much use in calling out apples for not being oranges. Bavinck, however, was no such professor. For all his introverted bookishness, he maintained a lifelong commitment to theological engagement with the church, and the general public—both audiences that needed the results of his *Dogmatics* (as, in his own words, "the theology needed by our age"), even if that meant repackaging his *Dogmatics* in a more easily digestible form.

For this reason, we find Bavinck devoting a great deal of time to the production of two shortened versions of the *Dogmatics*, one aimed at readers with a university-level education (albeit not in theology), and another pitched for senior high school students and new undergraduate students. The former, *Magnalia Dei*, has been available in English for some time, first under the title *Our Reasonable Faith*, and more recently under the much more accurate English title *The Wonderful Works of God*. The latter, however, his *Guidebook for Instruction in the Christian Religion*, lay forgotten for a century, and until now had never been made available in English translation. In it, Bavinck sets out to provide something for "all those who want to become acquainted with the chief content of our Christian, Reformed confession of faith through the means of a book that is not too long or too expensive."

This book shows us a side of Bavinck—the earnest Christian who was so committed to encouraging students in the faith—that has been largely forgotten in the century since his death. And beyond that, it gives us his presentation of the faith at a distinctive level, in all its simplicity and profundity. That it has laid untouched for so long was a significant omission in a now thriving effort to make his works available in translation. All of those who benefit from that effort now owe a debt of gratitude to Cameron Clausing and Greg Parker, one a PhD graduate, and the other a current PhD student, at the University of Edinburgh. The fruit of their labor is a timely one: in an age in which the church often struggles to see how its theology could be communicated to its younger members, Clausing and Parker have shown us Bavinck as a theologian passionate about bringing theology to teens and young adults in his own context, always recognizing (unbegrudgingly!) that times change, while the truth advances. I hope that this book will inspire many in our generation to do the same.

James P. Eglinton
Meldrum Senior Lecturer in Reformed Theology
University of Edinburgh

Preface

On Friday, November 30, 1618, the seventeenth session of the Synod of Dordt was held, and the discussion was dedicated to the best method of catechizing. After extensive deliberation and the distinguished opinions of various native and foreign theologians, the synod made a decision that is still worthy of examination and consideration.[1]

In the first place, the synod differentiated between three types of catechism: in the home by parents, in school by the teachers, and in the churches by pastors and elders. Furthermore, it divided the pupils into three groups: children (until the age of eight, according to the advice of the Hessians), boys and girls, and young men and women, and recommended for each of these groups very different subject matter.[2] Third, it emphasized

1. For an introduction to the Synod of Dordt, see Herman J. Selderhuis, "Introduction to the Synod of Dordt (1618–1619)," in *Acta et Documenta Synodi Nationalis Dordrechtanae*, vol. 1, ed. Donald Sinnema, Christian Moser, and Herman J. Selderhuis (Göttingen: Vandenhoeck & Ruprecht, 2015), xv-xxxii. The Synod of Dordt was an international assembly held by the Dutch Reformed Church in the city of Dordrecht (Dordt) in the Netherlands. The synod gathered to settle an intra-Reformed discussion on the relation between God's sovereignty and human responsibility. Bavinck's reference here to "native" theologians is a reference to those theologians from the Netherlands. The Synod of Dordt is uniquely the only international Reformed synod to have taken place, with twenty-six delegates from Great Britain, France, Palatinate, Brandenburg, Hesse, Swiss Cantons, Nassau-Wetteravia, Geneva, Bremen, and East Frisia.

2. For a full list of participants in the Synod of Dordt, see Fred van Lieburg, "The Participants in the Synod of Dordt," in *Acta et Documenta Synodi Nationalis Dordrechtanae*, lxiii-cvii, lxxxiii. Notably absent from the synod were the French delegates, as King Louis XIII would not permit them to attend the proceedings. The famous painting of the synod by Pouwel Weyts depicts the hall of the Kloveniersdoelen in Dordrecht with a long table in the middle. At the table sit the Remonstrant defendants, while the international accusers encircle them. The painting depicts one set of empty seats, which show them as empty to symbolize the French absence. The mention of the Hessians is a reference to the international delegates from Hesse. The invitation was sent on June 25, 1618, to the Count of

that the subject matter should be firmly imprinted in their memory; additionally, it strongly insisted on a supplementary explanation, so that the children understand what they are learning.

Meanwhile, times have changed and we have changed with them. Concerning catechizing in the home, due to lack of time, passion, and ability it is not practiced in many households. Church catechism is only moderately attended in many places. And in schools, the content and volume of social education is so extensive, there is hardly any time left for religious education. The previously mentioned synod had suggested two hours a day. Nowadays, one is pleased if there is biblical history daily in the primary school and one hour every week in the high schools set out for biblical history, church history, or doctrine.

The change of times has also had an influence on the subject matter. Many doctrines, which at the time of the Reformation demanded extensive treatment, for example concerning the sacraments, can now be dealt with much quicker; and other subjects, which then were barely mentioned or not at all—such as general and special revelation, common grace, and the nature of inspiration, the teachings of different churches and sects, the theory of evolution, etc.—have become so prominent that they cannot be passed silently. Furthermore, the Synod of Dordt correctly remarked that there is a distinction between catechism in church and in school; after all, the aim of preparing the children of the congregation is for full membership in the church. The synod regards religious instruction as one of the subjects of education that will introduce them to the knowledge of Christianity.

Out of that flows religious instruction at schools, which go beyond primary education. There is the desire to handle the subject matter not in the form of questions and answers but in a regular, systematic order, so that the mutually connected religious truths of faith will be clearly revealed; furthermore, to present this material in a manner that penetrates into the consciousness of the students and brings unity to all their ideas. [This necessitates] distinguishing [religion], [identifying its] coherence, and [ultimately] its significance for all other knowledge. Finally, to discuss the material in a scriptural sense: that it is not only revealed in its teaching

Hesse requesting him to send three or four theologians. On October 17, 1618, the Hessians announced they would send Georgius Cruciger, Paul Stein, Daniel Angelocrater, and Rodophus Goclenius; see *Acta et Documenta Synodi Nationalis Dordrechtanae*, esp. page 29 for the advice of the delegates concerning the catechism of children, youth, and young adults.

but also in its comforting character, and that it is applied to the heart and conscience. Religious instruction must be *education* in the true sense of the word, and it must be education in the *religion*—that is, in the most tender and sacred of what a human soul may possess.

In the composition of this guidebook, these demands have stood before me, the experience of which will show to what extent I have responded to them. Furthermore, in writing this guidebook, I had in mind the pupils in the highest classes of our Christian gymnasium,[3] public schools, in the education of teachers, and in normal schools, etc., and moreover those who desire to understand the main content of our Christian, Reformed confession of faith through a not too comprehensive or expensive book. I have with careful planning during the process intimately connected this book with the work that has gone under the title *Magnalia Dei* [4] for a few years by this same publisher, who saw clearly that if desired in the majority of cases, it is still possible to find an expansion and further explanations of the discussed subjects.

H. Bavinck
Amsterdam
September 1913

3. In the Netherlands in the nineteenth and early twentieth centuries, the gymnasium was a type of secondary school that emphasized the teaching of Latin and Greek. In Bavinck's 1902 lectures on the *Theological Encyclopedia*, a student's lecture notes suggest that "the Gymnasium is not meant to be an introduction to any particular subject; rather it is only to be the place where the community is founded, indiscriminately." Unknown student, Lecture Notes, *Encyclopaedie d. Theol.* (1902), courtesy of James Eglinton, University of Edinburgh 11, 14. [Dutch: Gymn. bedoelt niet in te leiden in bepaald vak, maar om alleen zonder ondersch. saam te plaatsen op gemeensch. grondslag.]. Drawing upon something similar to the German concept of *Bildung*, Bavinck perceives education of the entire community as a good thing; for an explanation of the German concept of *Bildung*, see Frederick Beiser, *The Romantic Imperative* (Cambridge: Harvard University Press, 2003).

4. Bavinck, *Magnalia Dei: onderwijzing in de christelijke religie naar gereformeerde belijdenis*. 2e druk (Kampen: J. H. Kok, 1931. For a translation of the first edition, see Bavinck, *The Wonderful Works of God: Instruction in the Christian Religion according to the Reformed Confession*, trans. Henry Zylstra (Philadelphia: Westminster Seminary Press, 2019); Bavinck, *Magnalia Dei: onderwijzing in de christelijke religie naar gereformeerde belijdenis*, 1e druk (Kampen: J. H. Kok, 1909).

Introduction

Herman Bavinck: A Theologian for the Church

Dutch Reformed theologian Herman Bavinck (1854–1921) was born December 13, 1854, in Hoogeveen, the Netherlands. The son of Rev. Jan Bavinck, *Dominee* (Minister) in the *Christelijke Gereformeerde Kerk* (Christian Reformed Church), and Gesina Bavinck. Herman was simultaneously enrolled in both Kampen and the University of Leiden during his university years. Upon completion of his studies at both institutions, Herman served as a pastor in the *Christelijke Gereformeerde Kerk* in Franeker for a year, before being appointed as professor of dogmatics at the *Theologische School* (Theological School) in Kampen. During his time in Kampen (1883–1902), he taught dogmatics, ethics, and the theological encyclopedia, among other courses.[1] In 1902, he succeeded Abraham Kuyper as professor of dogmatics at the *Vrije Universiteit* (Free University) of Amsterdam, where he taught for the remainder of his life. While in Amsterdam, Bavinck also served in the Dutch Parliament.[2] Throughout his life, Herman Bavinck remained an active preacher and churchman while endeavoring to be engaged in the larger society. He longed to be faithful to the Reformed tradition that had

---

1. With the rise of the modern university in Germany, new questions arose on how to bring together the various subdisciplines in theology (i.e., exegesis, history, systematics, and practical theology), how to connect theology to the other disciplines in the university (i.e., philosophy, history, natural science, etc.), and how to define the relationship between academic (scientific) theology and ecclesial theology. The "Theological Encyclopedia" aimed to answer these questions and others. Most encyclopedias took on "fourfold curricular pattern of exegesis, church history, dogmatics, and practical theology." See Zachary Purvis, "Education and Its Institutions," in *The Oxford Handbook of Nineteenth-Century Christian Thought*, ed. Joel D. S. Rasmussen, Judith Wolfe, and Johannes Zachhuber (Oxford: Oxford University Press, 2017), 309.

2. James Eglinton, *Bavinck: A Critical Biography* (Grand Rapids: Baker Academic, 2020).

been handed down to him, and he yet knew it had to answer the questions being raised in his day and in his context.

Early on in his years at Kampen, Bavinck began to prepare his own dogmatics and ethics. While he would neither complete nor publish his ethics, his dogmatics began to take shape, as evidenced in his lecture notes from the 1880s.[3] In 1895, the first volume of what became a four-volume set was published. In the foreword to the first edition, Bavinck put forward his aim: "To cherish the ancient simply because it is ancient is neither Reformed nor Christian. A work of dogmatic theology should not simply describe what was true and valid but what abides as true and valid. It is rooted in the past but labors for the future."[4] The second, third, and fourth volumes of his *Reformed Dogmatics* were published in 1897, 1898, and 1901, respectively.

In 1911, Bavinck finished his second edition of the *Reformed Dogmatics*. It was the culmination of another ten years of work, adding almost eight hundred pages to the first edition. Regarding its original reception, James Eglinton observes that reviewers of Bavinck's complete set of his dogmatics said it "was 'not a devotional book, but rather a study book that has only been written for the scientifically educated' and that 'the price of such a work means that it is certainly not within the reach of everyone's budget.' "[5]

Although he was an academic theologian of the highest order, Bavinck was deeply committed to making theology accessible to the church. This can be seen in at least three ways: (1) his frequent publications in popular-level periodicals and Christian magazines, such as *De Vrije Kerk*, *De Bazuin*, and *Stemmen des Tijds*;[6] (2) his participation in student societies in the Netherlands, NCSV (*Nederlandse Christen Studenten Vereniging*) and CSV (*Christen Studenten Vereniging*); and (3) the publication of book-length popular-level works that distilled his *Reformed Dogmatics* into a format palatable for the average churchgoer. Bavinck used the skills he had developed as a professional theologian and ethicist and turned them toward the life of the church. At the start of the twentieth century, he wrote popular-level

3. Eglinton, *Bavinck*, 174.

4. Herman Bavinck, " 'Foreword' to the First Edition of the *Gereformeerde Dogmatiek*," trans. John Bolt, *Calvin Theological Journal* 45 (2010): 10.

5. Eglinton, *Bavinck*, 259.

6. For an outline of the purpose and aims of *De Vrije Kerk*, see John Bolt, *Theological Analysis of Herman Bavinck's Two Essays on the* Imitatio Christi*: Between Pietism and Modernism* (Lewiston: Mellen, 2013), 80–82.

works such as *The Sacrifice of Praise*,[7] *The Certainty of Faith*,[8] *Magnalia Dei*, and the present work *Guidebook for Instruction in the Christian Religion*.[9] These works all aim to bring a rich theology to the pew and also demonstrates Bavinck laboring "for the future" or next generation of Christians.

The year prior to the publication of *Guidebook for Instruction in the Christian Religion*, Bavinck delivered a speech in central Amsterdam titled "Modernism and Orthodoxy."[10] Eglinton's biography on Bavinck offers an intuitive reading on this speech, which provides a foundation through which to interpret Bavinck's life and work.[11] Eglinton argues that in "Modernism and Orthodoxy," Bavinck positioned his work as not necessarily modern or orthodox but, more precisely, Reformed.[12] To be Reformed, for Bavinck, requires one to continually look backward and forward:[13] back to Scripture and the historical development of doctrine. In turning forward, one is looking at the future and addressing theology through the questions and issues of one's own age. Thus, one is always resting upon the foundation laid down by Scripture and the pillars of the church, while simultaneously developing from that foundation. Theology under the Reformed umbrella for Bavinck is attuned to development while also being grounded in the norming norm of Scripture.

According to Eglinton, in the latter years of Bavinck's life, he continued to focus on Reformed theology while also broadening his focus to the

---

7. Bavinck, *De offerande des lofs: overdenkingen vóór en na de toelating tot het heilige avondmaal*, 16e druk (Kampen: J. H. Kok, 1948); *The Sacrifice of Praise*, ed. and trans. Cameron Clausing and Gregory Parker Jr. (Peabody, MA: Hendrickson, 2019).

8. Bavinck, "De zekerheid des geloofs," *Tijdschrift voor Gereformeerde Theologie* 9 (1901–1902): 129–98; Bavinck, *The Certainty of Faith*, trans. Harry der Nederlanden (St. Catherines, ON: Paideia Press, 1980).

9. Bavinck, *Handleiding bij het Onderwijs in den Christelijken Godsdienst* (Kampen: J. H. Kok, 1913).

10. Bavinck, *Modernisme en Orthodoxie: rede gehouden bij de overdracht van het Rectooraat aan de Vrije Universiteit op 20 October 1911* (Kampen: J. H. Kok, 1911); Bavinck, *On Theology: Herman Bavinck's Academic Orations*, trans. and ed. Bruce Pass (Leiden: Brill, 2020), 146, 181, 22.

11. Eglinton, *Bavinck*, 259–65; see also Pass's introduction to *On Theology*, 22–29.

12. Eglinton, *Bavinck*, 261.

13. Neo-Calvinism/neo-Calvinist we take to be a historical term representative of Calvinist revivals in the late nineteenth century that perceived the theology of Calvinism as world and life encompassing. See Eglinton, *Bavinck*, 156–58, 184; Eglinton, *Bavinck*, 261.

Christian faith in general. Theology in this manner is both local and global, both Reformed and catholic, for both the young and the old. In this way, Bavinck attempted to confront secularism not by drawing further boundaries in the plurality of Christianity, but through drawing lines of connection.[14]

This idea of Bavinck, as a theologian, who strove to do Reformed theology while also laboring for a more ecumenical Christian faith, becomes clearer when compared with the larger *Magnalia Dei* (1909) published two years prior to the *Guidebook*. This volume displays his emphasis on strengthening Reformed theology within the Netherlands, but also his desire to edify all Christians in a shifting ideological landscape. Bavinck's *Magnalia Dei* is "*onderwijzing in de Christelijke religie naar Gereformeerde Belijdenis*" ("instruction in the Christian religion according to the *Reformed Confessions*"). Suitable for college-age students, perhaps those taking Bavinck's classes at the *Vrije Universiteit*, it contains numerous citations to the Belgic Confession, the Canons of Dordt, and the Heidelberg Catechism, which together compose the three forms of unity—the theological standards of the Dutch Reformed Church.

On the other hand, his *Guidebook* is more broadly "*onderwijs in den Christelijken Godsdienst*" ("instruction in the *Christian Religion*"). It is a more catholic (universal) undertaking—that is, an undertaking for the church universal. While the work bears the marks of a Reformed theologian (as Bavinck notes in the preface, it is "for those who desire to understand the main content of our Christian, Reformed confession of faith"), it should be earmarked as a more ecumenical endeavor. After all, in that quote, "Christian" precedes "Reformed." Moreover, *Guidebook* is intended for a younger crowd, those attending the equivalent to an American high school.

When we read *Guidebook*, we see that Bavinck is not constructing a novel theological system. He is at his best drawing on catholic theology while remaining firmly in the Reformed tradition that came out of Switzerland and landed in the Netherlands. *Guidebook* proves to be both theologically deep and accessible, remaining at a level of readability not found in his much larger *Reformed Dogmatics*. *Guidebook* is both profound and egalitarian in the truest sense of the words. In Bavinck's hierarchy of reads, *Guidebook* is for the young adult, *Magnalia Dei* is for the working professional, and *Reformed Dogmatics* is for the academic.

---

14. Pass, *On Theology*, 1–29. Pass makes a similar point through evaluating Bavinck's approach to secularism.

Throughout his *Guidebook*, Bavinck draws upon Augustinian themes. Indeed, Bavinck's more pronounced use of Augustine in *Guidebook* is remarkable compared to *Reformed Dogmatics*, although not altogether surprising. In an 1893 essay titled "Calvinistisch en Gereformeerde" ("Calvinist and Reformed"), Bavinck identifies several salient features to Protestantism;[15] the first of which is that Protestantism is "definitively Augustinian."[16]

At the outset of *Guidebook*, he beckons the reader to see that the highest good is "God, and God alone."[17] Throughout the work, God is routinely re-introduced as the highest good.[18] Bavinck informs the reader that the benefits of Christ include "the gift of the highest good, communion with God and all his blessings."[19] In Bavinck's formulation, this God—who is the highest good—makes himself known in the self-consciousness through the inner self.[20] Augustine viewed the world as a cosmic order in which the highest good for humans is to recognize and love the highest good, God. The soul must be directed toward the highest good. For Augustine, attending to the highest good happens through the inner self. This is also why Augustine places such high emphasis on finding trinitarian motifs within the inward man. This teaching is the basis of Augustine's attempts to discern the image of the Trinity in the soul and its activity.[21] Through this activity is the discovery of the highest good. As man seeks to understand himself, he is ultimately directed toward God. Bavinck closes *Guidebook* with God's

---

15. Bavinck, "Calvinistisch en Gereformeerd," review of *De Heidelbergsche catechismus en het Boekje van de breking des broods*, by M. A. Gooszen, De Vrije Kerk 19:2 (Februari 1893): 49–71. Bavinck was reviewing *De Heidelbergsche catechismus: textus receptus met toelichtende teksten* (Leiden: Brill, 1890) by Maurits Albrecht Gooszen (1837–1916), who was a Dutch Reformed theologian and professor at Leiden University.

16. Bavinck, "Calvinistisch en Gereformeerd," 56.

17. See p. 13.

18. See pp. 74, 94.

19. See p. 122.

20. Bavinck's weaving together of Augustine and Schleiermacher has been explored by Cory Brock and Nathaniel Sutanto. See "Herman Bavinck's Reformed eclecticism: On catholicity, consciousness, and theological epistemology," *Scottish Journal of Theology* 70.3 (2017): 310–32, esp. 320–23. See also Cory Brock, *Orthodox yet Modern: Herman Bavinck's Use of Friedrich Schleiermacher* (Bellingham, WA: Lexham Press, 2020).

21. The first trinity is that of mind, knowledge, and love. The mind comes to know itself, and in that, love itself. The same basic idea underlies the second trinity of memory, intelligence, and will.

declaration that all is very good in God's presence. All Christians become participants in the highest good in the kingdom of God. On this Augustinian path, Bavinck is a guide who directs us to God.

Another Augustinian theme of note is the restlessness of the human heart. Bavinck places God before the reader as the highest good because he is the only one who can satisfy the heart of mankind.[22] The aim of the mind seeking God in Augustine's *De Trinitate* is "to know as we are known" to see God "face to face."[23] In the opening chapter, Bavinck writes: "In Christ . . . we behold the Father himself in all of the fullness of his grace and truth (John 1:17; 14:9), so we may boast in humility, we know him because we are known by him; we love him because he first loved us (1 John 4:19)." The work closes, stating: "all will see God's face and be like him . . . all will know, as they are known."[24] In the end, the human heart is satisfied because it is truly known and truly loved by God, the highest good. *Guidebook* is definitively Augustinian.

Another influence that most readers quickly notice is that the title of the work closely resembles John Calvin's *Institutes of the Christian Religion*. The Dutch title of Calvin's work is *Institutie, of Onderwijzing in de Christelijke Godsdienst*, which is congruent with Bavinck's Dutch title *Handleiding bij het Onderwijs in den Christelijken Godsdienst*.[25] While the later editions (1536–59) of Calvin's *Institutes* increased in size, Bavinck worked at distilling his *Reformed Dogmatics* into a more concise form. *Guidebook* follows his rigorous academic work and is the *crème de la crème* of his theology. From the completion of his *Reformed Dogmatics* (1895–1901) and subsequent revision (1906–1911), to *Magnalia Dei* (which extracts the heart and

---

22. See pp. 28, 54, 96, 136.

23. Augustine, *De Trinitate*, trans. Edmund Hill (Hyde Park, NY: New City Press, 2013), 236–37; Book VIII, ch. 3; Book IX, ch. 3; Book XII, ch. 4.

24. See pp. 14–15, 194.

25. One reviewer suggested that Bavinck's title was also similar to *Kort begrip der Christelijke religie* (*Brief Understanding of the Christian Religion*) by Hermanus Faukelius (1560–1625). This was a short summary of the Heidelberg Catechism that was later republished as title *Onderwijs in de leer van den godsdienst, naar het kort begrip der Christen religie (Education in the Doctrine of Religion, according to the Brief Understanding of the Christian Religion)*. See Hermanus Faukelius, *Kort begrip der Christelijke religie* (Haarlem: Johannes Jacobus Beets, 1810); Faukelius, *Onderwijs in de leer van den godsdienst, naar het kort begrip der Christen religie* (Groningen: Doesburg, 1846). A connection to Calvin was also suggested in the same review that suggested Faukelius (G. Leestafel, *De Heraut voor de Gereformeerede Kerken in Nederland*, November 9, 1913, 3).

soul of Bavinck's dogmatics) to the accessible *Guidebook*, a refined catholic, Reformed lay-level, Augustinian book was born. This homage to Calvin should come as no surprise, as Bavinck is well known, alongside Abraham Kuyper, as the father of a retrieval and adaptation of Calvinism.

Reception of *Guidebook for Instruction in the Christian Religion*

When *Guidebook* hit the Dutch market in 1913, it was not alone in its genre or style as a manual to a field of study. The effects of the 1876 Higher Education Act were being felt in Dutch education as it shifted in a modern direction.[26] Therefore, there was an influx of guidebooks in the market to supplement the changing academic scene. A review of *Guidebook* written in *De Heraut* lamented the influx of these manuals (although Bavinck's work was an exception to this complaint). The reviewer perceived Bavinck as succeeding in his goal of setting forth a brief manual on the Christian religion. Notably, the reviewer also believed that it could fit into the new curriculum in the gymnasium.[27]

---

26. In 1814, the Van der Duyn van Maasdam Committee drafted a regulation for Dutch grammar schools and universities. This went into effect in 1815 and remained essentially unchanged until the Higher Education Act of 1876. A regulation in 1820 allowed for tuition-free study of theology (Reformed theology) at Dutch universities. In the aftermath of the Pan-European revolutions of 1848, the Dutch Parliament increasingly pushed in a liberal direction and adopted a constitution that cross-pressured theology departments across the Netherlands. This pressure finally reached its climax in 1876 with the passing of the Higher Education Act. This act allowed theology departments across the Netherlands to retain "theology" in the description of their departments, while the content they taught was to be called "religious studies." This wasn't the only shift. In education, the Higher Education Act of 1876 partnered with the Pre-Higher Education Act of 1876. The gymnasium up until this point had been classical in nature, including classic and modern languages, religion, etc. The act pushed the gymnasium in a modernist direction. In 1902, Bavinck lamented this shift in his lectures on the Theological Encyclopedia. Nine years later, he attempted to find a solution to supplement the shift in the gymnasium. See unknown student, "Lecture Notes Encyclopaedie d. Theol," 9–15; see also Kees Schuyt and Ed Taverene, *Dutch Culture in European Persepective: 1950, Prosperity and Wealth* (London: Palgrave Macmillan, 2004), 290–91.

27. G. Leestafel, *De Heraut voor de Gereformeerede Kerken in Nederland*, November 9, 1913, 3.

> And then also my other objection, which concerned the time available for the teaching of religion at our grammar schools and higher civic schools, is absent from this *Guidebook*, because it may be assumed that in the one hour a week, which is available there for this teaching, its §20 [chapters] can be sufficiently absorbed by the children of the higher classes, thus in two or three years.[28]

Harm Bouwman (1863–1933), a Dutch Reformed pastor and, at the time, professor at the *Theologische School* in Kampen, also wrote a positive review:

> Dr. Bavinck wrote this book for the students of the highest courses of our Christian gymnasiums, higher civic schools, training colleges, standard school, etc. and also for all those who would like to get acquainted with the main contents of our Christian Reformed confession by means of a not too comprehensive, or expensive book. In 20 short chapters, together 243 pages, he summarizes the contents. He does not deal with the subject matter in questions and answers, but in a regular and systematic order. . . . This booklet is excellent in its brevity and clarity.[29]

While most reviewers appreciated the contents of the book and its flexibility for use in various institutions, many desired that questions be included at the end of the chapters to aid students. This was true of Bouwman's review,

---

28. G. Leestafel, 3. [Dutch: En dat ook mijn andere bedenking, die op het stuk van den, voor het Godsdienstonderwijs aan onze gymnasia en hoogere burgerscholen beschikbaren tijd, tegenover deze Handleiding wegvalt is, omdat mag worden aangenomen, dat in het eene uur per week, hetwelk daar voor dit onderwijs beschikbaar is, haar 20§§ door de leerlingen der hoogere klassen, alzoo in twee of drie Jaren, voldoende kunnen opgenomen.] This reviewer also recommended reading *Guidebook* alongside the Bible and the Heidelberg Catechism. Interestingly, Jan Bavinck's second edition of his commentary on the Heidelberg Catechism was also released in 1913. See Jan Bavinck, *De Heidelbergsche Catechismus in 60 Leerredenen Verklaard*, 2e (Kampen: J. H. Kok, 1913).

29. Harm Bouwman, "Boekaankondiging," *De Bauzin: Gereformeerde stemmen uit de Christelijke Afgescheidene Kerk in Nederland-Kerk-Nieuws-en advertentieblad*, November 7, 1913. [Dutch: Dr. Bavinck schreef dit boek voor de leerlingen der hoogste klassen van onze christelijke gymnasia, hoogere burgerscholen, kweekscholen, normaallessen, enz. en voorts voor allen die door middel van een een niet te uitgebreid en niet te kostbaar boek kennis willen maken met den hoofdinhoud van onze Christelijke Gereformeerde Geloofsbelijddenis. In 20 korte hoofdstukkenm samen 243 bladzijden, vat hij den inhoud saam. Hij behandelt de leerstof niet in vragen en antwoorden, maar in geregelde en systematische orde. . . . Dit boekje munt uit door beknoptheid en duidelijkheid.]

"G's" review in *De Heraut*, and a brief review in *Het Oosten*.[30] The reviewer in *Het Oosten* wrote,

> The author has in mind with this guidebook the students in the highest classes of Gymnasia, H. B. S. [Hoogere Burgerscholen] schools of education, etc. . . . It is entirely in keeping [in style] with Bavinck's *Magnalia Dei*. . . . Question books are going out of fashion. But wouldn't it be advisable to have a very concise book of questions, referring to the chapters of the guidebook? In the spirit of Doedes with his *De Leer der Zaligheid* (*The Doctrine of Salvation*), I mean.[31]

A multiplicity of reviewers believed it would have been advantageous to include a series of questions in the book for students to study.

Concerning *Guidebook* and *Magnalia Dei*

The astute reader will notice that there is notable word-for-word overlap between Bavinck's Dutch titles: *Magnalia Dei: Onderwijzing in de Christelijke Religie naar Gereformeerde Belijdenis* (*Education in the Christian Religion according to the Reformed Confession*) and *Handleiding bij het Onderwijs in den Christelijken Godsdienst* (*Guidebook for Instruction in the Christian Religion*). Although *Magnalia Dei* was first published in Dutch in 1909 and the *Guidebook* in 1913, to say that the second work is largely a redacted version of the first would be an overstatement. Like a younger sibling, *Guidebook* cannot escape its resemblance to its older sibling, *Magnalia Dei*; nonetheless, *Guidebook* is a distinct book in its own right in the Bavinck corpus.

As editors, we chose to make references to the second Dutch edition (1931) of *Magnalia Dei*. In this respect, there are many notes, as we tracked areas of abridgement between the two works and what is unique to *Guidebook*. While these comments oriented toward mapping similarities between the two works do not exclusively make up the contents of our notes, they comprise a large percentage of them. Chapters 19 and 20 refer to the first

30. Bouwman, "Boekaankondiging," 3; G. Leestafel, 3.

31. "Over een en ander." *Het Oosten; wekelijksch orgaan der Weesinrichting te Neerbosch*, February 25, 1914. [Dutch: De schrijver heeft met deze handleiding op het oog de leerlingen in de hoogste klassen van Gymnasia, H. B. S., kweekscholen enz. . . . Zij sluit zich geheel aan bij Bavinck's "Magnalia Dei." . . . Vragenboekjes raken uit de mode. Maar was het niet aanbevelenswaardig om muist deze handleiding een heel beknopt vraagboekje te hebben, welks vragen verwezen naar de hoofdstukken van de handleiding? In den geest van Doedes met diens "Leer der Zaligheid," bedoel ik.] J. I. Doedes, *De Leer der Zaligheid Volgens het Evangelie in de Schriften Des Nieuwen Verbonds* (Utrecht: Kemink en Zoon, 1868).

edition of *Magnalia Dei* (1909), as there were notable changes between the first and second editions. The first (1913) and second (1932) editions of *Guidebook* are identical.

Three options are open to the reader for the notes: (1) Read the main text and ignore the notes; (2) glance at the notes to acknowledge unique features to *Guidebook*; or (3) read the notes in conversation with *Magnalia Dei*, which will help expand the reader in Bavinck's thinking. Although these expansions and redactions between *Magnalia Dei* and *Guidebook* make this text akin to a critical edition, calling it such is beyond our hope for the book.

For readers who want to follow the expansions and redactions, here are some helpful details: the numbers found in brackets [##] are references to the pagination in the 1913 Dutch edition of *Guidebook*. Likewise, references in the notes to *Magnalia Dei* are references to the pagination of the 1931 Dutch edition.

Readers may be surprised to see references to the Dutch *Magnalia Dei* and not to the most recent English edition, *The Wonderful Works of God*.[32] This is due to noteworthy errors that persist in Henry Zylstra's 1956 translation of the first edition of *Magnalia Dei*.[33] Coenraad Bavinck (Herman's brother) had released the second edition twenty-four years earlier, which included edits to the first edition as well as an additional chapter. The need for an updated edition of *Magnalia Dei* is evident for at least two reasons.

First, the heavy editorial hand of the translator negatively impacted the transmission of Bavinck's thought. Coenraad Bavinck had released the second edition twenty-four years earlier, which included edits to the first edition as well as an additional chapter. Moreover, within Zylstra's translation, he did not consistently translate key terminology and added and redacted from the text at will.[34]

---

32. Bavinck, *The Wonderful Works of God* (Glenside, PA: Westminster Seminary Press, 2020). This is a beautiful reprint of Henry Zylstra's translation. The addition of Bavinck's preface by Nathaniel G. Sutanto is the gem of the volume.

33. Henry Zylstra's (1909–1956) translation of *Magnalia Dei* was originally published by W. B. Eerdmans in 1956. After completing his PhD at Harvard University, Zylstra began teaching at Calvin College in 1941. In 1950, Zylstra was promoted to professor and chaired the English department at Calvin. In 1956, the same year as the publication of his translation, Zylstra lectured at the Free University in Amsterdam with a Fulbright grant. It is unclear to what degree Zylstra's Dutch colleagues influenced his translation.

34. See Gregory Parker Jr., "Review of *The Wonderful Works of God* by Herman Bavinck," *Reformation 21*, April 6, 2020, https://www.reformation21.org/blog/the-wonderful-works-of-god.

Second, the translator disconnected Bavinck from his Reformed sources by being inconsistent with the omission of citations to the Belgic Confession and the Canons of Dordt. This is an odd translation decision for a text intended to guide readers in the Reformed confessions! Since it was inconsistent, however, it is unclear if it was intentional.

In the current work, we have placed the occasional word in brackets. Although these words are not original to the text, they should facilitate a smoother reading experience. Added to this editorial decision, we have also chosen to include salient Dutch words in parentheses for the reader who wants to dive deeper.

Because of these and other similar issues, we decided the best way forward was to reference the Dutch edition of *Magnalia Dei*. This provides those with the interest and the ability the tools for tracking down references. In our (Lord willing) forthcoming English volume of *Magnalia Dei*, readers will be able to identify the page numbers [##] found in the notes in this book.

The End Purpose of *Guidebook*

While its specific intended use is to teach *instruction in the Christian faith*, this book may also serve an additional purpose: to be a primer to the theology of Herman Bavinck. For those who want to understand Bavinck, there may be no better place to begin. This *Guidebook* contains an ideal summation of Bavinck's theologically mature program. Reformed and catholic, vigorous yet concise, theological and comprehensible, it is a Bavinckian primer *par excellence*. For students interested in stepping into Bavinck, there is no better place to begin.

If we as translators had a singular goal in mind, it would be aligned with Bavinck's hope that he wrote in his preface: that the main contents of the Christian faith might be made known to the next generation of readers. The translation of theological books is akin to the handing down of family heirlooms.[35] In the pages that follow, Bavinck puts forth a clear articulation of the Christian religion. In typical Bavinck style, his writing is thoroughly

---

35. Herman Bavinck, "Reading, Thinking, Speaking," trans. Gregory Parker Jr., *Modern Reformation* vol. 30, issue 1 (January/February 2021): 14–16 (esp. 15). "It is our duty to collect treasures for ourselves and our posterity: to read, to interpret, to understand, to make the whole earth our domain; to subject nature to spirit, matter to thought."

saturated with Scripture. He traverses a path in which he attempts to bridge the gap between the theology in the academy and theology in the church. In doing so, he provides the pilgrim with a theology that is uniquely accessible. For those who found his *Reformed Dogmatics* alarmingly academic and his *Magnalia Dei* intimidatingly thick, *Guidebook* is the theological porridge that is "just right" for most readers.

This *Guidebook* can be easily synthesized with the four-volume *Reformed Dogmatics*. The first volume corresponds to chapters 1–5 with theological prolegomena (the organic knowledge of God, general and special revelation). The second volume correlates with chapters 6–9 on God and creation (God as Triune, and creation as a testimony in its unity-in-diversity to God's triunity); this includes creation, providence, and anthropology (the *macro* and *micro-cosmos*). Volume 3 corresponds to chapters 10–13 on sin and salvation (sin and death, the covenant of grace, and the person and work of Christ). Lastly, the fourth and final volume correlates with chapters 14–20 on the work of the Holy Spirit (effectual calling, the means of grace, the church, and the consummation of the world).

In his *Guidebook for Instruction in the Christian Religion*, Bavinck has given a gift to the church. The reader will likely find little that is groundbreaking or novel (as one regularly does in *Reformed Dogmatics*). However, this book supplies the theology of an academic concerned with the life of the church. It is an example of catechetical theology produced by one of the foremost academic theologians of his time.

Above all, we hope this translation helps fulfill Bavinck's hope for true theology: that it does not remain an object of the head but penetrates the heart and thus becomes an act of confession and praise. As he writes, "Dogmatics, therefore, is . . . a hymn of adoration and thanksgiving, a 'glory to God in the highest' (Luke 2:14)."[36] In this book, Bavinck gives us a songbook: setting God before us and calling us to sing God's praises.

36. Bavinck, *Reformed Dogmatics*, vol. 1, *Prolegomena*, ed. John Bolt, trans. John Vriend (Grand Rapids: Baker Academic, 2004), 112 [hereafter *RD* 1).

1

The Knowledge of God

1. [1] The highest good of man is God and God alone.[1] In the beginning, [man] was created according to God's image and likeness, and man can never wholly eradicate or destroy his divine origin and divine relationship. Even though [through sin] he has lost the attributes of knowledge, righteousness, and holiness, which were contained in this image, there are still some "small traces" present in him, which are not only sufficient to deny him all innocence, but which also bear witness to his former greatness and continually remind him of his divine calling and heavenly destination.[2]

In the entirety of the life and striving of man, he comes to this: that he does not have enough in the whole world. Along with the animals, he shares a sense perception and a sensual consciousness; but above this, he was equipped with intellect and reason, which gives him an awareness of things that are invisible and eternal. Likewise, along with the animals, man has sensual desires, the need for food and drink, light and air, work and ordinary [daily] rest. Moreover, man has received a will that, guided by reason and the conscience, extends to the unseen, spiritual, and eternal goods. The presentation of Holy Scripture roots both the intellect and the will in the heart of man, and in them God has laid eternity (Eccl. 3:11). Out of that are the springs of life; therefore, they must be preserved [2] for and above everything (Prov. 4:23). It does not benefit man, therefore, whether he gains houses and fields—yea, the whole world if he suffers the destruction of his soul (Matt. 16:26). No creature, however powerful, is capable of redeeming his soul (Ps. 49:7–8).[3]

---

1. *Magnalia Dei*, 7 [hereafter *MD* plus page number]. Bavinck admits in the preface that there will be a clear correlation between *Magnalia Dei* and *Handleiding*. In fact, they begin with the same sentence [Dutch: "Des menschen hoogste goed is God, en God alleen."]. Similarly, the second chapter of *MD* begins, "God is the highest good for man [Dutch: God het hoogste goed voor den mensch.]" (9).

2. *The Belgic Confession of Faith*, Article 14: The Creation and Fall of Humanity; cf. *MD*, 9.

3. For an expansion of this paragraph, see *MD*, 11–12.

This inability to satisfy the human heart applies not only to material treasures and sensual pleasures, but equally to those ideal goods that come under the name of science and art, of humanity, civilization, or culture.[4] For these [material, sensual, and ideal] goods are by no means despised in Holy Scripture. On the contrary, they are prized (Exod. 31:3; 35:31; 1 Sam. 2:3; Prov. 2:6, 8:11; James 1:17); but they only obtain their true value if the fear of God is their foundation (Prov. 1:7), they are connected with love (1 Cor. 13:2), and they are used to God's glory (1 Cor. 10:31).

As was said by Augustine, the heart of man is created for God and finds no rest until it finds it in God.[5]

2. In order for our hearts to find rest in God, naturally we must possess some knowledge of him, for the unknown is unloved. At present, there are many who completely deny the knowability of God; but Holy Scripture, with the rest of humanity, assumes that God, at least to some extent, can be known by man because [God] has revealed himself (for more: see chapter 2). According to Scripture, [God] has not only revealed himself in the works of nature (Rom. 1:19–20) but above all by the word of prophets and apostles in the person of Christ, who was the Father's only and much beloved Son (Matt. 3:17; John 1:14; Rom. 8:32; Heb. 1:3), the preeminent messenger (Matt. 11:27; John 3:16; 17:3), who [3] thus is able to perfectly convey the name of the Father and help us to know the true one (John 1:18; 17:6; 1 John 5:20). In the revelation of him, this Christ, the one sent, bears witness to the knowledge

---

4. In *MD*, he expands on this idea, writing of the heart of man as the physical point of origin and the main organ of bodily life, so it is also the spiritual and ethical source of the higher life of man; it is the seat of our self-consciousness, of our relationship to God, our bondage to the law in our whole moral and spiritual nature (11).

5. St. Augustine, *The Confessions* (London: Penguin Books, 1961), 1. In *MD*, Bavinck writes similarly, "Zoo blijft het woord van Augustinus, dat het hart des menschen tot God is geschapen end at het geen rust vindt, voordat het ruste vindt aan zijn vaderhart. Alle menschen zoeken Dan. ook eigenlijk naar God, getuidge dezelfde kerkvader, maar zij zoeken Hem niet op de rechte wijze, niet in den rechten weg, niet op de rechte plaats. Zij zoeken Hem beneden, en Hij is boven. . . . Zij voelen zich tot God aangetrokken en tegelijk door Hem afgestoon" (14). [English translation: So, it remains with the word of Augustine, that the heart of man was created for God and that it cannot find rest until it rests in his Father's heart. Then all men are really seeking for God, but they do not all seek him the right way, not in the right way, nor in the right place. They seek him down below, and He is up above. . . . They feel themselves attracted to God and at the same time repelled by him.]

of the one true God, who is eternal life (John 17:3).[6] From this it is apparent that the knowledge of God in Christ bears a wholly special character and differs from all other knowledge in origin and object and in essence and fruit.

In *origin* because knowledge of God is indebted to Christ. To a certain extent, we acquire all other knowledge through our own effort and research. But the knowledge of the only true God must be given to us, as children, through Christ. Apart from him, it is nowhere to be found; not in schools of science or in renowned philosophers. But Christ knows the Father and has revealed him to us. "No one knows the Son except the Father, and no one knows the Father except the Son and anyone to whom the Son chooses to reveal him" (Matt. 11:27).[7]

In *object* because although the knowledge of nature and history and of the whole world, especially in the last century, is so vast and multiplying, it is still not complete; it is about the creature and therefore is restricted to the finite and does not find the infinite.[8] There is, however, a revelation of God's eternal power and divinity in the works of creation, but the knowledge of God obtained from it is limited and insufficient for man, who is a sinner needing redemption (Rom. 1:20–23; 3:19–20). In Christ, however, we behold the Father himself in all of the fullness of his grace and truth (John 1:17; 14:9), so we may boast in humility that we know him because we are known by him; we love him because he first loved us (1 John 4:19).

In *essence* because Jesus speaks the Scripture above (Matt. 11:27) not out of an [impersonal] knowledge (*weten*), but as one who knows (*kennen*) God.[9] [4] There is a vast difference between them. One may know (*weten*) much about creatures, countries, or cultures from reading books, but this is much different from knowing (*kennen*) something from contemplation. It is this knowledge concerning God (*weten*) that consists only in

6. In *MD*, he writes of Christ as the midpoint and highpoint of revelation [Dutch: haar middel—en haar hoogtepunt"] (15).

7. For an extension of Christ as the origin of revelation, see *MD*, 17–18. In this section, Bavinck writes of the Son's intimate relation with the Father and roots his trustworthiness as a reliable revelation in his mission, as the one who is sent to deliver his people.

8. For a lengthening of Christ as the object of revelation, see *MD*, 18–19.

9. For an enlargement of Christ as the essence of revelation, see *MD*, 19–21. It will be helpful for the reader to know when Bavinck is utilizing two different ways of expressing "to know" with *kennen* and *weten*. They both express different kinds of knowledge; *kennen* indicates an intimate personal knowledge, while *weten* indicates impersonal knowledge.

the intellectual acceptance of another's witness, never reaching the heart, and therefore granting no salvation or peace, but rather makes judgment worse (Matt. 7:21; Luke 12:47–48; 1 Cor. 13:1–13; James 1:23; 2:19). Christ, however, intends a knowledge (*kennis*) of God, which rests on a personal relationship with (*kennismaking*) and experience of his being and virtues, of his righteousness and grace, and therefore can be possessed only by his children (Matt. 5:8; 18:3; John 3:15; 7:17).[10]

Finally, in *effect* and *fruit* because this knowledge (*kennis*) of God indeed gives at the same moment eternal life.[11] It is not a power like the English proverb ascribes to knowledge, nor does it give to us authority only of the mind over material objects, like contemporary culture and technology; rather it is life, pure life, eternal life. And this life, according to Holy Scripture, includes peace, joy, and salvation; it is a life that in principle already triumphs here on earth and hereafter perfectly upon all sin and death. "He who believes in me," Jesus said, "though he die, yet shall he live, and everyone who lives and believes in me shall never die" [John 11:25–26]. He who believes in the Son *has* eternal life (John 3:36).

3. In accordance with this teaching of the Holy Scriptures, the nature of this science (*wetenschap*) was developed in the Christian Church, and it soon received the name of "Theology," the study of God, and it retained this name until the present day. Theology was viewed as the science (*wetenschap*) that deduced, imagined, and recounted the knowledge of God from revelation under the guidance of his Holy Spirit. And a theologian is one who in a real sense is a scholar taught by God, who speaks of God, about God, and for the sake of the glory of God's name.

Like all other sciences (*wetenschapen*), in due course, theology wonderfully expanded so that a division was necessary. Typically, the theologian differentiates the science into four groups of study. The first group studies the origin, the collection, the text, and the interpretation of the books of the Bible; the second group concentrates on the church and seeks to understand its history and its present; the third group has the knowledge of God as its center (*middelpunt*), which is contained in revelation and thus includes all of those subjects that have to do with the truthful content of revelation; while, finally, the fourth group covers the offices in Christ's church and sets forth their work. But all these subjects are nevertheless masterfully con-

10. He introduces this sort of "knowing" (*kennen*) as the knowledge of faith in *MD*, 20.

11. For an expansion of the effect and fruit of revelation, see *MD*, 21–22.

nected to an organic unity and elevated to the position of an independent science by the idea of the knowledge of God, which supports them all. For this reason, theology is entitled to its own place in the sphere of the sciences, which are practiced at our colleges and compromise five so-called faculties: besides the faculty of theology, there exists that of law, medicine, mathematics and the field of the natural sciences, and literature and philosophy.

The third group of study in theological science has therefore a direct object for knowledge, which God has revealed of himself in nature and Scripture; and it endeavors to explain this to the human consciousness in such a manner that its truth and value clearly come to light. Naturally, however, this can occur, and it is fitting for it to [6] occur in a diversity of ways, depending on the persons in whose consciousness the truth of revelation is displayed. Holy Scripture itself speaks of milk for children and of solid food for adults (1 Cor. 3:2; Heb. 5:12–14; 1 Pet. 2:2); it distinguishes between children, youths, and fathers in Christ (1 John 2:12–14), and believers and unbelievers in the gathering of the congregation (1 Cor. 14:23–24). In his preaching to the Jews, Paul was a Jew, to the Greeks a Greek, and to all people all things that he might rescue some (1 Cor. 9:20–22). The word of God is indeed suitable for all kinds of purposes, for teaching and comforting, but also for reproof, admonishment, and punishment (2 Tim. 3:16; 4:2). Additionally, the true faith can be declared in a written or unwritten confession by the congregation over against the world. [The confession] may be explained by the servant of the word in the pulpit to adults, through catechism to children, and through the theologian via dogmatics, whether assertively (positively, thetical) or repudiatingly (elenctic, apologetic), according to scholarly demands. [The confession] may also be explained by a teacher in a simple guidebook or textbook, laid down for students of a secondary or preparatory school.[12]

Although the manner of presentation can be quite different in each of these cases, it is always the same truth. In this respect, there is no distinction between children and adults, between the simple and scholars; they all have one Lord, one faith, one baptism, one God and Father, who is above all, though grace is given to each of them according to the measure of Christ's gift (Eph. 4:5–7). In this spirit, Calvin began his catechism of Geneva with this question: "What is the chief end of human life?" The [7]

12. A description of the various faculties and theology's place among them is absent from *MD* as well as the content of this paragraph, which discusses the place of theology in the life of the believer.

answer rang clear and powerful: "That man might know God by whom they were created."[13] In the same way, the Westminster Catechism begins its education with the question: "What is the chief and foremost end of man?" It gave this short and profound answer: "Man's chief end is to glorify God and to enjoy him perfectly forever."[14] And the inscription above our Dutch Confession of Faith is: "True Christian confession, containing the principal teachings of God and the eternal salvation of souls."[15]

In the next four sections, we first highlight the sources from which our knowledge of God should be derived, after which we begin with a description of this knowledge of God itself. In this, we first concern ourselves with God himself as he has revealed himself, thus with his essence, his attributes, and his existence. Then we proceed to the treatment of his works, not in and of themselves (like in the other sciences of nature, history, etc.), but only as the works of *God* in their relation to him, as revelation of knowledge. These works fall into two large groups, the works of creation and providence, and that of re-creation and redemption. These works of re-creation and redemption have their objective foundation in the person of Christ and are brought about subjectively through the Holy Spirit in the congregation, until it is filled to all the fullness of God. Thus we, having proceeded from God through all his works, return to God; he is the Alpha and the Omega of all things; from through and to him are all things (Rom. 11:36; Rev.1:8).

---

13. John Calvin, *The Catechism of the Church of Geneva*, trans. Elijah Waterman (Hartford, CT: Sheldon & Goodwin, 1815), 9.

14. *The Shorter Catechism of the Westminster Assembly with Analysis and Scriptural Proofs*, ed. Edwin Hall (Philadelphia: Presbyterian Board of Publication and Sabbath-School Work, 1919), 5.

15. Cf. *MD*, 22.

2

Revelation (General)

4. [8] The knowledge of God is only obtainable for man, insofar as God freely wills to make himself known to man.[1]

This message from God himself is usually indicated with the name *revelation*. Scripture employs various names for this; it speaks of manifestations, speech, instruction, works, making himself known, etc. It therefore indicates that revelation does not always occur in the same way but takes place in very different forms. In fact, all the works of God are outward facing, either in word or in deed, components and elements of that one, great, all-encompassing and always ongoing revelation of God. The creating, maintaining, and ruling of all things, the calling and guiding of Israel, the sending of Christ, the outpouring of the Holy Spirit, the writing down of the word of God, the preservation and the propagation of the church, etc.—each of these together point to and from the ways by which the revelation of God comes to us. They each make something of God known to us. Whatever is and occurs can and should lead us to the knowledge of him, whom to know (*kennen*) is eternal life.

This revelation, whether general or special, always bears the following characteristics.[2]

First, revelation always proceeds freely from *God himself*. He is here, like everywhere, the sole actor; and in doing so, [9] he acts absolutely conscious (*volkomen bewust*) and free. It is true that many who reject the confession of a personal, self-conscious (*zelfbewust*) God still regularly speak of a revelation of God. However, this is a use of the word in conflict with its proper meaning. From the perspective of those who believe solely in an impersonal, unconscious (*onbewuste*), almighty force, one may yet speak of an unconscious, involuntary appearance of brute force; but they may no longer speak of revelation proper, since accordingly, revelation presup-

1. In *MD*, 22–25, he develops more fully the idea of God's freedom in revelation and our absolute dependence on him for knowledge of himself.

2. The previous two paragraphs are uniform with two paragraphs in *MD*, 24.

poses the absolute consciousness (*volkomene bewustheid*) and freedom of God. All revelation, which is correctly called so, is based on the idea that God exists personally (*persoonlijk*), that he himself is conscious (*bewust*), and that he can make himself known to creatures. The knowledge of God in man has its foundation (*grondslag*) and starting point (*uitgangspunt*) in the knowledge that God possess of himself. Without self-consciousness (*zelfbewustheid*) and self-knowledge (*zelfkennis*), no knowledge (*kennis*) of God is possible for humanity (Matt. 11:27).[3]

In the second place, all of God's revelation is *self*-revelation. God is the origin, and he is also the content of his revelation. This is true of the highest revelation that has come to us in Christ, for Jesus himself says that he has revealed to the people the name of the Father (John 17:6) and has declared God to us (John 1:8). Only this went beyond all prior revelation, which God issued forth from himself. All the works of God in nature and grace, in creation and re-creation, and in the world and history enable us to know something of the incomprehensible and lovely nature of God. They do not each do this in the same manner or to the same degree; there is endless diversity here. One work of God speaks more of his righteousness, and another of his goodness; here shines his omnipotence, and over there the wisdom of God is evident.[4] But all together, and each to its own degree, they proclaim to us the great virtues of God and make [10] known to us his properties and perfections, with his essence and self-differentiation (*zelfonderscheidingen*), with his thought and word, and with his will and pleasure.[5]

In the third place, revelation comes from God, has God as its content, and has *God himself* as its goal. It is from him, through him, and to him; God has worked everything for his own sake (Prov. 16:4; Rom. 11:36). Al-

---

3. This paragraph is nearly identical to one in *MD*, 24–25.

4. Apart from a brief expansion between John 17:6 and John 1:18, the current paragraph matches a paragraph in *MD*, 26. The sentences that remain in the current paragraph are separate paragraphs in *MD* and are identical.

5. In between these two paragraphs in *MD*, 25–26, Bavinck writes that while God's knowledge of himself is infinite, we know him through finite revelation. Therefore, both objectively (the world) and subjectively (our self-conscious), we are restricted to only a small glimpse of the fullness of God's being; nonetheless, this knowledge remains reliable because of its source, and man will never find existential rest until he finds it in the Father's heart. Bavinck, *Philosophy of Revelation: A New Annotated Edition*, ed. Nathaniel Sutanto and Cory Brock (Peabody, MA: Hendrickson, 2018), 23 [hereafter, *PoR*]. "In creation God manifests the power of his mind; in revelation, which has redemption for its center, he discloses to us the greatness of his heart."

though the knowledge of God, which is communicated in his revelation, is and remains essentially distinct from his self-knowledge, it is nevertheless so immensely rich, so broad, and so deep that it can never be fully absorbed in the consciousness (*bewustzijn*) of any reasonable creature. The angels far exceed man in understanding and see the face of the Father, who is in heaven daily (Matt. 18:10), but they are eager to see the things that have been announced to us by the preachers of the gospel (1 Pet. 1:12). And as men think more deeply of the revelation of God, they are compelled all the more to cry out with Paul, "Oh, the depths of the riches and wisdom and knowledge of God! How unsearchable are his judgments and how inscrutable his ways" (Rom. 11:33).[6] Therefore, revelation can be beautiful to man and have in mind his salvation (Mark 16:15–16; John 3:16, 3:36; Acts 17:27), yet also not have its final end in man but go far beyond him. In revelation, God composes praise for himself and glorifies his own name. Because revelation is from and through God, it also has his glorification for its destiny and end.[7]

5. This revelation is distinguished between general and special.

In general revelation, God reveals himself through the ordinary course of phenomena and the ordinary course of events; in special revelation, he often employs unusual means, appearances, prophecy, and [11] miracles to make himself known to men. The latter has especially the content of the attributes of God's omnipotence, wisdom, and goodness; above all, it reveals God's holiness and righteousness, mercy, and grace. The former addresses all people and opposes the outbreak of sin through common grace; the latter only comes to those who live under the gospel and are blessed by special grace in the forgiveness of sins and the regeneration of life.[8]

---

6. This paragraph is likewise identical to one in *MD*, 26, apart from the material that follows his citation of Rom. 11:33. Bavinck gives attention to each passage from Mark, John, and Acts, which he simply cites in the present work.

7. Following this paragraph, in *MD*, 27–28, Bavinck writes of revelation as having its mid- and high point in the person of Christ, and of the place of the word of God for the believer. The highest revelation, then, is the Son of God—the one who was with the Father from the very beginning, who took on flesh, and was sent in order to give the light of knowledge of the glory of God. This is the second occasion that Christ as the mid- and high point of revelation was dropped in the present volume. In light of the special place of this revelation, the believer is encouraged to trace out God in nature and history and recognize the true, the good, and the beautiful.

8. This paragraph is identical to a paragraph in *MD*, 28, apart from the first sentence, which Bavinck splits in the current work to become its own paragraph, just prior to this one.

However much they are distinguished, they are also closely connected with each other. Both have their origin in the free goodness and favor of God. General revelation is due to the Word, who in the beginning was with God, who made all things, and whose lights shines in the darkness, and coming into the world gives light to every man (John 1:1–9). Special revelation is due to the same Word, but that Word has become flesh in Christ and is presently full of grace and truth (John 1:14). Both revelations have grace for content—the latter general, the former special[9]—and they are both included in Holy Scripture. The latter, although originally from nature, is therefore incorporated into Scripture, because we (mankind) on account of the darkness of our understanding (*verstand*) could never deduce it purely from nature. But now Scripture spreads a light on our path through the world and gives us the true perception of nature and history.[10] Scripture causes us to become aware of God where we would otherwise not see him; through its light, we behold God's attributes, spread out in all of the works of his hands.

There is, according to Scripture, first of all the revelation of God in nature all around us.[11] "The heavens declare the glory of God, and the sky above proclaims his handiwork" (Ps. 19:1). "He makes his sun rise on the evil and on the good [12] and sends rain on the just and on the unjust" (Matt. 5:45); see further (Pss. 8, 65, 104, 145, 147; Isa. 40; Matt. 6:26–30; Rom. 1:19–20).[12]

Furthermore, there is a revelation of God in history.[13] Out of one blood, he has made all the families of mankind to dwell on the face of the whole earth (Acts 17:26). He wiped out the first generation of humanity in the flood and simultaneously preserved the house of Noah (Gen. 6–9). He

---

9. Up until this point, this paragraph is identical to one in *MD*, 28.

10. Interestingly, where Bavinck delves into a discussion on common and special grace in *MD*, in the present work he considers the impact of revelation on nature and history. "The more we penetrate in our thinking to the essence of history, as to that of nature, the more we grasp its idea and maintain it, the more it will manifest itself as rooted in *revelation* and as upheld by *revelation*; the more it will lift itself up to and approach that view of history which Christianity has presented and wherewith Christianity in its turn confirms and supports revelation in nature and history" (*PoR*, 111).

11. For an expansion of the revelation of God in nature, see *MD*, 29–32.

12. In the present work, the "six proofs" appear after "self-consciousness," and in *MD* before it. The thrust, however, remains the same.

13. For an expansion on revelation in history, see *MD*, 32–33.

confused the speech of man at the tower of Babel and spread them over the whole earth (Gen. 11:7–8). And when the Most High gave the nations (*volken*) their inheritance and divided the children of Adam, he appointed the seasons, and fixed their dwelling and the borders of the peoples according to the numbers of the sons of Israel (Deut. 32:8; Acts 17:26). Although he chose the people (*volk*) of Israel as the bearer of his special revelation and let the Gentiles walk according to their own ways (Acts 14:16), he did not lose sight of them (the Gentiles) nor leave them to their own destiny. On the contrary, "He has not left himself without a witness, for he did good by giving you rains from heaven and fruitful seasons, satisfying your hearts with food and gladness" (Acts 14:17). What is known of God, is made known to them, because God has revealed it to them (Rom. 1:19), "that they should seek out God, and perhaps feel their way toward him and find him" (Acts 17:27).

And finally, there is also a revelation of God in man himself, in his own heart and conscience (*geweten*), and in all the directions of his life.[14] Man was created in God's image and still bears traces of it; he is God's offspring (Acts 17:28). As God did not leave himself without a witness (Acts 14:17), so man feels (*voelt*) the impetus within himself to climb up to the invisible from the visible things through his understanding (*verstand*) and reason (*rede*) (Rom. 1:19) and subject all his movements to moral judgment [13] (Rom. 2:14–15). The fool may say in his heart, "There is no God" (Ps. 14:1)," but deep in every human soul is the feeling of absolute dependence (*gevoel van volstrekte afhankelijkheid*)[15] on an almighty power, a feeling (*gevoel*) of divinity—just as Calvin called it thereby; also a seed, a principle of religion and morality.

---

14. For more on revelation in man's self-consciousness, see *MD*, 33–34.

15. Friedrich Schleiermacher, *Christian Faith: A New Translation and Critical Edition*, ed. Catherine L. Kelsey and Terrence N. Tice, trans. Terrence Tice, Catherine L. Kelsey, and Edwina Lawler (Louisville, KY: Westminster John Knox, 2016), §4.2; §32–33. It is worth noting the phrase the "feeling of absolute dependence" (*gevoel van volstrekte afhankelijkheid*) is a clear reference to Schleiermacher. In *RD* 1.66, Bavinck writes, "For Schleiermacher the essence of religion lay in a feeling of absolute dependence" (*gevoel van volstrekte afhankelijkheid*). Likewise, in *RD* 1.278, he similarly pairs Calvin and Schleiermacher with this "religious feeling" or "sense of divinity." He suggests that man possesses an internal organ of perception that has a certain aptitude for perceiving the divine and corresponds with external revelation. For a condensed and stellar reading on Bavinck's modified appropriation of Schleiermacher, see Cory Brock, "Between Demonization and Dependence: Bavinck's Appropriations of Schleiermacher," *Ad Fontes* 2.7 (2018): 1–6.

In theology, people have tried to classify and divide all of these testimonies, which nature and history make concerning the existence and essence of God, into various groups. Thus [theologians] gradually began to speak of six proofs for the existence of God.

First, however great and powerful the world may be, it still bears witness in itself that it exists in the forms of space and time, that it bears a finite, coincidental, dependent (*afhankelijk*) character and thereby points away from itself to an eternally, necessarily existing, independent (*noodzakelijk*) being, who is the final cause of all things (cosmological proof).

Second, everywhere in the world, in its laws and structures, in its unity and harmony, in the organization of all its creatures, there is a purpose detected that, by every explanation from chance, impels ridicule and leads us to the recognition of an all-wise and almighty being, who with infinite intellect has established that purpose and by his omnipotent and omnipresent power aims at and achieves that aim (teleological proof).

Third, the consciousness (*bewustzijn*) of all people includes the awareness (*besef*) of a higher being, above which nothing higher can be thought, and at the same time is thought by all as necessarily existing. If such a being did not exist, the highest, absolute, and most necessary thought would be an illusion and man would lose faith (*vertrouwen*) in the testimony of his consciousness (*bewustzijn*) (ontological proof).

Thereby the fourth proof is immediately added to this: [14] Man is not only a reasonable but also a moral being. He feels (*voelt*) in his conscience (*geweten*) as bound to a law that is high above him and that demands from him unconditional obedience. That law points to a holy and righteous lawgiver, who can deliver and destroy (moral proof).

To these four proofs are added two more, derived through the consensus of nations (*volken*) and from the history of humanity. It is a remarkable phenomenon that there are no nations (*volken*) without religion. Some have argued the contrary, but historical investigation has been increasingly unsuccessful; there are no atheist tribes or nations (*volken*). This phenomenon is of great significance, for the absolute universality shows the necessity of [religion] and thus puts forth one of two conclusions for us to adopt: either that the whole of humanity suffers from a foolish imagination on this point; or that the knowledge and the grace of God, although in corrupted forms, occurs in all peoples and is grounded on its existence.

Even so, considered in the light of Scripture, the history of humanity displays a plan and course that refers us to a supreme being who reigns over all things. Nevertheless, this observation is true: All sorts of objections and difficulties arise in the life of the individual as well as the life of the nations (*volken*). But it is remarkable that everyone who studies history consciously (*bewust*) or unconsciously (*onbewust*) begins their journey with the assumption that history is a guide through thought and design and focuses on the discovery of this thought. History and the contemplation of the past are founded on belief in the providence of God.[16]

6. The content of general revelation and the grace given it provides us with deep insight into the [15] great value it possesses for the world and humanity.[17] For God did not abandon his creation after the entrance of sin, but in Christ redeemed and restored it. He has not only blessed it with special grace, but he has also extended his common grace over the whole of creation's length and breadth: for the continued existence of the world and man; the glory of God's name over the whole earth; the revelation of his eternal power and divinity in the works of his hands (Rom. 1:19); the labor of man and the fertility of woman[18] (Gen. 3:19–20); the beginning of culture (Gen. 4:20–22); following the judgment of the flood, the Noahic covenant (Gen. 8:21–22); for the stability of the natural order (Gen. 8:22, Jer. 33:20, 25, etc.); the restoration of the blessing of creation (Gen. 9:1, 7); dominion over the animal world (Gen. 9:2); the prohibition against the murder of man (Gen. 9:5–6); for the spread of humanity over all the earth (Gen. 11:8, Deut. 32:8; Isa. 45:18; Acts 17:26); the fruitfulness of nature with food and the mirth of the heart (Matt. 5:45; Acts 14:16–17); and religion and morality (Rom. 1:19–20; 2:14–15). All these are due to common grace in connection and in service of special grace. In a word, "every good gift and perfect gift is from above, coming down from the Father of lights, with whom there is no variation or shadow due to change" (James 1:17).

However, we should not be guilty of overestimating or underestimating this general revelation. Earth is not hell, but it is also far from being heaven. Optimism is equally as one-sided as pessimism. Although there is much that is good and delightful in the world, evil casts its dark shadow everywhere. The earth is full of the loving kindness of the Lord, but it is often still a stage [16] of disaster and calamities; the history of humanity

---

16. The previous seven paragraphs are identical to paragraphs in *MD*, 30–32.

17. For more on the importance of general revelation, see *MD*, ch. 4, "The Value of General Revelation."

18. Given the Genesis citation, Bavinck is most likely referring here to the judgments rendered on Adam and Eve (which are bifurcated in that direction). Compared to his peers, Bavinck was forward-thinking regarding women's rights and, contra Kuyper, promoted suffrage in the Netherlands.

testifies to God's guidance, but it is, at the same time, a history of blood and tears, of injustice and misery. Think of the devastation in our Christian society that is daily caused by the sins of alcohol, prostitution, and crime. It gives you an account of the poverty and idleness, of the wickedness and anger, which dwells in the heart of man, even if it is covered under the cloak of civilization and decency. You will agree with the word of Scripture that the intention of the heart of man is evil from his youth (Gen. 8:21).

This very same judgment touches all the religions found in the human world. The sense (*besef*) of the divine and the seed of religion hidden therein are thanks to God's general revelation and redound as an unfathomable blessing to the human race. But the manner in which this religious sense (*besef*) within manifests itself in representations (*vorstellingen*) and affections (*aandoeningen*), and in outward acts of worship, is counterfeited and corrupted everywhere. Paul says that the Gentiles, although knowing God from his general revelation in nature, have not glorified him or given him thanks as God; but they have been frustrated in their thoughts, and their foolish hearts have been darkened (Rom. 1:21–23). Impartial historical research of the religions of the people (*volken*) has led to the same conclusion. One can veil the seriousness of this conclusion from the mind of man with the help of a false philosophy and multifarious forms of the elusive essence of religion. But the fact remains the same: In the long course of its civilization, humanity has not glorified God nor given thanks to God. In the first place, in all nations (*volken*), we find idolatry and the production of graven images [17]. Alongside this idolatry, then, are all sorts of false conceptions (*vorstellingen*) about humanity and the world, sanctification and sin, and about the present life and the life to come. Third, all religions distinguish themselves as religions separate from Christianity through the endeavor of the individual to acquire salvation through the effort of human strength. Idolatry is always accompanied by superstition in faith, fortune-telling (divination), and magic (witchcraft).

And the so-called larger religions—whereby we particularly think of the religions of Zarathustra in Persia (seventh century BC), of Confucius in China (sixth century BC), of Buddha in India (fifth century BC), and of Muhammad in Arabia (seventh century AD)—do not, at least in practice, provide an exception. Indubitably, in many ways, these religious founders were elevated above the superstitions they saw around them; yet they, even if they cut off some wild branches from false religions, have still not cut off the root of it.[19] Thus the words of Paul the apostle remain: that the world with all its wisdom has not known God (1 Cor. 1:21). "The light shines in the darkness, and the darkness has not overcome it" (John 1:5). "The Word [the Logos] was in the world, but the world has not known [*gekend*] him" (John 1:10).

General revelation awakens and nourishes the need for a special revelation. If there is to be salvation for mankind and the world, then general revelation illuminates its necessity. It is already entwined within this special revelation; it will be a work of redemption, an act of special grace. No people (*volk*) and no religion have been satisfied with the general revelation of God in nature and history. All of them felt the need for another, further disclosure of God than that which comes to them from nature.

---

19. For Bavinck's elaboration on this section, see *MD*, 48–50.

3

Revelation (Special)

7. [18] Through special revelation, in which God spoke to us first through the prophets and then through the Son God, he meets the need he himself aroused [in the human heart] (Heb. 1:1). This special revelation is always closely related to general [revelation], but it is nevertheless necessarily distinguished from it.[1] This distinction is particularly evident in the way it occurs, in the content it contains, and in the goal it seeks.

As far as the *manner* is concerned, this is not always one and the same; it is distinguished according to the means (*middelen*) by which God himself works in his special revelation and is called by various designations: appearing (*verschijnen*), revealing (*openbaren*), uncovering (*ontdekken*), making known (*bekend maken*), speaking (*spreken*), proclaiming (*verkondigen*), teaching (*onderrichten*), etc.[2] In many places in the Holy Scriptures (for example, Gen. 2:16, 18, 4:6f., 6:13f., 12:7, 13:14, etc.), it is simply said that the Lord appeared, spoke, said, commanded, etc., without regard to the way it happened, but little more is explained. Oher texts shed more light on this and enable us to distinguish between the two kinds of means (*middelen*) that God uses.

To the first kind of these belong all those means (*middelen*) that bear an objective (*voorwerpelijk*) character and through which God, as it were, comes from outside of man and appears to him and speaks to him.[3] This is then not to be understood in the general sense, in which he is revealed and speaks in all the works [19] of creation and providence (Ps. 29:3–9; 33:6,

1. "As a disclosure of the greatness of God's heart, special revelation far surpasses general revelation, which makes known to us the power of the mind. General revelation leads to special revelation, and special revelation points back to general revelation. The one calls for the other, and without it remains imperfect and unintelligible. Together they proclaim the manifold wisdom of God, which God has displayed in creation and redemption" (*PoR*, 25).

2. Bavinck addresses the *manner* of special revelation with its own chapter in *MD*, ch. 5.

3. Bavinck adds *voorwerpelijk* as an explanatory term to clarify *objectief.*

9); special revelation has a particular meaning. For example, God often appeared to Abraham, Moses, and the people of Israel on Mount Sinai, or above the tabernacle and the holy of holies, or in the clouds of smoke and fire as signs of his presence (Gen. 15:17; Exod. 3:2; 13:21; 19:9; Lev. 16:2; etc.). Or he also made known what he said to people by angels (Gen. 18:2; 32:1; Dan. 8:13; Zech. 1:9f.; Matt. 1:20; etc.); or in particular, by the angel of the covenant who bears the name of the Lord within himself (Exod. 23:21). Furthermore, he frequently worked by lots to declare his will amid Israel (Prov. 16:33) and from Urim and Thummim (Exod. 28:30). A few times, he spoke with an audible voice (Exod. 19:9; Deut. 4:33; 5:26; Matt. 3:17; 2 Pet. 1:17), or he himself wrote his law on the tablets of testimony (Exod. 31:18; 23:16).[4]

Also included in this group of the means of revelation are miracles, which take up a large and distinguished place in Scripture but in the present day are subject to fierce attacks from all sides. It is futile to defend the miracles of Scripture against those who have utterly rejected the worldview (*wereldbeschouwing*) of Scripture in the first place. For if God does not exist, as atheism and materialism teach; or if he does not have his own independent personal existence but is one essence with the world, as pantheism imagines; or if he withdrew from the world after creation and surrendered it to its own destiny, as deism puts forth; then it goes without saying that miracles are impossible. If the impossibility of miracles is established beforehand, then it is no longer necessary to argue about their reality [20].[5]

But Scripture presents a different idea of God, of the world, and also of the relationship that exists between them. It first teaches that God is a conscious (*bewust*), willing, and almighty being, who has called the entire world with all of its forces and laws into existence, yet he has not therefore absolutely exhausted his full power. He retains and possesses in himself an infinite fullness of life and power. There is nothing too wonderful for him (Gen. 18:14); for him, all things are possible (Matt. 19:26).[6] Moreover, [Scripture] regards the world as one great organic whole that includes the richest diversity of creatures, forces, and laws, and that no moment in time exists in itself but constantly lives and moves in God (Acts 17:28). Now if God with his omnipresent and almighty power in all times works through his creatures as his means (*middelen*), then how could he not then by that

4. This paragraph is identical to one in *MD*, 56.

5. This paragraph is identical to one in *MD*, 56–57.

6. Up until this point, this paragraph is identical to one in *MD*, 57.

same power work in a different way and by another means (*middelen*) distinct from the normal course of nature and history to be known to us? Miracles are not, therefore, a breaking from the laws of nature. For these occur within Scripture, even if it does not sum them up or formulate them, they are fully recognized; after all, the ordering of all of nature stands fixed according to the covenant of nature that God made with Noah (Gen. 8:22). But just as man with his intellect (*verstand*) and will subdues the earth and through his cultivation governs nature, so God has the power to make this created world subservient to the execution of his council. Miracles prove that *the Lord* is God, not the world.

All these objective means of revelation reach their high point (*hoogtepunt*) and have their center (*centrum*) in the person of Christ, who is the supreme image of God (John 14:9), the fully expressed Word of God (John 1:14). This is not only through the miracles, which he and later [21] his apostles did, but especially on account of the redemptive miracles in his own person (conception, life, death, resurrection, ascension, etc.)—the absolute miracle, the miracle of history.

With this first kind of means (*middelen*), which are all objective (*voorwerpelijk*) and external, comes a second group, which bears a more subjective (*onderwerpelijk*) character and includes all the modes of revelation, of which God operates *in* man himself.

The first place is occupied by the unique revelation that fell to Moses as the mediator of the Old Testament. This is described as one in which the Lord spoke to Moses, face to face like a man speaks to his friend (Exod. 33:11). Moses took an entirely different place in the Old Testament and also was exalted high above all of the prophets. God spoke to him, not through means (*middel*) of a vision or in obscure words, but by word of mouth; he did not see the Lord in a vision, but he saw his likeness, his form, not his being or his face, but still the afterglow of the glory of God passed before his eyes (Num. 12:8; Exod. 33:18–23).

Furthermore, among these means (*middelen*) of revelation is the dream (Num. 12:6; Deut. 13:1–6). A vision or hallucination is a condition wherein the physical eye is closed to the outside world and the eye of the soul is opened to the view of divine things (Num. 12:6; Deut. 13:1–6)—especially the inspiration or voice of God's Spirit in human consciousness (*bewustzijn*) (Num. 11:25–29; 2 Sam. 23:2; Matt. 16:17; Acts 8:29; 1 Cor. 2:12; 2 Pet. 1:21). This last revelation through means (*middel*) of a voice in the human consciousness (*bewustzijn*) also occurs several times in the Old Testament, but there it is always represented as an activity of the Holy Spirit, who comes from [22] above and for a moment overcomes a prophet. But in the New Testament, when the Holy Spirit is poured out, inspiration not only becomes a more common form of revelation but also takes on a more organic and enduring character.

These two kinds of means of revelation can be summarized under the names of "manifestation" and "inspiration." However, it must be remembered that the content of manifestation does not entirely and only exist in deeds but is also in thought and words. Also, one must not lose sight that the meaning of inspiration here is distinguished from the activity of the Holy Spirit, which prophets and apostles enjoyed in the inscripturation of revelation (inspiration or *theopneustie* of the Holy Scriptures), as well as from the internal illumination (*illuminatie*), which all believers possess.[7]

8. The *content* of special revelation is best known to us through a short overview of its history.[8] It did not begin with Abraham first, but it took its inception immediately after the Fall (Gen. 3:15) and then flowed for a time with general revelation, as it were, in one stream. Yet already division came about in this emerging humanity (Cain and Abel, Cainites and Sethites), and this separation became absolutely necessary when special revelation threatened to be lost through the mixing of the church (*kerk*) and the world.[9] Even after the judgment of the flood and the division of humanity, idolatry and superstition increased hand in hand (Gen. 15:16; 18:1f.; Exod. 18:9–12; Josh. 24:2, 14–15; etc.).

In order for humanity now not to sink into superstition and iniquity, nor to break to the covenant of nature with Noah and for God's purpose with humanity not to be thwarted, God took a different path with [23] Abraham. He could not destroy the human race again in a flood; but he could allow the other nations (*volken*) to walk in their own ways, [while] establishing a covenant with one person [Abraham]; and in that one person with one people (*volk*); and by means of that covenant, extend and fulfill his promise; and when the fulfillment had come, it would expand again to all

7. The previous four paragraphs have nearly identical counterparts in *MD*, 60–61, apart from a slight difference in the first of the four paragraphs.

8. Bavinck provides a separate chapter (ch. 6) for the content of special revelation in *MD*.

9. It is interesting that Bavinck describes the fledgling community of the faithful (the line of Seth) as the church (*kerk*). This is in line with his general understanding of God's promises extending to include Israel (see also pp. 99–100).

of humanity [through Jesus].[10] With Abraham, therefore, a new age in the history of revelation began.

The revelation in this period is characterized in this way: God made a covenant with Abraham, with him and his seed, to be *their* God. The heart and center (*kern*) of the religion of the Old Testament lies not therefore in so-called monotheism, in the recognition of one God who is not only omnipotent but also righteous and holy, although this certainly forms a part of Israel's religion. Its essence lies in the one great promise that encompasses every other act of salvation: "I will be your God and you will be my people" (Gen. 12:1–3; 13:14–17; 15:1f.; 15:17–21; 17:1f.; 18:10; 22:17–19). This promise extends through the people (*volk*) of Israel to Christ, and in Christ to all of humanity and to the entire world. Not law but gospel, not demand but promise is the center (*kern*) of revelation, even in the days of the old covenant, to which man's part is to respond in faith and in the walk of faith (Gen. 17:1), just as Paul in Romans 4 and Galatians 3 understood the revelation of God to Abraham.

The promise of the covenant of grace to Abraham remains the content of all subsequent revelations of God in the Old Testament, although naturally it is elaborated and developed therein. Another era was entered with the covenant-making at Sinai and then the setting-up of a legal system given by God. But the promise, which was previously made to Abraham, was by no means annulled by this later [24] lawgiving (Gal. 3:15f). The law now comes to the promise and is added to it, but it was not originally joined to it. Following the promise, many years elapsed before the law was published. And when it came to the promise, it carried a provisional, momentary character. While the promise of the covenant of grace is eternal, the law endured only until the time when the proper seed of Abraham—namely, the Christ—would appear to those to whom the promise was substantively made and must receive the contents of the promise and dispense them (Rom. 5:20; Gal. 3:17–19).

The reason, however, that God added the law for a time to the promise was, according to Paul, because of transgressions (Gal. 3:19): that is, not only to prohibit and inhibit sin but also to make much of it, and to reveal sin, every sin—for instance, covetousness (Rom. 7:7)—as a violation of a positive law. By doing so, the law only increasingly highlighted the necessity of the promise. It proved in the history of Israel—which continually fell away and was guilty of all sorts of transgressions—that if

10. Up until here, this paragraph is nearly identical with one in *MD*, 62–63.

there could be justification of a sinner, then a righteousness apart from their works would have to be applied (Gal. 3:11); namely, a righteousness of faith. Indeed, far from being against the promise, the law served as a suitable means (*middel*) in God's hands to bring the promise ever closer to its fulfillment. The law took Israel into custody as a prisoner who lacked the freedom of movement. As a "pedagogue," it took Israel by the hand, accompanied them, and did not let them go for a moment. As a guardian and caregiver, it kept Israel under its supervision, so that they would learn to know and love the promise in its necessity and glory. Without the [25] law, so to speak, nothing would have come of the promise and its fulfillment. Then Israel would soon have sunk into paganism and lost both the revelation of God with its promise and their own religion and place among the nations (*volken*). But now the law has kept Israel protected, isolated, preserved for a long time in their solitude, and therefore created and marked out a circle in which God kept his revelation; that is, he kept his promise pure—extending, developing, and increasing it to bring it closer to its fulfillment. The law served to fulfill the promise. It placed everything under the wrath of God and under the sentence of death, and it decreed that all are under sin, so that the promise given to Abraham and fulfilled in Christ would be given to all believers and all would receive the adoption of children (Gal. 3:21–4:7).[11]

Therefore, the whole of revelation from the Old Testament results in Christ, not as a new law or teaching or institution but in the person of Christ. A *man* is the perfect revelation of God; the Son of Man is also the special, only begotten Son of God. Old and New Testament do not stand side by side as law and gospel, but together they relate as promise and fulfillment (Acts 13:12; Rom. 1:2), as shadow and body (Col. 2:17), as a picture and reality (Heb. 10:1), as shaken and unshaken things (Heb. 12:27), as obligation and freedom (Rom. 8:15; Gal. 4). And because Christ was the true content (*inhoud*) of Old Testament revelation (John 5:39; 1 Pet. 1:11; Rev. 19:10), he is also the keystone (*sluitsteen*) and crown in the allocation of the dispensation of the new covenant. He is the fulfillment of the law and all righteousness (Matt. 3:15; 5:17); all promises of the whole covenant, which is now confirmed in his blood (Matt. 26:28), are yea and amen in him (2 Cor. 1:20). The [26] people (*volk*) of Israel themselves—with their history, their offices and institutions, their temple and altar, their sacrifices and

11. For an expansion of the role of the law's relationship to promise, see *MD*, 68–70.

ceremonies, and their prophecy, psalmody, and wisdom teachings—attain in him their destiny and purpose. Christ is the fulfillment of all of this: first in his person and appearance, and then in his words and deeds; in his birth and life, in his death and resurrection, in his ascension and session at the right hand of God.

Since he has therefore appeared and accomplished his work, the revelation of God can no longer be supplemented or increased; it can only, through apostolic testimony in the Scripture, be professed and made the possession of all humanity. While everything in the Old Testament was in preparation for Christ, everything now stems from him. Christ is the turning point (*keerpunt*) of time.[12] The promise made to Abraham extends now out to all nations (*volken*).

9. At present, it is not necessary to say much more about the purpose of special revelation; it is evident enough from its content. Whereas general revelation by itself is able to restrain sin, special revelation must—which has Christ with the fullness of grace and truth as its content—utterly destroy sin in a single person, in humanity, and in the whole world, along with all the terrible consequences of misery and death, which sin drags after it. Thus far, the history of humanity presently has certainly not advanced. But we live in the dispensation of the fullness of time, in which everything is gathered together under Christ as head (Eph. 1:10; 2:14–15), and "according to his promise we are waiting for new heavens and a new earth in which righteousness dwells" (2 Pet. 3:13). The promise of the covenant of grace was from the beginning: "I will be your God, and you will be my people." That promise will be fulfilled [27] continually, until it reaches its perfection in the new Jerusalem (Rev. 21:3). Thus the victory over sin and death, the complete redemption of the world and humanity, the glory of God's unfathomable mercy and of his manifold wisdom is the glorious purpose of his special revelation.

---

12. Bavinck also refers to Christ as the *keerpunt* of time in "The Science of Holy Theology," in *On Theology*: "Or to put it differently, in the ages before Christ everything was being prepared for Christ. The ages were leading toward him, who is the turning point of the times." See also *MD*, 82.

4

Holy Scripture

10. [28] Concerning revelation, both general and special, we are informed by Holy Scripture.

It is important presently to clearly see the distinction and connection that exist between revelation and Scripture. On the one hand, there is considerable difference between the two. Sometimes, revelation arrived a long time before it was written down (*beshrijving*). Before Moses, for example, there was revelation but there was no mention of Scripture yet. This revelation also often contained much more than was recorded later in writing; the books of the prophets—for example, Amos—are only a brief summary of what they spoke to their contemporaries. Many prophets in the Old Testament and many apostles in the New Testament, who were all instruments of special revelation, left behind nothing in writing; and even Jesus, whom we are expressly told performed many other signs—so many that if they were each individually described, the world itself could not contain the books that would be written (John 20:30; 21:25). On the contrary, God may reveal something to his prophets and apostles in the course of writing that they themselves did not know beforehand and therefore could not previously have preached to others. For example, that is at least in part the case with the revelation John received on Patmos concerning the future.[1]

1. Bavinck's conception of revelation is both prior to and broader than Scripture. At first glance, this paragraph seems to present contradictory information if this idea is not maintained. We have, on the one hand, revelation that is not recorded in Scripture and, on the other hand, revelation that is given in Scripture. For the first, he mentions apostles and prophets who "left behind nothing in writing" yet were instruments of revelation. We might think of the apostle Barnabas and his wide-spanning public ministry across the ancient world. Bavinck contests here that Barnabas's ministry (of which we have little knowledge two thousand years later) was a form of revelation. For the second, in the revelation given in Scripture, we have something distinct from this" It is "special" revelation, in that it is knowledge of God that may not have been delivered yet to God's people, at least not in this form. Therefore, Scripture is not synonymous with revelation, but it is a form of revelation.

[29] Therefore, Scripture is not revelation itself but its *record* (*beschrijving*), a document (*oorkonde*) from which it can be known. However, when one calls Scripture the written document of revelation, one must still be aware of another error—namely, there are some who not only distinguish revelation and Scripture, but they also separate and disconnect each from the other. They acknowledge truly, then, that God has worked in a special way in revelation prior to Scripture, but they further present it as if the writing of this revelation was left entirely to the people themselves and apart from God's special providence. Scripture is then still a record of revelation but an accidental, fallible one; so that with great effort we might learn from Scripture, whether it belongs to special revelation or not. For such an approach, one makes a great distinction between the word of God and Holy Scripture and prefers to use the expression that Holy Scripture is not the word of God but that the word of God is *contained* in the Holy Scripture.

This idea (*voorstelling*) is itself very unlikely. For in addition to interpreting the relationship between word and writing (*shrift*) too mechanically, it also forgets that when God wanted to give a special revelation—which as we saw in the previous paragraph is in the seed of Abraham, that is in Christ, intended for all humanity—he also had to take special steps to preserve and make that revelation generally available by means of writing. To this end, writing also renders its service to the public. The written word is distinguished from the spoken, in that it does not die in the air but remains; it is not falsified like oral tradition but preserves its purity; and it is not limited in its scope to a few who [30] hear it, but rather it can extend to all peoples and into all times. Writing preserves the spoken word, frees it from falsification, and makes it public.

But we no longer need to stand by this human reasoning. The idea that special revelation is from God but that the Scriptures would have come about outside of his special care is, according to the testimony of Holy Scripture itself, out of bounds. It repeatedly and emphatically declares that *Scripture* is the word of God. Scripture has been distinguished from the preceding revelation, but it is not separate from it. It is not a human, accidental, arbitrary, addendum to revelation, but is itself an element of revelation. It is the seal (*afsluiting*) and the completion (*voltooïing*), the corner (*hoek*) and the keystone (*sluitsteen*) of it.

11. In order to see this, one only has to pay attention to the following clear testimonies that are contained in Scripture.

First, God often instructs the prophets to communicate the revelation they received, not only orally but also to record it in writing. In Exodus 17:14, Moses receives the command from the Lord to write down the story of the battle and victory over Amalek—which for Israel was of great significance—to be memorialized in the book of the redeeming work of God. In Exodus 24:3–4, 7, and 34:27, he is commanded to write down the statues and laws according to which God had made his covenant with Israel. And when Israel finished its wanderings in the wilderness and arrived opposite Jericho in the fields of Moab, it is explicitly said that Moses wrote down the journeys of the children of Israel to the mouth (*naar den mond*), that is, by the commandment of the Lord (Num. 33:2).[2] Certainly also [31] the song Moses sings in Deuteronomy 32, through the instruction of the Lord, must be written down and placed in the mouths of the children of Israel, that it may later be a witness against them in days of apostasy (Deut. 31:19, 22). Such commands to write down received revelation also appear later in the prophets (Isa. 8:1; 30:8; Jer. 25:13; 30:2; 36:2, 27–32; Ezek. 24:2; Dan. 12:4; Hab. 2:2). Even if these commands only apply to a small portion of the Holy Scriptures, they nevertheless indicate that God—who strongly demands that his words should not be added to or done away with (Deut. 4:2; 12:31; Prov. 30:6)—likewise extends his special care to the written record of his revelation.

In the second place, Moses and the prophets were well aware that they were not only speaking but also writing the word of God. Thus Moses is not only called in a special way to be a guide for the people (*volk*) of Israel (Exod. 3), but the Lord also spoke to him face to face like a man with his friend (Exod. 33:11) and made known to him all his laws and statutes. Every time and in every particular law, this introductory expression is found: And the Lord spoke, or the Lord said to Moses (Exod. 6:1, 9, 12, etc.). The whole law is ascribed to God in the books of Moses and throughout the whole of Scripture. He made his word known to Jacob, to Israel his statutes and judgments; so, he has not left his people (*volk*) without knowledge of his laws (Pss. 103:7; 147:19, 20. Likewise, the prophets were not only aware that they were called by the Lord (1 Sam. 3; Isa. 6; Jer. 1; Ezek. 1–3; Amos 3:7–8; 7:15) and received their revelation from him (Isa. 5:9, 6:9, 22:14, 28:22; Jer. 1:9, 3:6, 20:7–9; Ezek. 3:16, 26–27; Amos 3:8; etc.), [32], they were also convicted by what Amos said: "For the Lord God does nothing without

2. The phrase "*naar den mond*" is a direct quote from the Dutch Statenvertaling edition of the Bible, in which Num. 33:2 reads, "En Mozes schreef hun uittochten, naar hun reizen, *naar den mond* des HEEREN; en dit zijn hun reizen, naar hun uittochten."

revealing his secret to his servants the prophets" (Amos 3:7; cf. Gen. 18:17). They also knew that they did not write their own word but proclaimed the Lord's word; like the law of Moses always introduced his specific prophecies with the formula: Thus says the Lord, or the word of the Lord came to me, or the vision, the word (the voice of God), the burden of the Lord (Isa. 1:1; 2:1; 8:1; 13:1; Jer. 1:2, 4, 11; 2:1; 23:33; Ezek. 1:1; 2:1; 3:1; Dan. 7:1; Amos 1:3, 6, 9; etc.).[3]

Third comes the testimony of the New Testament. Jesus and the apostles repeatedly, when quoting the Old Testament, spoke under the name of Moses, Isaiah, David, or Daniel (Matt. 8:4; 15:7; 22:43; 24:15). But no less often did they use the formula: it is written (Matt. 4:4), or Scripture says (John 7:38), or God says (Luke 12:20), or the Holy Spirit says (Heb. 3:7), etc.[4] By this manner of quotation, they clearly indicated that the Scriptures of the old covenant, although composed of different parts and originating from different writers, nevertheless constitutes one organic whole, which in its written form also has God as its author. Jesus and the apostles expressed this conviction not only indirectly but also directly in clear terms. Jesus declared that the Scriptures cannot be broken—that is, separated. It cannot be stripped of its authority (John 10:35), and he did not personally come to abolish the law and the prophets, but to fulfill them (Matt. 5:17; Luke 24:44).[5] The apostle Peter says that the prophetic word is a firm and reliable a light upon our path. That is why, since the prophecy—which is contained in the Scriptures of the Old Testament—is not based on a prophecy and prediction of the future that was developed by the prophets themselves. [33] Indeed, prophecy in former times was not produced by the will of a man; moved by the Holy Spirit, the holy people of God spoke (2 Pet. 1:19–21; cf. 1 Pet. 1:10–12). In the same sense, Paul states that the Holy Scriptures,

---

3. Absent from Bavinck's citations is Jer. 23:33, where the prophet is asked if the Lord has burdened him: "When one of this people, or a prophet asks you, 'What prophecy has the LORD burdened you with now?' You must reply, 'You are the burden! The LORD says he will abandon you!'"

4. Bavinck uses Matt. 12:26 as evidence for his claim that "God says," but this verse reads: "And if Satan casts out Satan, he is divided against himself. How then will his Kingdom stand?" In principle, Bavinck is correct; however, since the writers of the New Testament do in several places refer to Scripture as "God says," we have replaced the Matt. 12:26 with Luke 12:20.

5. Although Bavinck cites Luke 16:27, this does not seem to be the correct passage to which he is alluding. We have therefore replaced it with the correct citation of Luke 24:44.

which together compose the Old Testament, are able to make us wise unto salvation; indeed, if we search and read them by faith—that is, in Christ Jesus. For all Scripture, which is included in those Holy Scriptures, is inspired (*ingegeven*) by God (*theopneustos*, breathed out by God, breathed through him), and for that reason is also profitable for teaching, for reproof (conviction and discipline), for correction, and for training in righteousness (2 Tim. 3:15–16).

Finally, and fourthly, concerning the Scriptures of the New Testament, Jesus himself refrained from writing; rather he chose, called, and trained his apostles to act as his *witnesses* (*getuigen*) in the midst of the world, especially after his departure (Matt. 10:1; Mark 3:13; Luke 6:13; 9:1; John 6:70). He equipped them with special gifts and powers (Matt. 10:1, 9; Mark 16:15f; Acts 2:43; 5:12; Rom. 15:19; Heb. 2:4), particularly with the Holy Spirit, who would remind them of all that Jesus told them (John 14:26); he will also proclaim to them the things to come and therefore guide them into all truth (John 16:13). So then, it is not really the apostles themselves who witness to Christ, but it is the Holy Spirit who acts in and through them as Jesus' witness (John 15:26–27). Just as the Son came to glorify the Father (John 17:4), so the Holy Spirit came to glorify the Son; therefore, everything he proclaims and does, he receives from the Son (John 16:14).

The apostles did not bring this testimony of Christ [34] solely to their people (*volks*) and contemporaries in Jerusalem, Judea, and Samaria, but to all creation and to the ends of the earth (Matt. 28:19; Mark 16:15; Acts 1:8). This mandate to go out to the whole world also contained, not explicitly but implicitly, the command to testify of Jesus in writing. But if the promise made to Abraham was to come to mankind in Christ, then the gospel could not reach this end unless it was subsequently also written down and preserved for all ages and extended to all nations (*volken*). The apostles in their missionary work were also guided by the Holy Spirit, that they took hold of the pen themselves, and also testified through their Gospels and letters of the fullness of the grace and truth that appeared in Christ. Not only in their oral preaching but also in their writings, they were consciously (*welbewust*) concerned with unfolding the truth that God revealed in Christ and made known to them by his Spirit.

Matthew writes the book of generations—that is, the story of Jesus Christ, the Son of David (Matt. 1:1). [In his Gospel,] Mark displays how the gospel (*evangelie*) begins with Jesus Christ, the Son of God, and takes the origin of his narration from him (Mark 1:1). Luke, after diligent investigation and through detailed narrative, writes to provide Theophilus with assurance about the things that, in the circle of believers, were absolutely certain on the grounds of the testimony of the apostles (Luke 1:1–4). John writes his Gospel so that we believe that Jesus is the Christ, the Son of God, and that by believing we may have life in his name (John 20:31). He says likewise in his first letter that he proclaims that which he has seen, heard, beheld, and touched with his hands concerning the Word of life, that we may have fellowship with the apostles, and that this [35] fellowship is also with the Father and with his Son Jesus Christ (1 John 1:1–3). Paul is convinced that he is not only called to be an apostle by Jesus Christ (Gal. 1:1) and has received the gospel from him through revelation (Gal. 1:12; Eph. 3:2–8; 1 Tim. 1:12), but also that he proclaims the word of God by his mouth and pen (1 Thess. 2:13; 2 Thess. 2:15; 3:14; 1 Cor. 2:4, 10–13; 2 Cor. 2:17), so that anyone who preaches another gospel is accursed (Gal. 1:8). And just as all the apostles attach to the acceptance or rejection of their word the eternal life or eternal death of man, so the apostle John in the last chapter of his Revelation threatens with severe judgment anyone who appends or deducts from the words of the prophecy of this book (Rev. 22:18–19).

12. The special activity of the Holy Spirit by which revelation is written down is usually indicated by the name of inspiration (*ingeving*) (inspiration, *theopneustie*) (2 Tim. 3:16). What this consists of becomes clearer by comparing it with nature and through further explanations in Scripture. In general, a person is susceptible to have thoughts of others in his consciousness (*bewustzijn*) and be guided by others in his thinking; all education and training is based on this susceptibility, and all knowledge (*kennis*) and science (*wetenschap*). Usually, this communication of thoughts from others to us takes place by means of signs (*teekenen*) or gestures, spoken or written words. On our part, these thoughts are then incorporated with our consciousness (*bewustheid*) and intention (*opzet*), often also with great exertion recorded in our ideas (*voorstellen*) and thinking (*denken*) and made an element of our inner life (*zieleleven*). But the phenomena of hypnotism, the suggestion, etc., prove that without any work on our part, ideas (*vorstellingen*) and thoughts (*gedachten*) can be brought [36] into our consciousness (*bewustzijn*), and like a forceful ruler, influence our will and actions. In this way, people can be reduced to will-less tools, which simply carry out what others (the hypnotist) command of them. Scripture and experience, likewise, teach that man is susceptible to influences and workings of evil spirits, so that he no longer speaks and acts as himself but is controlled in his thinking and doing by the evil spirit: in Mark 1:24, for example, the

unclean spirit who speaks through the possessed [man] recognizes Jesus as the Holy One of God.[6]

Another phenomenon (*verschijnsel*) that can serve the purpose of clarifying the inspiration (*ingeving*) of the Holy Spirit, is the so-called inspiration (*inspiratie*) among artists. All the great thinkers and poets have learned by experience that the best and most beautiful that they have delivered are not on account of their own efforts but to sudden striking thoughts. Naturally, such an experience does not rule out the previous research and reflection; genius does not make effort and diligence superfluous. Although study as a rule is indispensable for gaining such experiences, they are not the logical conclusion or the ripe fruit of it. In the genius there is always a mysterious force that is not susceptible to calculation. Nietzsche wrote in a letter to his sister:

> You cannot imagine the violence of such creations; one is full of passionate zeal, delight and tension, one hears and sees nothing, one takes. The ideas fall as lightning. Everything happens involuntarily to the highest degree, a feeling of freedom (*vrijheidsgevoel*) as in a tempest, of independence (*onafhankelijkheid*), of power, of divinity (*goddelijkheid*); that is my experience of inspiration.[7]

---

6. The previous thirteen paragraphs are nearly identical to those in *MD*, 83–89.

7. This paragraph is also found in *MD*, 89, but is split into two paragraphs. Quote from Friedrich Nietzsche, *The Complete Works of Friedrich Nietzsche*, vol. 11, ed. Oscar Levy and Robert Guppy (New York: The Macmillan Company, 1914), xxi-xxiii. Bavinck condenses the original quote, which is in a letter from Friedrich to his sister Elizabeth Förster-Nietzsche. Below is Elizabeth's framing of the quote:

> [Friedrich] says in a letter to me: "You can have no idea of the vehemence of such composition," and in "Ecce Homo" (Autumn 1888) he describes as follows with passionate enthusiasm the incomparable mood in which he created Zarathustra:

> "Has anyone at the end of the nineteenth century any distinct notion of what poets of a stronger age understood by the word *inspiration*? If not, I will describe it. If one had the smallest vestige of superstition in one, it would hardly be possible to set aside completely the idea that one is the mere incarnation, mouthpiece or medium of an almighty power. The idea of revelation in the sense that something becomes suddenly visible and audible with indescribable certainty and accuracy, which profoundly convulses and upsets one—describes simple the matter of fact. One hears—one does not seek; one takes—one does not ask who gives: a thought suddenly flashes up like lightning, it comes with necessity, unhesitatingly—I never had any choice in the matter. There is an ecstasy such that the immense strain of it is sometimes relaxed by a flood of tears, along with which one's steps either rush or involuntarily lag, alternately.

When such phenomena (*verschijnselen*) already occur in the ordinary life of people or artists [37], there is no basis for combating the influence of God on the thinking (*denken*) and willing (*willen*) of his creatures. Yet God, by his Spirit, inhabits all creation (Gen. 1:3; Pss. 33:6; 104:30) and particularly man, who is made alive by the Spirit of God and quickened by the breath of the Almighty (Job 33:4; Ps. 139:1–16f.). "In him we live and move and have our being" (Acts 17:28). Thinking, willing, and acting, also in man's sinful ways, stands under the dominion of God; nothing happens outside his foreknowledge and counsel (Eph. 1:11). The king's heart is a stream of water in the hand of the Lord; he turns it wherever he will (Prov. 21:1). He weighs the hearts and the plans of mankind (Prov. 5:21; 16:9; 19:21; 21:2). In a different and much more intimate way, God lives by his Spirit in the heart of his children; by that Spirit, he brings them to the confession of Christ as Lord (1 Cor. 12:3), he causes them to know (*kennen*) the things that have been given to them (1 Cor. 2:12; 1 John 2:20; 3:24; 4:6–13), he imparts to them gifts of wisdom and knowledge (*kennis*) (1 Cor. 12:8), and he works in them both willing and working, according to his good pleasure (Phil. 2:13).

All these actions of God's Spirit in the world and in the congregation are not identical with the inspiration (*ingeving*) that came to the prophets and

---

There is the feeling that one is completely out of hand, with the very distinct consciousness of an endless number of fine thrills and quivering to the very toes; there is a depth of happiness in which the painfullest and gloomiest do not operate as antitheses, but as conditioned, as demanded in the sense of necessary shades of color in such an overflow of light. There is an instinct for rhythmic relations which embraces wide areas of forms (length, the need of a wide-embracing rhythm, is almost the measure of the force of an inspiration, a sort of counterpart to its pressure and tension). Everything happens quite involuntarily, as if in a tempestuous outburst of freedom, of absoluteness, of power and divinity. The involuntariness of the figures and similes is the most remarkable thing; one loses all perception of what constitutes the figure and what constitutes the simile; everything seems to present itself as the readiest, the correctest and the simplest means of expression. It actually seems to use one of Zarathustra's own phrases, as if all things came unto one, and would fain be similes: 'Here do all things come caressingly to thy talk and flatter thee, for they want to ride upon thy back. On every simile dost thou here ride to every truth. Here fly open unto thee all being's words and word-cabinets; here all being wanteth to become words, here all becoming wanteth to learn of thee how to talk.' This is *my* experience of inspiration. I do not doubt that one would have to go back thousands of years in order to find some one who could say to me: It is mine also!"

apostles but can still serve to clarify and explain. If not only in name, but indeed and in truth, the Spirit of God dwells and works in every creature; if that same Spirit dwells in a special sense in God's children, then all the reasons for that peculiar activity, which are indicated by the name of inspiration (*inspiratie*), should not be considered impossible or unlikely. But then again, it is necessary to see the distinction between the working of God's Spirit in the world and the church and that which is in the prophets and apostles. [38] This distinction especially comes to light when we compare Romans 8:14 with 2 Peter 1:21. In the first place, Paul says that many who are *led* (*geleid*) by the Spirit of God are children of God; but Peter declares in the cited text, that the holy men of God—namely, the prophets—were *carried along* (*gedreven*) by the Holy Spirit and thereby produced prophecy. The leading of the Spirit is the portion of all believers and consists in an illumination (*verlichting*) of the mind (*verstands*) and a reign and control of the will and affections (*genegenheden*), by which they receive knowledge, desire, and strength to do that which is pleasing to God. But the carrying of the Holy Spirit was given only to the prophets and apostles and consisted in an encouragement and admonition to make known to the people the revelation of the counsel of God.

The character of the inspiration (*ingeving*) is further determined through the frequently occurring formula: that which is written in the Old Testament is spoken *from* the Lord *by* (through means of) the prophet (Matt. 1:22; 2:15, 17, 23; 3:3; 4:14, etc.). In Greek, a preposition is used with "Lord" that denotes him as the origin (*oorsprong*) of that which is spoken; but the preposition used by the prophets indicates that they are the means (*middelen*), the *organs*, by which God has spoken. This is even more pronounced when it is said that God spoke *by the mouth* of his prophets (Luke 1:70; Acts 1:16; 3:18; 4:25). The doctrine, which Scripture gives us, then, is that God or his Spirit is the actual spokesman or speaker of his word. Nevertheless, he speaks by his prophets and apostles who served as his organs.

We would, however, entirely misunderstand the Scriptures if from this idea (*vorstelling*) we concluded that the prophets and apostles had been unaware and unwilling (*bewust -en willooze*) organs in the hand of the Holy Spirit, only serving as a mouthpiece. [39] For not only does God always honor his own work and never manipulates his reasonable creatures, as if they were irrational beings, but the Holy Scripture also decisively protests this "mechanical" conception of inspiration. After all, although the prophets were carried along by the Holy Spirit, they *themselves* also spoke (2 Pet. 1:21). The words they have written down are also quoted several times as *their* own words (Matt. 22:43, 45; John 1:23; 5:46; Rom. 10:20; etc.). Usually they are separated, prepared, and qualified for the office of prophet or apostle (Jer. 1:5; Acts 7:22; Gal. 1:15). Just as in the receiving, so they remain also in the writing down of revelation entirely conscious (*bewust*) of themselves. Their own activity is not suffocated by the Spirit but comforted, empowered, and purified. They themselves are diligent in the investigation (Luke 1:3). They contemplate and remember the revelation, which they received in former times (John 14:26; 1 John 1:1–3). They make use of historical sources (Num. 21:14; Josh. 10:13, etc.). They find, for example, the psalmists in their own experiences the material for their songs; and in all the writings, from which the Bible is composed, come the particular aptitude and character, the particular development and upbringing, and the particular language and style of the many writers. The study of Scripture teaches us not only the one word of God but also the various individuals who wrote the Bible. What a difference there is between the books of the Kings and those of the Chronicles, between Isaiah and Jeremiah, between Matthew and Luke, between John and Peter and Paul![8]

Here too, as in all of God's works, out of unity emerges diversity and from diversity emerges unity. If God has spoken to us through the prophets and apostles, then he has engaged their whole personality, [40] which he himself formed, to be taken into his service as a self-conscious (*zelfbewust*) and self-acting (*zelfwerkzaam*) organ of his inspiration (*inspiratie*). This inspiration (*inspiratie*), therefore, does not bear a mechanical character but rather an "organic" one.[9] This does not prohibit the investigation into the origin of the collection of the biblical books; rather, it arouses and insists on it according to the text and from the sense of Scripture. That is why early in the Christian church, a rich theological science (*theologische wetenschap*) arose.

13. On this inspiration of Scripture rests the properties that were ascribed primarily through the Reformation, in opposition to Romanism and the Anabaptists. The former departs from Protestants at various points in the doctrine of Scripture. In addition to including in the Bible the apocryphal books of the Old Testament, they teach that the authority of Scripture is not founded on its own testimony but on that of the church; that Scrip-

---

8. The previous four paragraphs are identical to those in *MD*, 89–90.

9. Up until this point, this paragraph is identical to one in *MD*, 90. This paragraph is missing from the Zylstra's translation of *MD*. (See Bavinck, *The Wonderful Works of God*, 87.)

ture is not necessary, only useful, because God has entrusted his truth to the church and gave it an infallible magisterium in the pope; that Scripture is opaque and can only be interpreted infallibly by the church and therefore must be withheld from the layman, other than with the permission from the ecclesiastical authorities; and that the Scripture is finally not perfect and sufficient but requires supplements from tradition. In the same way, the Anabaptists and many related movements also shift the center of gravity (*zwaartepunt*) from Scripture to the congregation—now, not as with Rome into the institutional church, but more mystically in the individual or collection of believers; the inner (*inwendig*) word, spoken by God's Spirit in their hearts, is then exalted above the external (*uitwendig*) word written in the Bible, which is then referred to as a dead letter.

On the other hand, the Reformation attributed to Scripture the [41] four properties of authority, necessity, clarity, and sufficiency or perfection. The first property suggested that Scripture did not derive its authority from the church but from itself, and that it should be believed (*autopistie*).[10] Scripture does not rest on the church but rather the church on Scripture (Isa. 8:20; John 5:39; Eph. 2:19–21). The property of necessity indicated that the tradition cannot be kept pure in a wandering and lying world, but only the written word can survive unadulterated (2 Tim. 3:16). By clarity it was meant that the truth, the knowledge (*kennis*) of which was necessary for salvation, is presented so simply and comprehensibly in Scripture that anyone who is earnest can easily find it without guidance from a church or priest (Ps. 119:105, 130; John 5:39; Acts 17:11). In the property of sufficiency, it was said that special revelation appeared fully in the person of Christ and was described in Scripture and therefore did not require any further addition by mankind and fallible traditions (Isa. 29:13; Matt. 15:4–9; 1 Cor. 4:6).[11]

10. Here, Bavinck adds *autopistie*.

11. These final two paragraphs are unique to *Handleiding*.

5

Scripture and Confession

[42] 14. There was in the time of the apostles and thereafter no absence of difference concerning the essence of Christianity and the relationship in which it stood to Judaism and paganism. Nevertheless, more astonishing is the unanimity with which Scripture was accepted as the word of God in the whole Christian church.

This applies in the first place to the Old Testament. In the teaching of Jesus and the apostles, it was always mentioned and drawn upon. Surreptitiously, and as if it were the most natural thing in the world, with the teachings of Jesus and the apostles, the Old Testament of the Jewish church passed into the Christian congregation. The gospel brought with it the Old Testament, and it could not have been adopted and acknowledged without this. For the gospel is always the fulfillment of the promises of the Old Testament and without it dangles in the air; and the Old Testament is the pedestal on which the gospel rests, the root from which it grows. As soon as the gospel found its way somewhere, the Scriptures of the Old Testament were accepted as the word of God with it and therein at the same time without any objection. The New Testament community, therefore, did not exist for a moment without a Bible; from the very beginning, it was in possession of the Law, the Psalms, and the Prophets.

Soon came the writings of the apostles. In part, these writings—such as the [43] Gospels and the general epistles—were intended for the whole church; in part, like other letters, they were addressed to a particular congregation in Rome, Corinth, Colossae, etc. Obviously, all these writings, as coming from apostles and apostolic men, were from the beginning held in great respect by Christian churches; they were read in gatherings and also sent to other congregations to be read. Thus the apostle Paul himself requests that the letter he writes to the church of Colossae, after it has been read there, also be read to the church at Laodicea; and also conversely that the Colossians should take note of the letter, which he wrote for Laodicea, which is likely the letter to Ephesus (Col. 4:16). In addition, Peter not only makes mention of a letter, which his readers have received a short-time back from Paul; but he also speaks of another letter from this apostle, which indeed contains the same teachings as that which Peter presents but is sometimes difficult to understand and, through ignorant and unstable men, is distorted (2 Pet. 3:15–16).[1] From this, it cannot be inferred that a collection of Paul's letters already existed; it only clearly shows that the writings of Paul were known in a much wider circle than the local churches to which they each were specifically addressed.

Of course, the congregations in an earlier time drew their knowledge of the gospel for the most part from the oral preaching of the apostles and their disciples. However, when these men passed away and their proclamation ceased, the writings of the apostles naturally grew in value. From testimonies from the middle of the second century, we know also that the Gospels and later also the epistles were read regularly in [44] the assembly of believers, quoted as evidence of some truth, and aligned with the writings of the Old Testament. By the end of the second century, the Scriptures of the New Testament, along with those of the Old Testament, stood as "the whole Scripture," as "the foundation and pillar of the faith," as *the* Scripture that is to be regularly read in the assembly of believers. Regarding some of the writings (Hebrews, James, Jude, 2 Peter, 2 John, 3 John, Revelation; the letters of Barnabas, the Shepherd of Hermas, etc.), there was still some dispute for a while as to whether they could be counted among the Holy Scriptures. Nevertheless, gradually, there was also clarity and unanimity about this; the universally recognized writings were summed up under the name of "canon" ("rule of truth" or "rule of faith") and recorded and established as such at the Synod of Laodicea in the year 360, at Hippo Regius in Numidia in the year 393, and at Carthage in 397.

These Scriptures of the Old and New Testaments form the foundation of the prophets and apostles, on which all Christian churches in communion with one another place, or at least claim to place, themselves. All churches have, in their official confession of faith, recognized the divine authority of Scripture and accepted it as a reliable rule for faith and life. There has never been a difference or conflict between Christians churches concerning this dogma; the struggle against Scripture as the word of God came from the outside, from the side of pagan philosophers—such as Celsus and Porphyry in the second century—but within Christianity, the first dates are from the eighteenth century.[2]

---

1. The previous portion of this chapter is identical to three paragraphs in *MD*, 102–3.

2. The previous two paragraphs match a section of *MD,* 103–4. Celsus was a second-century philosopher opposed to Christianity. Porphyry was also a second-

15. However, the congregation has not received this Scripture from God to rest on it—much less to bury this treasure in the earth. It [45] has, on the contrary, the calling to preserve, to explain, to proclaim, to apply, to interpret, to spread, to praise, to defend this word of God; that is, cause them to triumph over the thoughts of humanity.[3] As soon as a congregation begins to discharge this calling, however, a difference soon becomes apparent over the meaning of the word of God. Even though the Holy Spirit has been promised to the church and given as a guide into all truth, the congregation, neither as a whole nor in specific members, is equipped with the gift of infallibility. Already in the apostolic church, there were all kinds of errors that originated either in Judaism or paganism. These are the two cliffs, through all the centuries, where the church constantly runs the danger of going wrong and which it therefore must avoid with utmost vigilance and caution.

In the face of these errors on the right and left sides, the church of Christ is positively and unequivocally compelled to say that which is the truth, entrusted to it by God in his word. This is what the church does by gathering together in small and large assemblies (synods) and determining there what—on one or another point according to its conviction (*overtuiging*)—is divine truth and thus stands as a doctrine of the church (dogma). Therefore, the truth laid down in Scripture leads, on its own accord, everyone who believes and embraces it to confession. Confession is the calling of all believers and also the impulse of their hearts. Whoever truly believes, with all his heart and soul, cannot do otherwise but confess (that is, bear witness to) the truth that has set him free and the hope of this truth that has been planted in his heart (Matt. 10:32; Rom. 10:9–10; 2 Cor. 4:13; 1 Pet. 3:15; 1 John 4:2–3). Every believer and every congregation [46] therefore confess, as truly as the testimony of the Holy Spirit testifies, that God's word is the truth. As the errors take a finer form, the congregation is urged to give a more careful account of the content of the truth they confess, and also to express in clear and unequivocal terms what they believe. Therefore, the

century philosopher. His two most famous works are *Philosophy from Oracles* and *Against Christians*. Bavinck also refers to these two in his 1912 work *Het Christendom*. See Bavinck, *Het Christendom* (Baarn: Hollandia-Drukkerijk, 1912) 7; Bavinck, *What Is Christianity?* trans. Gregory Parker Jr. (Peabody, MA: Hendrickson, 2022), 6. Bavinck describes Celsus and Porphyry as having been convinced by the slander brought forth about Christ.

3. The remainder of this paragraph is identical to a paragraph in *MD*, 104–5. In between these two identical sections in *MD* is a short section that expands on the importance of the church to not discharge its calling.

oral confession on account of the urgency of the circumstances develops into the written confession (creed or confession).

From various sides, objections to the composition and preservation of ecclesiastical confessions as such have now been raised. The Remonstrants here in this country [the Netherlands], for example, were of the opinion that a confession was in conflict with the exclusive authority of Holy Scripture, robbed freedom of conscience, and inhibits the growth of knowledge. But these objections are based on misunderstanding. The confessions do not serve to reduce Scripture but rather uphold and protect it against the arbitrary will of the individual. They do not violate but support the freedom of conscience (*vrijheid des gewetens*) against all kinds of false spirits who try to seduce the souls of the weak and ignorant. They do not oppose the development of knowledge, but keep and guide it in the right direction, and they themselves at all times are tested and revised by Holy Scripture, which is the only rule of faith.

16. The Apostles' Creed (the twelve articles) is the oldest symbol (*symbool*). It was not composed by the apostles but arose at the beginning of the second century and developed from the Trinitarian baptismal command that Christ himself had given (Matt. 28:19). Originally, it was slightly shorter than the present form we know; but for all intents and purposes, it is the same short summary—namely, of the great facts upon which Christianity rests—and as such, still the common ground and the unbreakable [47] bond of all Christendom. To this apostolic creed (*symbool*) are added four other confessions that bear an ecumenical (universal) character and are accepted by many churches, namely: the confession of the Council of Nicaea in 325, which is in Article 9 of our Netherland confession, called the Nicene Creed;[4] this latter creed [the Niceno-Constantinopolitan Creed] incorporates and expands upon the earlier creed of Nicaea;[5] then the confession of the Council of Chalcedon in 451; and finally, albeit incorrectly titled the Creed of Athanasius, which can also be found in article 9 of the Netherland confession as an accepted creed (*symbool*).[6] Since all of these

4. Bavinck is referring here to Article 9 of the Belgic Confession.

5. Bavinck is distinguishing between the creed produced at the First Council of Nicaea (325) and the creed produced at the First Council of Constantinople (381). This latter creed is also referred to as the Nicene Creed or, more accurately, the Niceno-Constantinopolitan Creed. The Niceno-Constantinopolitan Creed incorporates and expands the earlier Nicene Creed.

6. The previous three paragraphs are identical to paragraphs in *MD*, 105–6. In *MD*, Bavinck more clearly differentiates Christianity and Judaism by virtue of the Trinity.

creeds (*symbolen*) set forth the doctrine concerning Christ, they thereby set forth those in connection with the Trinity, and the councils that accomplished this great work established a fundamental confession for all of Christendom.[7]

But upon this common foundation, all kinds of disagreement and schism soon arose in the Christian church. The practice of discipline led to the secession of Montanism (second half of the second century), Novatianism (mid-third century), and Donatism (fourth century). Much more serious was the schism that gradually occurred between the church in the East and in the West, which in 1054 was fully completed. In both churches, unity was further damaged by all kinds of sects; and in the Reformation of the sixteenth century, there was such a fundamental break that the hope of the restoration of the unity of Christ's church has been removed indefinitely. In and after the sixteenth century up until the present day, the divisions and schisms have continued and multiplied. There are countless churches, sects, groups, and movements. Of the more than 1.5 billion people, who by ordinary estimations inhabit the earth, there are about 10 million Jews, 175 million Muslims, [48] 214 million Hindus, 120 million Buddhists, 300 million Confucians, 140 million Shintoists, and 173 million Polytheists. Christians together only make up a third of the inhabitants of the earth: approximately 534 million, and are split into 254 million Roman Catholics, 106 million Greeks, 165 Protestants, and divided into many other groups and sects.[8]

Nonetheless, we continue to believe that Christ is gathering his people from all races and languages, from all people (*volken*) and nations (*natien*); he will bring them all and they will hear his voice. And "there will be one flock, and one shepherd" (John 10:16).[9]

---

7. The confessions that Bavinck puts forth as universal are the Apostolic, Nicene (325), Nicene (381), Chalcedon, and Creed of Athanasius; cf. Bavinck, *What Is Christianity?*, 21.

8. Bavinck provides a similar set of statistics in *MD*, 113.

9. The final line of ch. 8 in *MD* and the present work are identical (see 113). See Bavinck, *The Sacrifice of Praise* (Peabody, MA: Hendrickson, 2019), 85. Here, Bavinck writes of the unity of confession in Christ: "The unity of confession, accordingly, is the purpose of the history of the world. One day, angels and devils, the righteous and the ungodly will agree acknowledging that Christ is the firstborn the Son of the Father and, therefore, the heir of all things. Then every knee shall bow, and every tongue confess, that Jesus Christ is the Lord."

6

The Essence of God

17. [49] Having established the sources from which we may derive knowledge (*kennis*) of God, we go now to a description of him. But as soon as we consider what it means that we, futile, finite, sinful creatures should know (*kennen*) and may speak of him, not only does a holy shyness take hold of our soul, but it also raises the question in our hearts: Is this knowledge (*kennis*) not too wonderful for man? Is not God infinitely beyond man? Is he—the invisible, the eternal, and infinite one—truly knowable by our weak, human-bound sense perception (*zinnelijke*)?

There have been many in the past who have given a negative answer to these questions. We, as well, should be doing the same if we did not believe that God has, out of free grace, made himself known (*kenbaar*), and through his revelation given us the right and boldness to think and speak about him. We should, of course, always do this with holy reverence and childlike fear, for in knowledge of him (*kenbaarheid*), he remains exalted and incomprehensible; but still, we may do it, because according to his own good pleasure he is knowable (*kenbaar*) with a knowledge (*kennis*) that is eternal life (John 17:3).

There is no book in the world that, in the same manner and in the same way as Holy Scripture, maintains the incomprehensibility [50] of God, his absolute transcendence (*volstrekte verhevenheid*) above all creatures and at the same time combines that with the knowledge of God and the intimate relationship of the Creator with his reasonable creatures.[1] Already on the first page of the Bible, there is the absolute transcendence (*volstrekte verhevenheid*) of God above all of his creatures. Without need or becoming tired, he brings forth the whole world through his word alone. "Through the word of the Lord the heavens were made, and by the Spirit of his mouth all their hosts" (Ps. 33:6).[2] "For he spoke, and it came to be; he commanded,

---

1. The introduction to the chapter up until this point is unique to *Handleiding*, but the remainder of the paragraph is identical to one in *MD*, 117–18.

2. "Door het Woord des HEEREN zijn de hemelen gemaakt, en door den Geest Zijns mond al hun heir" (Ps. 33:6).

and it stood firm" (Ps. 33:9). He does according to his will with the host of heaven and the inhabitants of the earth, and there is no one who may turn his hand or say to him, "What are you doing?" (Dan. 4:35). The nations (*volkeren*) are like a drop in a bucket and are accounted as dust on the scales. He cannot be compared to anyone, and no likeness can be ascribed to him (Isa. 40:15–18). Who can be compared to the Lord? Who is like the Lord among the children of the strong? (Ps. 89:6). There is no name by which he can truthfully be called: his name is wonderful (Gen. 32:29; Judg. 13:18; Prov. 30:4). When the Lord speaks to Job out of the whirlwind and spreads the greatness of his works before him, Job humbly bows his head and says, "Behold, I am so small, how can I answer you; I cover my mouth with my hand" (Job 39:37). "God is great, and we know him not" (Job 36:26). The knowledge (*kennis*) of God is too wonderful for us; it is high; we cannot reach it (Ps. 139:6).

And yet, that same high and exalted God stands in an intimate relation to all his creature, even the smallest and least. Scripture does not provide an abstract conception of God, as philosophy does, but it presents before our eyes the true, living God and causes us to see him in all the works of his hands. Lift [51] up your eyes and see who created all these things. Everything was created (*geshapen*) by his hand; everything has been brought forth (*voortgebracht*) according to his will and council; everything is preserved by his power. Therefore, everything bears the imprint of his virtues, the mark of his goodness, wisdom, and power. And among all creatures, man was created in his image and likeness; he alone is called God's "offspring" (Acts 17:28).[3]

On account of this intimate relationship, God may be known also by his creatures, and he may be spoken of in humanly ways. The same Scripture, which portrays in the loftiest ways God's incomparable greatness and majesty, speaks simultaneously of him in analogies (*gelijkenissen*) and images that sparkle with life. It speaks of his eyes and ears, hands and feet, mouth and lips, heart and bowels. It attributes to him all kinds of virtues, wisdom (*wijsheid*) and knowledge (*kennis*), will (*wil*) and might (*macht*), righteousness (*gerechtigheid*) and mercy (*barmhartigheid*), and also attributes to him affections (*aandoeningen*) of joy (*vreugde*) and sorrow (*smart*), fear (*vrees*) and grief (*verdriet*), zeal (*ijver*) and jealousy (*aloerschheid*), repentance (*berouw*) and wrath (*toorn*), hatred (*haat*) and vengeance (*wraak*). It mentions

3. This paragraph is identical to one in *MD*, 118. Bavinck utilizes "man" here inclusively. "Man" is representative for humanity, both male and female.

his searching (*onderzoeken*) and thinking (*denken*), hearing and seeing, smelling and tasting, sitting and standing, visiting and forsaking, remembering and forgetting, blessing and disciplining, etc. And it likens him to the sun and light, a fountain and spring, a rock and hiding place, a tower and buckler, a lion and an eagle, a hero and warrior, an artist and a builder, a king and judge, a farmer and shepherd, a husband and father. Everything in the whole world that man can find for support and protection and help is to be found originally, perfectly, and abundantly in God. From him, every family in heaven and on earth is named (Eph. 3:15). He is the "Sun of being" and all creatures are "his radiating rays" (Da Costa).[4]

[52] In the knowledge (*kennis*) of God, it is always vital to hold equally these two sets of statements about the divine being and to do justice to them both. If we abandon the absolute transcendence of God to all his creatures, we fall into polytheism (the pantheon of Gods in paganism) or pantheism (everything is God), which according to history mutually relate to one another and tend to blend together. And if we abandon the relationship of God to his creatures, we are stranded on the cliff of Deism (belief in one God without revelation) or atheism (the denial of the existence of God), which likewise in different ways correspond with one another. Scripture holds both of these together [God's transcendence and immanence] and Christian theology followed in its footsteps. God actually does not have a name by which we can truly name him, and yet he calls himself and permits us to call him by many, many names. He is the infinitely exalted one and at the same time the living one, the God who cares for all his creatures. His attributes (*deugden*) are in every respect incommunicable (*onmededeelbaar*) and in another sense communicable (*mededeelbaar*). Our intellect (*verstand*) cannot fathom this. There is not an adequate (equivalent) concept of God (*Godsbegrip*). A definition, an explanation that explains his being is not given by God. A name that fully expresses what he is cannot be found. But one does not conflict with the other. Truthfully, because God is the

4. Isaac Da Costa, *Da Costa's Kompleete Dichtwerken*, ed. J. P. Hasebroek (Leiden: A. W. Sijthoff, 1863), 43–51. Although Bavinck references this poem in *MD*, he does not disclose the source of this poem until later in *Handleiding*, where he references his favorite poet, Willelm Bilderdijk. Unfortunately, to our knowledge, Bilderdijk never published anything containing this phrase. However, Bilderdijk's contemporary and good friend Isaac Da Costa mentions it in his hymn "Voorzienghied" (English: "Providence") when he says, "You are the sun of being; we are your radiating rays!" (Dutch: "Gy zijt de zon des zijns; wy, uw vergankbre stralen!") This paragraph is identical to one in *MD*, 118.

one who is high and lifted up, who dwells in eternity, he also lives with him who is of a contrite and lowly spirit (Isa. 57:15). God did not reveal himself, so that from his revelation we might construct a philosophical concept of God (*wijsgeerig Godsbegrip*), but so that we might receive, acknowledge, and confess him, the one true, living God, as our God. For these things have been hidden from the wise and understanding, but they are revealed to children (Matt. 11:25).

[53] The knowledge (*kennis*), which we acquire from God in this way, is therefore a knowledge of faith (*kennis des geloofs*); it is inadequate, it is not equivalent to God's being, for God is infinitely exalted above all of his creatures; it is also not merely symbolic, that is to say, expressed in phrases that have been arbitrarily formed by us and do not at all correspond with reality (*werkelijkheid*). Rather, it is ectypal or analogical, because it rests on likeness and kinship, which in spite of God's absolute transcendence (*volstrekte verhevenheid*), nevertheless, exists between him and the works of his hands. The knowledge God provides us of himself in nature and Scripture is limited, finite, piecework (*stukwerk*), but it is pure and true. Therefore, God has revealed himself, in a way in his word, particularly in and through Christ; and thus it is God alone who meets the needs of our heart.

18. The attempt to consider all of the teachings of Scripture on the doctrine of God, and therefore to maintain both God's transcendence (*verhevenheid*) and his relationship to the creature, led the early church to the distinction of two groups of attributes (*eigenschappen*) in the divine being. These two groups have traditionally been referred to by different names: Roman theology still prefers to speak of negative and positive (apophatic and cataphatic), the Lutherans of quiescent and operative (resting and working), and the Reformed of incommunicable and communicable attributes. However, in each division the substance remains the same. It always has the purpose of maintaining the transcendence (God's distinction from and exaltation above the world) and the immanence of God (his communion with and his dwelling in the world). The Reformed designation of incommunicable and communicable [54] attributes facilitates this meaning clearer than those in use by the Romans and Lutherans. The assertion of the former attributes protects us against polytheism (the multiplicity of deities) and pantheism (everything is God); and the assertion of the second group of attributes protects us against deism (belief in God apart from revelation) and atheism (the denial of the existence of God).[5]

5. The previous five paragraphs are identical to paragraphs in *MD*, 118–20.

There is no convincing objection, despite the inadequacy of the designations, to not continue to utilize the Reformed terms. Only we must remember that the two groups of the incommunicable and communicable attributes are not separable and divorced from each other. Of course, we cannot treat both at the same time, and we must speak of one before the other. Nevertheless, the purpose with the division is that we should always remind ourselves that God possess all his communicable (*mededeelbare*) attributes in an absolute (*volstrekte*) manner, in an infinite and therefore in an incommunicable (*onmededeelbare*) manner. God's knowledge, wisdom, goodness, righteousness, etc. have some similarities to those same attributes in creatures, but they are God's own in an independent, unchanging, eternal, omnipresent, simple—in a word, an absolute-divine (*volstrekt-Goddelijke*) way. Therefore, in creatures, we can truly make distinctions between their essence (*wezen*) and their attributes (*eigenshappen*); a man can lose his arm and his leg, he can even in sleep or sickness lose his consciousness, without ceasing to be a man. But that is not possible with God. His attributes (*eigenschappen*) coincide with his being. Every attribute (*eigenschap*) *is* his being. He is not only wise and true, good and holy, righteous and merciful, but he is wisdom, truth, goodness, holiness, righteousness, and mercy itself, and therefore also the origin and fountain of all those virtues present in creatures. [55] He *is* all that he *has* and the source of all that creatures have, the abundant fountain of all goods.[6]

19. The incommunicable (*onmededeelbare*) attributes, therefore, are understood as those perfections or virtues that are meant to demonstrate that all that is in God exists in an absolute-divine (*volstrekt-Goddelijke*) way—that is, to a degree not susceptible to being shared with creatures. This group of attributes maintains the absolute transcendence (*volstrekte verhevenheid*) and incomparability of God and finds its clearest rendering in the name Elohim, God. It is true that the name "god" is also given to creatures. Not only does the Holy Scripture sometimes speak of the idols of pagans as gods, it forbids us, for example, to have other gods (Exod. 20:3); it also says that Moses is a god to Aaron (Exod. 4:16) and to Pharaoh (Exod. 7:2), it designates the judges as gods (Ps. 82:1, 6), and Christ calls upon this in his self-defense (John 10:33–35). But this use of language is metaphorical and derivative. The name of God originally and essentially belongs to God alone. With this name, we always connect the idea to an infinite power that is personal but nevertheless transcendent above all creatures. God alone is God.[7]

6. This paragraph is nearly identical to two paragraphs in *MD*, 120–21.
7. This paragraph is broken into two paragraphs in *MD*, 121.

As such, he possesses incommunicable (*onmededeelbare*) attributes. They are proper to him alone; they do not occur in creatures and cannot even be communicated to any creature. For all creatures are dependent (*afhankelijk*), changeable (*veranderlijk*), composed (*samengesteld*), and subject to time and space. God is *independent* (*onafhankelijk*) in an absolute sense from everything; as such, he is determined by nothing (Acts 17:25; Rom. 11:36); *unchangeable* (*onveranderlijk*), so that he remains the same forever and all changing falls to the side of the creature and in the relationship in which this creature stands before [56] him (James 1:17); *simple* (*eenvoudig*), so that he is free of all composition of spirit and matter, thought and extension, essence and attributes, mind and will, etc. He is perfectly free, and he *is* everything he *possesses*, pure truth, life and light (Ps. 36:9; John 5:26; 1 John 1:5); *eternal* (*eeuwig*), so that he is exalted above all time and yet penetrates every moment of time with his eternity (Ps. 90:2); *omnipresent* (*alomtegenwoordig*), so that he is exalted above all space and yet bears every point of space with his omnipotent and omnipresent power (Ps. 139:7–8; Acts 17:27–28);[8] and finally also the *one* and the *only* God (Deut. 6:4; Mark 12:29; John 17:3), because no one and nothing is above or beside him, nor can anything under him but that which he alone is.

These incommunicable attributes are presently of the utmost importance not only for thought but also for religious life; for only if God is independent (*onafhankelijk*) and unchangeable (*onveranderlijk*), eternal (*eeuwig*) and omnipresent (*alomtegenwoordig*), can he be the God of our unconditional faith, of our absolute trust (*vertrouwen*), of our perfect salvation.

But if this is true, we do not have enough in these incommunicable (*onmededeelbare*) attributes. What would it profit us to know (*weten*) that God is independent (*onafhankelijk*) and unchangeable (*onveranderlijk*), eternal (*eeuwig*) and omnipresent (*alomtegenwoordig*), if we thereby must lack the knowledge that he is merciful (*barmhartig*) and gracious (*genadig*), and of great loving-kindness (*goedertierenheid*)? The incommunicable (*onmededeelbare*) attributes light the *path* in which everything in God exists

8. Up until this point, this paragraph is identical to one in *MD,* 121. The remainder of the sentence is unique to *Guidebook*, although a similar sentence is found in *MD*, 122. "God is the one God and the only God as no one or nothing above, beside, or under him can be what he is." [Dutch: Alleen Dan. is God de eene en de eenige God, wanneer niemand of niets boven, naast of onder Hem zijn kan, wat Hij is.]

(*bestaat*) in him; but they leave us in the dark concerning the *content* of the Divine Being. But the communicable (*mededeelbare*) attributes come with it; and they tell us that God, who is infinitely high and exalted, yet inhabits all his creatures and possess all those attributes, which are also within creatures in a limited and qualified way. He is not only a God from afar, but he is also near. He is not only independent (*onafhankelijk*) [57] and unchangeable (*onveranderlijk*), eternal (*eeuwig*) and omnipresent (*alomtegenwoordig*), but he is also wise and omnipotent, righteous (*rechtvaardig*) and holy, gracious, and merciful. He is not only Elohim; he is also Jehovah (Yahweh);[9] not merely *El-Shaddai*, the Almighty (Gen. 17:1; Exod. 6:2), but also the God of the covenant and of promise, who gives himself to and binds himself with his people forever, whose name, whose *own* name is Jehovah, the Lord (Exod. 3:14–15; Isa. 42:8; 43:10–15; 44:6; 48:11).

20. These communicable (*mededeelbare*) attributes are so abundant that a complete summary is impossible.[10] However, the first thing the Holy Scripture seeks to provide here with all the names of God is certainly this: that they will give us a profound, indelible impression of God, who is absolutely transcendent and yet merciful to the people (*volk*) of his covenant; the true, the real, the *living* God. The idols of the pagans and the idols of philosophers (pantheism and polytheism, Deism and atheism) are the work of man's hands; they do not speak, they do not see, they do not hear, they do not feel, they do not move. But Israel's God is in heaven and does whatever he pleases. He is the only (Deut. 6:4) true (John 17:3), eternal living God (Deut. 5:26; Josh. 3:10; Dan. 6:27; Acts 14:15; 2 Cor. 6:16; 1 Tim. 3:15, 6:17). People desire to make God a dead God, in order to be able to deal with him according to their pleasure. But the Holy Scripture calls to man: You have gone astray; God exists. He is the true God; he *lives*, now and forever. And "it is a fearful thing to fall into the hands of the living God" (Heb. 10:31).

As such a living God, who is pure life and the fountain of all life (Ps. 36.9; Jer. 2:13), he is *Spirit* (John 4:24), without body, although all kinds of bodily parts and actions are ascribed to him (Deut. 4:12, 16), [58] and therefore formless (Deut. 4:15–17) and invisible (Exod. 33:20; John 1:18; 6:46; 1 Tim. 6:16). As Spirit, moreover, he has *consciousness* (*bewustzijn*), absolute knowledge (*volmaakte kennis*) of himself (Matt. 11:27; 1 Cor. 2:10), and from and through himself also absolute knowledge (*volmaakte kennis*)

9. Up until this point, this paragraph is identical to one in *MD*, 122.

10. Up until this point, this paragraph is unique to *Handleiding*. What follows can be found in *MD*, 124–25.

of all things that will be or will happen in time, however obscure or puny the creature may be (Isa. 46:10; Jer. 11:20; Matt. 10:30; Heb. 4:13). Furthermore, he has a *will* whereby he does all that pleases him (hidden will or decretive will; Ps. 115:3; Prov. 21:1; Dan. 4:35) and also determines what is the rule for our conduct (revealed will or will of the command; Deut. 29:29; Matt. 7:21; 12:50). And he has *power* by which—despite all the opposition can execute what he has purposed—nothing is impossible for him (Gen. 18:14; Jer. 32:27; Zech. 8:6; Matt. 19:26; 1 Tim. 6:15).[11]

But this knowledge (*kennis*), will (*wil*), and power (*macht*) are not capricious, but are in all parts morally determined. This is already reflected in the *wisdom* attributed to God in Scripture (Prov. 8:22–31; Job 28:20–28; Rom. 16:27; 1 Tim. 1:17) and by which he organizes and directs everything in accordance with the purpose he has established for creation and re-creation (Ps. 104:24; Eph. 3:10; Rom. 11:33). Furthermore, this is clearly and plainly expressed in the *goodness* and *grace*, on the one hand, and in the *holiness* and *righteousness*, on the other hand, which are attributed to God. God is not only the all-knowing and all-powerful but also the all-good, the only (Matt. 10:18), perfect (Matt. 5:48), and source of everything good in creatures (Ps. 145:9). This goodness of God extends over the whole world (Ps. 145:9; Matt. 5:45) but changes according to the objects upon which it focuses and then takes on, as it were, various forms. It is called *long-suffering* when it reveals itself to sinners (Rom. 3:25); *grace* when it is shown [59] to the guilty who receive forgiveness of sins (Eph. 2:8); *love* when God communicates and imparts himself to his creatures (John 3:16; 1 John 4:8); *kindness* when the goodness of God demonstrates itself to his saints (Gen. 39:21; Num. 14:19; Isa. 54:10; Eph. 2:7); and *pleasure* when it is emphasized that this goodness with all of its benefits is a free gift (Matt. 11:26; Luke 2:14; 12:32; 2 Thess. 1:11).[12]

The goodness and grace of God go hand-in-hand with his holiness and righteousness. God is called the *Holy One*, not only because he is exalted above all creatures as creatures (*alle schepsel als schepsel*), but above all because he is separated from all unrighteousness and impurity in the world. Therefore, he demands that his people (*volk*), whom out of free grace he declared to be his possession, be holy (Exod. 19:5–6; Lev. 11:44–45; 1 Pet. 2:9) and he himself sanctifies them through Christ (Eph. 5:26–27), who

11. This paragraph is identical to one in *MD*, 125.

12. This paragraph is nearly identical to one in *MD*, 125–26. The first two sentences have minor differences.

himself was sanctified for their sake, so that they also might be sanctified in truth (John 17:19). Closely connected with the holiness of God is his *righteousness*. For the Holy One cannot have fellowship with sin; he hates it (Ps. 45:7; Job 34:10), is angry with it (Rom. 1:18), is jealous for his honor (Exod. 20:5), and therefore in no way can the guilty be considered innocent (Exod. 20:5–7). His holy nature demands that he upholds the law outside of himself in the world of creatures, that without respect of persons everyone might be held accountable for their work (Rom. 2:2–11; 2 Cor. 5:10).[13]

According to this remarkable teaching of Scripture on account of the same righteousness, he not only punishes the wicked but also grants salvation to the faithful. It is true that the pious, considered alone [apart from Christ], are sinners and no better than the others. While the wicked hide or disguise their sins, they who are just acknowledge and [60] confess their guilt. But this is precisely what makes the difference. Although *personally* guilty and unclean, they stand, as far as the *matter* is concerned, on the side of God and against the world. They may, therefore, plead on the promise of his covenant of grace, on the truth of his word, and on the righteousness God himself has applied in Christ. According to this righteousness, we may say with reverence, God is obligated to his people to forgive their sins and grant eternal life (Pss. 4:1; 7:10; 31:2; 34:22; 35:23; 51:16; 103:17; 1 John 1:9). And when God often delays and the pious are tested in their faith, the *truthfulness* and *faithfulness* of God come to light more brilliantly in their perfect salvation (Gen. 24:27; 32:10; Josh 21:45; 2 Sam. 7:28; Pss. 57:4; 105:8). The Lord will accomplish it for his people (*volk*); his mercy is forever (Ps. 138:8). He is merciful and gracious, long-suffering, and great in kindness (Exod. 34:6; Pss. 86:15; 103:8; 145:8).[14]

Indeed, some boast in chariots and some in horses, but we will boast in the name of the Lord our God (Ps. 20:7; Jer. 9:23–24; 1 Cor. 1:31; 2 Cor. 10:17). “For this is God, our God forever and ever; He will guide us forever” (Ps. 48:14).[15] He is a *blessed* and a *glorious* God (1 Tim. 6:15; Eph. 1:17). And blessed is the people whose God is the Lord (Ps. 33:12).[16]

---

13. This paragraph is contained within one in *MD*, 126.

14. This paragraph is three paragraphs in *MD*, 126–27.

15. This is a direct quote from Ps. 48:15 in the Statenvaling [Dutch: “Want deze God is onze God eeuwiglijk en altoos; Hiz zal ons geleiden tot den dood toe”].

16. This paragraph is identical to one in *MD*, 127.

7

The Trinity

21. [61] Richer and more glorious than in the attributes, the eternal being of God meets us in the revelation of his Triune (Trinity) existencc.[1] At the same time, this revelation did not occur in and through the proclamation of a single formula; rather, it had a long historical progression and expanded over centuries. That God exists as Father, Son, and Holy Spirit became manifest earlier and even clearer in God's works than in his spoken word.

Of course, in the beginning, God's unity stood opposed to idolatry and image worship, to which paganism and Israel often succumbed. That the Lord is Israel's God, and the only God, was first of all deeply impressed upon the soul (Gen. 17:1; Exod. 3:6, 14–15; 20:2–5; Deut. 4:35, 39; 6:4–5; 32:39; Josh 22:22; 2 Sam. 7:22; 22:32; Isa. 45:5, etc.). Yet in the progress of revelation, the fullness of the Divine Being came to light in the diversity, and in the unity of God the personal self-distinction. Already the name by which God in Hebrew is ordinarily called has some significance here. For this name, Elohim, is a plural form and does not denote, as formerly often thought, the three persons in the Divine Being; but yet as a so-called intensive plural, it points to the fullness of life and power that is present in God. Undoubtedly, this is also connected with the plural form [62] of which God occasionally speaks of himself, and by which he makes distinctions within himself, which bear a personal character (Gen. 1:26–27; 3:22; Isa. 6:8).[2]

Of more significance is the teaching of the Old Testament, that God accomplishes all things in creation and providence through his Word and

1. Chapter 10 in *MD*, 127, on "De Drieëenheid Gods" begins similarly, but they diverge after the opening sentence. English: "Richer and more vibrant still than the attributes, the eternal being of God meets us in the revelation of his Triune existence." [Dutch: "Rijker en levendiger nog Dan. in de eigenschappen, treedt het Eeuwige in de openbaring van zijn drieëenig bestaan ons te gemoet."]

2. The same passages of Scripture are referenced in *MD*, 131, though the composition of the paragraph is unique to *Handleiding*.

Spirit.[3] Through his Word, he only has to speak and it is there (Gen. 1:3f.; Pss. 33:6, 9; 29:3–10; 147:18). His word is a commandment (Ps. 33:9), and his voice possesses power (Ps. 29:4). And that word also, precisely as a Word, is conscious (*bewust*) and full of wisdom—the wisdom, which was forever with him, through which he made the whole world (Job 28:20–28; Prov. 8:22–31; Ps. 104:24; Jer. 10:12; 51:15). Likewise, he created everything through his Spirit. Similarly, God *is* wisdom, and at the same time he *has* wisdom, so that he can communicate it and display it in his works. So, he *is* himself in his being Spirit (Deut. 4:12), and he *has* a Spirit, by which he dwells in the world (Ps. 139:7).

Without anyone having been his counselor, the Lord has brought forth everything by his own Spirit (Isa. 40:13). This Spirit hovered over the waters in the beginning (Gen. 1:2) and remains active in all created things. Through this Spirit, God adorns the heavens (Job 26:13); he renews the face of the earth (Ps. 104:30); he gives life to man (Job 33:4); he keeps breath in his nostrils (Job 27:3); he gives him understanding and wisdom (Job 32:8); he also makes the grass whither and the flowers fade (Isa. 40:7). In a word: through the word of the Lord, the heavens were made, and by the Spirit of his mouth all their hosts (Ps. 33:6).[4]

This self-distinction of God comes out even richer in the works of re-creation. Then it is not Elohim, but Jehovah, not God in general, but the Lord, the God of the covenant, who reveals himself, making himself known in miracles [63] of redemption and salvation. As such, he redeems and guides his people (*volk*) not merely through his word, which he speaks or brings to them, but he also sends the angel of the covenant (the angel of the Lord), who already in the history of the patriarchs appeared to Hagar (Gen. 16:6f), Abraham (Genesis 18f.), and Jacob (Gen. 28:13f.), but especially in the deliverance of Israel from the house of slavery from Egypt, manifesting his grace and power (Exod. 3:2; 13:21; 14:19; 23:20–23; 32:34; 33:2; Num. 20:16). This angel of the Lord does not stand with the created angels but is a special revelation and appearance of God. On the one hand, he is clearly distinguished from God, who speaks of him as his angel; and yet on the other hand is with God himself in name, in power, in salvation and blessing, in worship and honor. He is called the God of seeing (Gen. 16:13), the God of Bethel (Gen. 31:13); he is called God or Lord himself (Gen. 32:28, 30; Exod. 3:2–4), bears the

3. This sentence is identical to a sentence in *MD*, 132, although the remainder of the paragraph is different.

4. This paragraph matches a portion of a larger paragraph in *MD*, 132–33.

name of Lord within him (Exod. 23:21), redeems from all evil (Gen. 48:16), delivers Israel from the hand of the Egyptians (Exod. 3:8), spreads the waters and makes the sea dry (Exod. 14:21), protects the people of God on their way, brings them safely to Canaan, and makes them to triumph over their enemies (Exod. 3:8; 23:20). He must be fully obeyed as God himself (Exod. 23:20) and always surrounds those who fear the Lord (Ps. 34:7; 35:5–6).[5]

Just as in the re-creation, Jehovah exercises his redeeming activity through his angel of the covenant, so by his Spirit he imparts all kinds of gifts and powers to his people (*volk*). The Spirit of the Lord in the Old Testament is the source of all life, salvation, and ability. He gives courage and strength to the judges Othniel (Judg. 3:10), Gideon (6:34), Jephthah (11:29), and Samson (14:6; 15:14); artistic skills to the workers of the priestly garments, the tabernacle, and the temple [64] (Exod. 28:3; 31:3–5; 35:31–35; 1 Chron 28:12); understanding and wisdom to the elders who bear, with Moses, the burden of the people (Num. 11:15, 25); the gift of prophecy to the prophets (Num. 11:25, 29; 24:2–3; Mic. 3:8; etc.); and renewal, sanctification, and guidance to all God's children (Pss. 51:12; 143:10).[6]

In a nutshell: the word, the promise, the covenant the Lord made with Israel when he brought them out of Egypt, and the Spirit he bestowed to Israel, remained with them throughout the ages and even after the exile on the day of Zerubbabel amid the people, so that they did not have to fear (Hag 2:5–6). When the Lord led Israel out of the land of Egypt, he became to them a redeemer. And from this comes, therefore, the belief of God in respect to his people (*volk*) that in all their distress he himself was afflicted (considering the sufferings of his people as his own sufferings); that he therefore sent the angel of his countenance to them to deliver them; that they would be redeemed by his love and grace, and lifted them up and carried them all the days of old; and that he also granted them the Spirit of his holiness, to guide them in the ways of the Lord (Isa. 63:9–12). The Lord, in the days of the old covenant, through the high priest set down his threefold blessing upon the people (*volk*) of Israel, the blessing of the protection, grace, and peace of the Lord (Num. 6:24–26).[7]

Thus in the history of God's guiding of Israel, the threefold distinction in the essence and operation of the Divine Being becomes clearer and clearer. However, the Old Testament also contains the promise that a higher

5. This paragraph is identical to one in *MD*, 133.
6. This paragraph is identical to one in *MD*, 133.
7. This paragraph is identical to one in *MD*, 133–34.

and richer revelation will follow in the future. Israel rejected the word of the Lord and grieved his Holy Spirit (Isa. 63:10; Ps. 106:29). The revelation of God in the angel of the covenant and in the Spirit of the Lord proved [65] to be insufficient; indeed, for God to confirm his covenant and fulfill his promise, another higher revelation was needed.

And this was announced by the prophets. In the future, in the last days, the Lord will raise up from the midst of Israel a prophet like Moses, in whose mouth the Lord will put his words (Deut. 18:18); a priest, who will be a priest forever according to the order of Melchizedek (Ps. 110:4); a king from David's house (2 Sam. 7:12–16); a shoot, which shall come forth from the stump of Jesse (Isa. 11:1); a branch, who will reign as king and execute justice and righteousness on the earth (Jer. 23:5). He shall be a man, the son of a virgin (Isa. 7:14), without form or glory (Isa. 53:2f); but at the same time, he will be Immanuel (Isa. 33:16), the angel of the covenant (Mal. 3:1), the Lord himself, who appears to his people (*volk*) (Pss. 45:8; 110:1; Hos. 1:7; Mal. 3:1), bearing the name of Wonderful, Counselor, Mighty God, Everlasting Father, Prince of Peace (Isa. 9:6).[8]

This appearance of the servant of the Lord will be followed by a richer administration of the Holy Spirit. The Spirit will rest upon the Messiah in an extraordinary measure as the Spirit of wisdom and understanding, of counsel and strength, of the knowledge and fear of the Lord (Isa. 11:2; 42:1; 61:1); but then he will be poured out on all flesh, on sons and daughters, old and young, servants and maidservants (Joel 2:28–29; Isa. 32:15; 44:3; Ezek. 36:26–27; Zech. 12:10), and he will give all a new heart and a new spirit, so that they will walk in his statues, keep his commandments, and do them (Ezek. 11:19–20; 36:26–27; Isa. 31:31–34; 32:38–41).

Thus the Old Testament itself points toward the full [66] revelation of God, which will consist in the revelation of his Triune being.[9]

22. The fulfillment in the New Testament corresponds to this promise and prophecy. Here, too, the unity of God is the starting point of all revelation (John 17:3; 1 Cor. 8:4; 1 Tim. 2:5). However, from this unity, the diversity of the Divine Being now manifests itself more clearly; first of all, in the great acts of salvation, the incarnation (*vleeshwording*), satisfaction (*voldoening*), and outpouring (*uitstorting*), and then also in the teachings of Jesus and his apostles.[10]

---

8. The previous two paragraphs are a single paragraph in *MD*, 134.
9. The previous two paragraphs are identical to four paragraphs in *MD*, 134–35.
10. This paragraph matches a portion of a larger paragraph in *MD*, 135.

Already the conception of Christ shows to us a threefold activity of God. For as the Father gives the Son to the world (John 3:16), and the Son himself descends from heaven (John 6:38), he is conceived in Mary by the Holy Spirit (Matt. 1:20; Luke 1:35). At the baptism, Jesus is anointed with the Holy Spirit and declared publicly by the Father as his beloved Son, in whom he is well pleased (Matt. 3:16–17). The works that Jesus does are shown to him by the Father (John 5:19; 8:39) and are accomplished by him in the power of the Holy Spirit (Matt. 12:28). In his death, he offered himself to God without blemish through the eternal Spirit (Heb. 9:14). In the resurrection, Jesus is raised by the Father (Acts 2:24) and at the same time by his own action, by which he is powerfully proven to be the Son of God according to the Spirit of holiness (Rom. 1:3–4). After his resurrection, on the fortieth day he ascends to the heavens in the Spirit, who made him alive, and with angels, authorities, and powers having been subjected to him (1 Pet. 3:19, 22).[11]

With this comes the corresponding teaching of Jesus and the apostles. Jesus came to earth to proclaim the *Father* and to make his name known to the people (John 1:18; 17:6). The Father's name as [67] Creator of all things was common for the Gentiles, and this meaning also has support in the Scriptures (Luke 3:38; Acts 17:28; Eph. 3:15; Heb. 12:9). Furthermore, the Old Testament points to God several times as Father in his (theocratic) relationship with Israel, because he has created and preserved [Israel] through his wonderful power (Deut. 32:6; Isa. 63:16).

But in the New Testament, a glorious new light rises over our understanding of the name of God as Father. Jesus always makes an essential distinction between the relationship in which he stands before the Father and in which others, the Israelites or disciples, stand. When he, for example, teaches his disciples to pray, he places "Our Father" on their lips and explicitly says, "When *you* pray, speak thus" (Luke 11:2); and likewise, after the resurrection when he announces to Mary Magdalene his imminent ascension to heaven, he says, "I am ascending to my Father and your Father, to my God and your God" (John 20:17). God is, namely, his *own* Father (John 5:18). He knows the Son and loves him in a way and to a degree as, again, only the Son and Father mutually know and love (Matt. 11:27; Mark 12:6; John 5:20). By the apostles, therefore, God is always called in a special sense the Father of our Lord Jesus Christ (Eph. 1:3). This relationship between Father and Son (Christ) did not begin in time but is from eternity (John

11. This paragraph is identical to one in *MD*, 135.

1:1, 14; 17:24). God is, therefore, in the first place Father because he is the Father of the Son in a wholly unique sense; this Fatherhood is his original, special, personal property.[12]

In a derivative sense, then, God is further called the Father of all creatures because he is their Creator and Sustainer (1 Cor. 8:6; Eph. 3:15; Heb. 12:9)—of Israel because through election and calling, it is the work of his hands (Deut. 32:6; Isa. 63:16; 64:8), and of the church and all believers because the love of the Father toward the Son passes through [68] Christ upon them (John 16:27; 17:25), and they are adopted as his children and born of him through the Spirit (John 1:12; Rom. 8:15).[13]

Therefore, the Father is always the *Father*, the First Person, who in essence is God, who takes the initiative in the counsel of God, and in all external works, in creation and preservation, redemption, and sanctification. He granted the Son to have life in himself (John 5:26), and the Spirit proceeds forth from him (John 15:26). It is according to his purpose, election, and good pleasure (Matt. 11:26; Eph. 1:4, 9, 11). From him originates creation and preservation, redemption and restoration (Ps. 33:6; John 3:16). To him in a special sense belong the kingdom, the power, and the glory (Matt. 6:13). He bears in a unique way the *name* of God, in distinction from the *Lord* Jesus Christ and from the Holy Spirit (1 Cor. 8:6; 2 Cor. 3:13). Indeed, Christ himself as mediator calls him not only his Father but also his God (Matt. 27:46; John 20:17), and he is called the Christ of God (Luke 9:20; 1 Cor. 3:23; Rev. 12:10). In a word, the First Person of the of the Divine Being is the *Father* because *from* him are all things (1 Cor. 8:6).[14]

23. If God is Father, then implied in this is that there also is a *Son*, who received life from him and shares in his love. Now the name of the Son of God was already in use in the Old Testament for the angels (Job 38:7), for the people of Israel (Deut. 1:31; 8:5; 14:1; 32:6, 18; Hos. 11:1), and especially for the theocratic king (2 Sam. 7:11–14; Pss. 2:7; 82:6–8). But in the New Testament, this name receives a much deeper meaning. For Christ is the Son of God in the complete sense of the name; he is exalted above angels and prophets (Matt. 13:23; 21:27; 22:2) and says himself that "no one knows the Son except the Father, and no one knows the Father except [69] the Son" (Matt. 11:27). In distinction from angels and men, he is his own Son

---

12. The previous two paragraphs are identical to a section of *MD*, 135–36.

13. This paragraph is nearly identical to a paragraph in *MD*, 136. In *Handleiding*, Bavinck includes Isa. 63:16 in his Scripture references.

14. This paragraph is identical to one in *MD*, 136.

(Rom. 8:32), the beloved Son, in whom the Father is well pleased (Matt. 3:17), the only begotten Son (John 1:18) to whom the Father granted to have life in himself (John 5:26).[15]

This whole relationship between the Father and the Son did not commence in time, by the supernatural conception of the Holy Spirit, or by the anointing at baptism, or through the resurrection and ascension, as many have claimed, but it has existed from all eternity. After all, the Son, who assumed a human nature as Christ, existed from the beginning with God as the Word (John 1:1), and was already in the form of God (Phil. 2:6), rich and clothed with glory (John 17:5, 24), the radiance of God's glory, and the express image of his nature (Heb. 1:3); he could, therefore, be sent out in the fullness of time and given to the world (John 3:16; Gal. 4:4; Heb. 1:6). Hence, creation (John 1:3; Col. 1:15), preservation (Heb. 1:3), and the acquisition of all of salvation (1 Cor. 1:30) are also attributed to him. He is not, like the creatures, made or created but is the firstborn of all creatures; that is, the Son who possesses the primacy and the rights of the firstborn over all creatures (Col. 1:15). Likewise, he is the firstborn from the dead, the firstborn among many brethren, and thus among all and in all things the first (Rom. 8:29; Col. 1:18).

Although in the fullness of time, though he was in the form of God, he also took the form of a servant; and he is equal to God the Father in everything (Phil. 2:6), in life (John 5:26), in knowledge (Matt. 11:27), in power (John 1:3; 5:21, 26), and in honor (John 5:23). He is himself God, above all worthy of praise for all eternity (John 1:1; 20:28; Rom. 9:5; Heb. 1:8–9). [70] As all things are *from* the Father, so are they are also all *through* the Son (1 Cor. 8:6).[16]

24. Both Father and Son unite and join together in the *Holy Spirit* and dwell through him in all creatures. Indeed, God is Spirit according to his being (John 4:24) and also holy (Isa. 6:3), but the Holy Spirit is clearly distinguished from God as Spirit. As by comparison, man is spirit in his invisible side and also has a spirit by which he knows himself; so God himself is Spirit, and he also has a Spirit who examines the depths of that being (1 Cor. 2:11). As such, it is called the Spirit of God or the Holy Spirit (Ps. 51:12; Isa. 63:10–11) in distinction from the spirit of an angel or a man or any other creature. But though distinguished from God, from the Father and the Son, he is still in the most intimate communion with them both. He is called the

15. This paragraph is identical to one in *MD*, 136–37.

16. The previous two paragraphs are a single paragraph in *MD*, 137.

breath of the Almighty (Job 33:4), the breath of his mouth (Ps. 33:6). He is sent by the Father and the Son (John 14:26; 15:26) and proceeds from both—not only from the Father (John 15:26) but also from the Son, for he is also called the Spirit of Christ or the Spirit of the Son, as well as the Spirit of the Father (Rom. 8:9).[17]

Because the Holy Spirit in this way is given or sent, poured out or proceeds from the Father and the Son, he often manifests as a power or as a gift that enables men to fulfill their calling and office. Such is the case with the Holy Spirit in Acts 8:15; 10:44; 11:15; 15:8; 19:2. One may also think of the gift of *glōssolalia* (speaking in tongues) or prophecy. But from this, many wrongly conclude that the Holy Spirit is nothing other than a gift or power of God. For clearly, he acts elsewhere as a person who bears a personal name and has personal properties and does personal works. Thus says [71] Christ in John 15:26 and 16:13–14, although the Greek word is neuter, in our language it nonetheless has a masculine pronoun: *he* will bear witness of me and glorify me; and he calls him in the same place with the name of Helper and elsewhere Comforter, which is also used of Christ in 1 John 2:1 and translated into Dutch as *Voorspraak* (Advocate). In addition to these personal names, the Holy Spirit also possess all kinds of personal properties, such as I-ness (Acts 13:2), self-consciousness (Acts 15:28), self-determination or will (1 Cor. 12:11). All kinds of personal activities are attributed to him such as examining (1 Cor. 2:11), hearing (John 16:13), speaking (Rev. 2:7), teaching (John 14:26), interceding (Rom. 8:27), etc. This is all clearly and supremely understood when he is placed in line with the Father and the Son, who are indubitably persons (Matt. 28:19; 2 Cor. 13:13).[18]

This last point, however, already contains more and indicates that the Holy Spirit is not only a person but that he is also truly God. And in this respect also, Scripture offers all the data which is necessary for this weighty confession. One must keep in mind that, in spite of the distinction shown above that exists between God and his Spirit, yet both at every turn in Scripture is interchangeable with the other so that the same God is at work whether God or the Spirit says or does something. In Acts 5:3–4, lying to the Spirit is called lying to God; in 1 Corinthians 3:16, believers are called God's temple because the Spirit of God dwells within them. In addition, an assortment of divine attributes such as eternity (Heb. 9:14), omnipresence

17. This paragraph is identical to one in *MD*, 137–38.

18. This paragraph is split into two paragraphs in *MD*, 138.

(Ps. 139:7), omniscience (1 Cor. 2:11), omnipotence (1 Cor. 12:4–6), as well as various divine works in creation (Ps. 33:6), preservation (Ps. 104:30), [72] and re-creation (John 3:3) are as much ascribed to the Holy Spirit as to the Father and the Son. Therefore, and with them, he also shares in the same honor; alongside the Father and the Son, he is also the cause of salvation (2 Cor. 3:13; Rev. 1:4). In his name we are baptized (Matt. 28:19) and blessed (2 Cor. 13:13). And blasphemy against the Holy Spirit is even an unpardonable sin (Matt. 12:31–32). While all things are *from* the Father and *through* the Son, they all exist and rest *in* the Holy Spirit.[19]

25. All these elements of Trinitarian doctrine that are spread throughout Scripture are, as it were, summarized by Jesus in his baptismal command and by the apostles in their prayer for blessing. After his resurrection and before his ascension, Christ commands his apostles to go and make disciples of all nations, and to baptize them in one name in which three different subjects have nevertheless revealed themselves. Father, Son, and Spirit are in their unity and distinction the perfect revelation of God. Likewise, according to the apostles, all salvation and blessing for man lies in the love of the Father, the grace of the Son, and the communion of the Holy Spirit (2 Cor. 13:13; 1 Pet. 1:2; 1 John 5:4–6; Rev. 1:4–6). Good pleasure, foreknowledge, power, love, the kingdom, and the power are of the Father. The mediation, the atonement, the grace, and the salvation are of the Son. Regeneration, renewal, sanctification, and communion are of the Spirit. The relationship Christ has with the Father fully corresponds to that which the Holy Spirit has with Christ. Just as the Son speaks and does nothing from himself but receives everything from the Father (John 5:26; 16:15), so the Holy Spirit receives everything from Christ (John 16:13–14). Just as the Son [73] testifies and glorifies the Father (John 1:18; 17:4, 6), so the Holy Spirit testifies of the Son and glorifies him (John 15:26; 16:14). Just as no one comes to the Father except through the Son (John 14:6), no one confesses "Jesus is Lord" except by the Holy Spirit (1 Cor. 12:3). Through the Spirit, we have fellowship with the Father and the Son themselves. In the Holy Spirit, God himself through Christ dwells in our hearts. If this is all true, then the Holy Spirit with the Son and the Father is the only true God, to praise and glorify forever.[20]

In its confession of the Trinity, the Christian church has said yes and amen to this teaching of Scripture. The church did not arrive at this rich

---

19. This paragraph is identical to one in *MD*, 138–39.
20. This paragraph is identical to one in *MD*, 139.

and glorious confession without a hard and long struggle of the spirits,[21] fighting and combatting on the one hand the threat of Arianism and on the other hand that of Sabellianism, that is both deism and pantheism. To do this, Christian theology had to utilize words and expressions such as being, persons, Trinity, personal properties, eternal generation, etc., which do not occur in the text of Scripture. This is nothing to disapprove of, for otherwise all reflection on the truth of God would be impossible. However, we must still keep in mind that all these words are of human origin, defective, and fallible, and that therefore it is the matter (*de zaak*) more than the name that is important.

This matter (*zaak*), however, is of the greatest importance for the life of the church. For in the confession of the Trinity the absolute (*volstrekt*) unity and the richest diversity of the Divine Being is preserved, Judaism. Islam, and Paganism are avoided, and the transcendence of God and his immanence are confessed. The three persons are not [74] merely forms of revelation but self-distinctions and modes of existence in the Divine Being. Father, Son, and Spirit possess one and the same divine nature and attributes; they are one in essence.[22] But they each have their own name; they each have special properties by which they are distinguished from one another: to the Father belongs Fatherhood, to the Son generation, and to the Spirit procession (*uitgang*) from both.

The order of existence in the Divine Being corresponds the order of the three persons in all the divine works. It is the Father *from* whom, it is the Son *by* whom, and it is the Spirit *in* whom all things exist. From the Father through the Son and the Spirit come all things in creation and re-creation, and in the Spirit and through the Son they all return to the Father. So, we thank the Father in particular for his electing love, the Son for his redeeming grace, and the Holy Spirit for his regenerating and renewing power.[23] The Triune God is the true God of the covenant, who is *above*, *for*, and *in* us.[24] In the love of the Father, the grace of the Son, and the communion of the Holy Spirit lie all blessings and salvation for man.[25]

21. Up until this point, this paragraph matches one in *MD*, 139–40.

22. Up until this point, this paragraph is unique to Guidebook. The remainder of the paragraph is identical to a section of a paragraph in *MD*, 142.

23. This section is identical to a paragraph in *MD*, 142.

24. This sentence is unique to *Handleiding*.

25. The final sentence of this chapter is identical to the final sentence of the chapter in *MD*, 144.

8

Creation and Providence

26. [75] While the God of revelation is the true, living God, he is also the *working* God. He cannot help but work; he always works (John 5:17); for all life and therefore especially the full, infinite life of God, is power, energy, and activity. As is the maker, so is his work. Because God is the maker, the Creator of all things, his works are great and wonderful (Pss. 92:5; 139:14; Rev. 15:3); true and faithful (Pss. 33:4; 111:7); righteous and kind (Ps. 145:17; Dan. 9:14). Yet among those works are the creation and preservation of all things, heaven and earth and humanity, the miracles of Israel and the works performed by his servants (Gen. 2:2–3; Exod. 34:10; Job 34:19; Isa. 19:25; John 9:4; etc.). And all these works exalt him (Ps. 145:10). Yes, the Lord makes himself glad in them (Ps. 104:31). He is the rock whose work is perfect (Deut. 32:4).[1]

Moreover, all these works by God are not reckless or compulsory but freely and consciously established. This has therefore already become clear to us in that speaking he brings everything to be through a single, powerful word and with the highest wisdom. But this same thought is also expressed elsewhere in Scripture: that God accomplishes everything according to his *counsel*. Only this is more clearly and powerfully expressed: that all the works of God, both in creation and [76] re-creation, are not only a revelation of his thought but also a product of his will. For, humanly speaking, all the external works of God proceed from a prior understanding and decree of the will. Therefore, the name of the counsel of the Lord varies. For example, "definite plan" (Ps. 33:11; Prov. 19:21; Isa. 46:10; Acts 2:23) occurs elsewhere with that of "decree" (Gen. 41:32; 2 Chron. 25:16; Ps. 2:7; Isa. 10:23; 14:27), "determined" (Jer. 51:12; Rom. 8:28; 9:11; Eph. 1:11; 3:11; 2 Tim. 1:9), "predestined" (Acts 10:42; 13:48; 17:26, 31; Rom. 8:29–30; Eph. 1:5, 11), and "favor" (Isa. 49:8; 53:10; 60:10; 61:2; Matt. 11:26; Eph. 1:5, 9), and Paul speaks of the counsel and good pleasure of God's will (Eph. 1:5, 11).

1. The first sentence is nearly identical to a sentence and the remainder of the paragraph is included in a larger paragraph in *MD,* 145.

From this counsel of God, the Scripture teaches further that he is great and wonderful (Isa. 28:29; Jer. 32:19), independent (*onafhankelijk*) (Matt. 11:26), immutable (Heb. 6:17), indestructible (Isa. 46:10), and that he reigns over all things (Eph. 1:11, even, for example, the transgression of the unrighteous to affix and kill Christ on the cross (Acts 2:23; 4:28). Because things and events, even the sinful thoughts and deeds of men, are eternally known and fixed in this counsel of God, they are not deprived of their character but rather are established and guaranteed all in their own kind and nature and in their context and circumstances. In this counsel of God is included sin and punishment, but also freedom (*vrijheid*) and responsibility (*verantwoordelijkheid*), the sense of obligation (*plichtsbesef*) and the conscience, the law (*wet*) and justice (*recht*). All that is and happens does so according to the counsel of the Lord, in the same connectedness as that in which reality appears and, to a greater or lesser degree, is known by us. The circumstances (*voorwaarden*) are as determined as the effects (*gevolgen*), the means (*middelen*) as well as the ends, the ways as well as the outcome (*uitkomsten*), the prayers as well as the hearings (*verhooringen*), the faith as well as the justification [77], the sanctification as well as the glorification.

Thus understood, in the sense of Scripture and according to the mind of the Spirit, the confession of the ever-wise counsel of the Lord is a source of rich consolation. For by this, we know that there is no blind chance, no dark destiny, no unreasonable and unholy will, no inescapable force of nature controls the world and humanity, but that the governance of all things rests in the hand of an all-powerful God and merciful Father. Certainly, it takes faith to understand this. For we often do not see, and in riddles man walks about on the earth; yet it is faith that sustains us in the struggles of life, enables us to trust (*vertrouwend*), and provides hope to withstand the future. For the ever wise and powerful counsel of the Lord stands eternally.[2]

27. The creation of the world was the beginning of the execution of this counsel of God. Just as Scripture alone teaches us to know the counsel of God, it is also through Scripture alone, which speaks of God's creative omnipotence, that we discover the origin of all things.[3] Science and philosophy cannot give an answer to the question of where everything comes from, and therefore in turn take the hypothesis of materialism or pantheism, of an eternal being or of eternal becoming (evolution). Scripture, on the

2. The previous three paragraphs are identical to three paragraphs in *MD*, 145–47.

3. The first two sentences of this paragraph are in *MD*, 147.

other hand, proceeds from the idea that God alone is eternal and unchangeable, the *being* who is and who was and who will be (Exod. 3:14), and by his order the world *became* and is always *becoming* (Pss. 90:2; 102:26–28). In other words, [the difference between *being* and *becoming*] is the principal and fundamental difference between Creator and creature.

[78] As creation, the whole world has its origin in God alone. There is no matter and no eternal power alongside God, but heaven and earth and all things are called into being by him. That is what Scripture expresses through the word *creation*. In a broad sense, this word is also utilized for the work of preservation (Ps. 104:30; Isa. 45:7), but in a narrow sense, it denotes the concept that God has brought forth all things out of nothing. True, the expression that God created all things *out of nothing* (*ex nihilo*) does not come from Scripture but appears first in 2 Maccabees 7:28; this term can also give rise to misunderstanding.[4] For *nothing* is not something and cannot be the principle or the origin from which all things originated; indeed, nothing can come from nothing. Scripture, on the other hand, states that the world was called into being by the *will* of God (Rev. 4:11) and "that what is seen was not made out of things that are visible" (Heb. 11:3). However, the expression "from nothing" can be understood in a good sense and also serve to dispel all kinds of errors, such as if the world was formed from some substance or power that existed eternally beside God. According to Scripture, God is not merely the former but also the Creator of the world. Humanly speaking, he first existed alone, and then the whole world was produced according to his counsel and by his will. The existence of the world was completely nonexistent beforehand, and so one can correctly say that God created the world out of nothing.[5]

This is the explicit teaching of Scripture: that God has existed from eternity (Ps. 90:2), but that the world had a beginning (Gen. 1:1). Frequently, it has been declared that God has done something prior to the foundation of the world; for example, elected and loved (John 17:24; Eph. 1:4). He is so powerful that he only needs to speak for something to be (Ps. 33:9), and to make the things [79] that are not as if they were (Rom. 4:17).

4. Many Bibles today do include the Maccabees and other books known as the apocrypha or inter-testament books. Bavinck's conception of the canon is typical for most post-Reformation theologians. "I beg you, my child, to look at the heaven and the earth and see everything that is in them and recognize that God did not make them out of things that existed. And in the same way the human race came into being" (2 Macc. 7:28 NRSV).

5. This is nearly identical to a paragraph in *MD*, 149.

Solely by his will does he give the world existence (Rev. 4:11). He has made everything—the heavens and the earth and all that is in them (Exod. 20:11; Neh. 9:6); from, and through, and to him are all things (Rom. 11:36). That is why he is also the almighty possessor of heaven and earth (Gen. 14:19, 22), who does everything that pleases him, to whose power there is no limit, on whom all creatures are completely dependent (*afhankelijk*) so that they cannot stir or move without his will (Ps. 115:3; Dan. 4:35). Scripture knows nothing of an unformed, eternal material alongside God; he is the only, absolute cause of all that is and happens, so that what is seen was not made out of things that are visible, but the whole world is prepared by the word of God (Heb. 11:3).[6]

This same distinction between Creator and creature is also maintained by Scripture in answering the question: *Why* or *for what purpose* did God create the world?[7] Philosophers have often said that the world is necessary for God, either to deliver him from his abundance or to meet some lack in him. But according to Scripture, God is the completely blessed in himself; he is in no way dependent on the world, but the world is dependent (*afhankelijk*) on him in an absolute sense (Job 22:2–3; Acts 17:25; Rom. 11:36). Creation was a completely free act of God; by his will all things and all beings were created (Rev. 4:11). However, that will is not arbitrary but contains the highest wisdom; all the work of God proceeds from and rests upon the counsel of God and is a work of the Trinity.[8] Before creation, he consulted wisdom (Job 28:20f; Prov. 8:22f,). And in time, he created all things by the Word, which in the beginning was with God and was God (John 1:1–3; Eph. 3:9; Col. 1:16; Heb. 1:2); and in the Spirit who searches the depths of God, he brought the creatures [80] to life and adorned the heavens (Job 26:12, 33:4; 1 Cor. 2:10). "How great," therefore, the psalmist cries out, "O Lord, how manifold are your works! In wisdom have you made them all; the earth is full of your creatures" (Ps. 104:24).

---

6. This is identical to a paragraph in *MD*, 149–50.

7. Cf. *MD*, 177. [Dutch: "Als God, die het eeuwige en volzalige wezen is, de wereld door zijn wil geschapen heeft, komt vanzelf de vraag op, *waarom* en *waartoe* Hij haar in het aanzijn geroepen heeft."] English: If God, who is the eternal being full of bliss, created the world by his will, the question automatically surfaces, *why* and *for what purpose* has he called it into being. *Handleiding* [Dutch: "Ditzelfde strenge onderscheid tusschen Schepper en schepsel wordt door de Schrift ook gehandhaafd bij het antwoord op de vraag: *waarom* en *waartoe* God de wereld schiep."]

8. The remainder of the paragraph is also a portion of a paragraph in *MD*, 151.

Thereby, Scripture also teaches us that God has created, maintains, and reigns over all things for his own glory. The purpose for which creatures have been created cannot, of course, lie in this alone, because the establishment of the end precedes the means. In general, Scripture also states that just as everything is from God, so also everything is through and to him (Rom. 11:36). And on this, Scripture further elaborates when it proclaims that the heavens declare the glory of God (Ps. 19:1), that God glorifies himself in Pharaoh (Exod. 14:17) and in the man born blind (John 9:3), that he grants all the benefits of grace for the sake of his own name (Isa. 43:25; Eph. 1:6), that Christ came to glorify the Father (John 17:4), and that every knee shall bow and acknowledge his glory (Phil. 2:11). It is God's good pleasure to reveal all his attributes to creatures, and thereby to prepare glory and honor for himself from all creatures. God does not require the world for this glorification, for it is not the creature who increases his glory autonomously (*zelfstandig*) and independently (*onafhankelijk*), but it is always God himself who, with or without the creature, glorifies his own name and delights in himself. Therefore, God never seeks out the creature, as if this could give him something he lacks or take something he already possesses. But the whole world in its breadth and length is a mirror to him by which he makes known his attributes. He always remains in himself as the highest good and remains eternally blessed by his own glory.

28. [81] As for the order in which God accomplished the work of creation, the first thing to note is that—according to Genesis 1:1 as regards their basic components—the heavens and earth were created in the beginning when there was neither time nor space, but time and space began to exist in the same moment and in the same form when the heavens and earth began to exist. Second, the earth then was for an unknown time in a state not of devastation but of wildness and emptiness—that is, in an unformed and formless state in which there was still no separation between light and darkness, water and waters, land and sea, and also no adornment with plants, animals, and humanity. Third, the works of six days are clearly divided into two groups, each of three days. The first group of works is introduced with the creation of light and brings distinction and separation, form and shape, color and tone; the second group of works begins with the formation of the bearers of light—sun, moon, and stars—and then subsequently, to fill the earth and provide those would inhabit it—birds and fish, animals and people. Fourth, the work of creation, according to the repeated testimony of the Scriptures (Gen. 2:1–2; Exod. 20:11; 31:17), was accomplished in six days.

Yet there has always been great freedom of thought and remarkable difference of opinion about the concept of these days. None other than Augustine held the view that God had created everything all at once and in the same moment, and that six days were not consecutive parts of time but only viewpoints from which the rank and order of the creatures could be contemplated. And from another side, there are more than a few who believe the days of creation to be much longer ages than twenty-four hours.[9] Be that as it may, the six days remain the creation week in which the [82] heavens and the earth and all their hosts were brought forth.[10] They point to the temporal order whereby the creatures one after another were brought into existence, and they contain an indication of the relationship of rank in which they relate to each other. This corresponds to reality, just as we still observe it daily. No scientific research can destroy this. For in rank and order, the formless precedes the formed, the inorganic precedes the organic, the plant precedes the animal, the animal precedes man. Man is and remains the crown of creation; the seasons of the earth were prepared for him. This is why the Scriptures also say so little about the creation of heaven and angels, and it is primarily about the earth. In an astronomical sense, the earth may be small and insignificant; in mass and weight, it may be surpassed by thousands of planets, suns, and stars; in a religious and moral sense, it remains the center (*middelpunt*) of the universe. It and it alone has been chosen as the dwelling place for man; a wrestling arena in which the great battle is fought against the powers of evil; a place of establishment for the kingdom of heaven.

In Scripture, all of creation is contained under the name of heaven and earth and all their host (Gen. 2:1), or also summarized as the "world." The original words, which are rendered in our Bibles by "world," now more often understood as a globe or circle (1 Sam. 2:8; Prov. 8:31), and then also as the dwelling place of man, insofar as it is inhabited by humanity (Matt. 24:14; Luke 2:1); occasionally, it draws more attention to the world in its temporary, changing, and transient state (Ps. 49:1–2; Luke 1:70; Eph. 1:21); and then also it points together to the unity of the world and the wholeness of all creatures together (John 1:10; Acts 17:24). These last two meanings [83] especially possess a rich content. The world, as it were, can always be

9. Up until this point, this paragraph is identical to a portion of a paragraph in *MD*, 154.

10. From this point onward, the paragraph is identical to a portion of a paragraph in *MD* 155–56.

viewed from these two points of view; it can be considered in its breadth and in its length.[11]

In the first case, it demonstrates an immensely rich diversity of creatures, which may be perceived as distinct, coexisting *beside* one another, giving the impression of wonderful harmony. Under the second point of view, the world is an age-old process by which, under the providence of God, it gradually becomes what it should be. However it is looked at, they remain *one* in spite of the thousands and millions of planets from which it is composed, *finite* despite the endless spaces in which it expands, and also *good* not only because it was brought into existence by the hand of God (Gen. 1:31), but also because it is still preserved and reigned over by his hand and, with or against his will, will be made subservient to his honor.

29. All of these considerations automatically lead from creation to providence. As a matter of fact, from the very first moment when the world as a whole or each of its creatures is called into being by the creative act of God, they pass at once and immediately into the hand of God's providence. There is no gradual transition here, much less a division or split. For just as creatures on account of them being creatures do not come *from* themselves into *existence*, likewise they cannot for a moment *through* themselves continue to *exist*.[12] Providence is immediately wed to creation, and creation passes directly and immediately into providence.[13]

This reveals the close relationship that exists between them both. And it is of utmost importance to hold the coherence of creation and providence before the face of deism.[14] The Scriptures accomplish this when [84] they make the work of providence a quickening (Job 33:4; Neh. 9:6), a renewal (Ps. 104:30), a preservation (Ps. 36:7), a speaking (Ps. 33:9), a will (Rev. 4:11), a work (John 5:17), upholding by the word of his power (Heb. 1:3), a care (1 Pet. 5:7), indeed even a creating (Ps. 104:30; Isa. 45:7; Amos 4:13). Implied in all these expressions is the truth that God did not leave the world to itself after creation and does not observe it from afar. The word *providence* must not be understood in this way, nor may it ever serve to push the living God and his operations aside or into the background. Providence

---

11. This paragraph is uniform with a paragraph in *MD*, 156.

12. There is a little bit of wordplay in the Dutch that is lost in English. [Dutch: "Want evenals de schepselen juist omdat zij schepselen zijn, niet *uit* zichzelf *ont*staan; zoo kunnen zij ook geen enkel oogenblik *door* zichzelf *be*staan."]

13. This paragraph is identical to one in *MD*, 159–60.

14. In *MD*, Bavinck engages Darwinism, Kant, and Pelagianism (each of which are absent from this chapter).

does not solely mean that God foresees things (that he sees them beforehand though they go their own way), but it also implies that God provides all that is necessary for the world (Gen. 22:8; 1 Sam. 16:1; Ezek. 20:6; Heb. 11:40). It is an act, not only of God's intellect but also of his will, an execution of his counsel, an operation by which he sustains the world from moment to moment. According to the beautiful description of the Heidelberg Catechism, "God's providence is his *almighty* and *ever-present power*."[15]

Preservation, which is ordinarily called the first operation of providence, is not a passive watching nor a *leaving* it be and walking away; it is an *active* subsistence, a *preservation*, a maintaining in the realest sense of the word.[16] It proceeds from God's power out of his almighty power; just as in the beginning it made the world to arise, it keeps the world turning (Pss. 33:9; 104:30; 107:26; 147:15; Rev. 4:11); that power does not work from afar but from close by. It is an omnipresent power. God is present with his being in all creatures (Ps. 139:7; Jer. 23:23; Acts 17:27), and all creatures, without exception, [85] live and move and exist in him (Acts 17:28), exist through him (Rom. 11:36), are sustained by the power of the Son (Heb. 1:2–3; Col. 1:17), and are created and renewed by God's Spirit (Ps. 104:30).

However, this intimate relationship between creation and providence must not be mixed with pantheism. This distinction cannot be overlooked. That there is such a distinction is evident from the fact that after the completion of the work of creation, God rested (Gen. 2:2; Exod. 20:11; 31:17). For although this rest is not a cessation of all work (Isa. 40:26–28; John 5:17), it is nevertheless cessation of a peculiar work, which is designated by the word *creation*; for creation is a production out of nothing (in the sense described above), and the work of preservation maintains that which has been brought into existence.[17]

For through creation the world does not become independent, for an independent creature is an inner contradiction, but it does nevertheless receive a being and existence distinct from the being of God. God and the world are distinct in name, in form, and in essence from each other; they

---

15. Heidelberg Catechism, Lord's Day 10. In *MD*, 161, the Heidelberg Catechism receives its own discussion.

16. This sentence is uniform with one in *MD*, 161. The remainder of the paragraph is an abridgement of *MD*, 161–62.

17. This paragraph is unique to *Handleiding* though it is similar in content to paragraphs in *MD*, 161–62. In *MD*, Bavinck discusses "voortgaande schepping" (continuous creation) and goes into greater depth engaging deism, which are both absent from the discussion above.

differ from each other as eternity and time, as infinity and finiteness, as Creator and creature.[18]

30. In itself, it is already of the utmost importance to retain this essential difference between God and the world. For whoever disbelieves or denies this distinction destroys religion, fashions God as a creature, and in principle performs that same sin Paul denounced of the Gentiles when he says, "For although they knew God, they did not honor him as God or give thanks to him" (Rom. 1:21). But there is an additional consideration that makes it necessary to never lose sight of the distinction between God and the world, between creation [86] and providence.[19]

For if God is, as it were, identical with the world and therefore not essentially distinguished from humanity, then all thought and action of mankind is immediately and directly an account of God; then sin is his work, and there is actually no sin anymore. Now, on the one hand, Scripture speaks as strongly as possibly that man, with all his thoughts and deeds and with all his sins, is under God's government. Humanity never becomes independent (*onafhankelijk*) of God. "The Lord looks down from heaven; he sees all the children of man. . . . He who fashions the hearts of them all and observes all their deeds" (Ps. 33:13, 15). He determines their dwellings (Deut. 32:8; Acts 17:26), establishes his steps, (Prov. 5:21; 16:9; Jer. 10:23), "and he does according to his will among the host of heaven and among the inhabitants of the earth" (Dan. 4:35); they are in his hands as in the hand of the potter and as a saw in the hand of one who hews (Isa. 29:16; 45:9; Jer. 18:6; Rom. 9:20–21).

When man becomes a sinner, he does not therefore free himself of God, but rather his dependence (*afhankelijkheid*) only takes on a different character: it loses its rational and moral nature and becomes creaturely subjection. The man, who becomes a slave of sin, lowers himself in God's hand into a pure instrument. And thus Scripture can say that God hardens, blinds, and makes stubborn (Exod. 4:21f.; Deut. 2:30; Josh. 11:20; Rom. 9:18), that he sends a lying spirit in the mouth of the prophets (1 Kings 22:23), that he appoints David through Satan to count the people (2 Sam. 24:1; 1 Chron 21:1), that he commands Shimei to curse David (2 Sam. 16:10), that he gives people over to their sins (Rom. 1:24), that he sends "a powerful delusion" (2 Thess. 2:11), and that Christ not only possesses a rising but also a falling of many (Luke 2:34).[20]

---

18. This paragraph is identical to a portion of a larger paragraph in *MD*, 162.

19. This paragraph is uniform with a paragraph in *MD*, 162.

20. This paragraph and the previous paragraph are a single paragraph in *MD*, 163.

[87] And yet, however much God's providence proceeds alongside of sin, Scripture nonetheless asserts as firmly and decisively that sin does not have its origin in God but in man, and it is not because of God, but only on account of man. The Lord is righteous and holy and far from wickedness (Deut. 32:4; Job 34:10), a light in whom there is no darkness (1 John 1:5), tempting no one (James 1:13), and he is the abundant fountain of all things good and pure (Ps. 36:9; James 1:17). He forbids sin in his law (Exod. 20) and in the conscience (*geweten*) of every man (Rom. 2:14–15); he has no desire for wickedness (Ps. 5:4) but hates it, and his wrath is against it (Rom. 1:18), and he threatens it with temporal and eternal punishment (Rom. 2:8).[21]

These lines of Holy Scripture—in which, on one hand, from beginning to end sin is under God's governance and yet, on the other hand, sin arises on account of man—can only be connected to one another if God and the world are not divorced from each other, and yet in essence they are distinct from each other.[22] That is what theology attempts to do when in its account of God's providence it mentions *cooperation* as a second piece along with that of preservation. For by this, one attempts to indicate that God is the *first* cause of all that is and happens, but that the creatures under, in, and through him also act as the *second* cause, who cooperate with the first cause.[23] Certainly, this applies to all of humanity, who are created by God as rational creatures and are always considered and treated by him as such. God and the world are never separated, and yet they are always distinguished. That is the way in which God's work and man's responsibility can be maintained and reconciled.

---

21. This paragraph is uniform with one in *MD*, 163.

22. Bavinck desires to wedge his theological position between pantheism and deism. God is not the world; therefore, he cannot be held accountable for man's sin. God is also not detached from the world; therefore, he is providentially engaged in governing the world. That man is responsible for his sin and that God governs all things, including sin, are two ideas Bavinck believes can be held together if one attends to the scriptural account of God.

23. Up until this point, this paragraph is identical to one in *MD*, 163–64. What remains is unique to *Handleiding*. The point Bavinck is making about first and secondary causes is in line with the Reformed tradition—that is, that God as the first cause does not entail that God is responsible for the activity of his creatures, but rather God pursues his own goals through the secondary causes of his creatures, that is by allowing them to have their own power of producing effects and their own freedom of activity.

Thus the doctrine of providence also becomes a rich source of comfort for the Christian. For in spite of the presence of sin and misery in the world, [88] in the end it is not the devil but God, the Almighty, the Father of our Lord Jesus Christ, who created the world and yet by his providence preserves and rules it. He not only preserves it, but he also rules and reigns over it; and he does so in such a way that the world turns and cooperates with the end he has determined.[24] The *governance* of God is implied as the third part, alongside preservation and cooperation of the providence of God. God reigns. He is the King of kings and the Lord of lords (1 Tim. 6:15; Rev. 19:6), and his kingdom lasts forever (1 Tim. 1:17). No coincidence and no fate, no arbitrary will and no compulsion, no capricious mood and no iron necessity rules nature, history, and the destiny of the children of man. For behind all secondary causes lies the will of an all-powerful God and faithful Father.

24. Cf. *MD*, 165. The remainder of the paragraph is identical to one in *MD*, 165.

9

Origin, Essence, and Destiny of Mankind

31. [89] The story of the origin of heaven and earth in the first chapter coincides with the creation of man. The creation of the other creatures, of heaven and earth, of sun, moon, and stars, of plants and animals, is reported in short words and the creation of the angels is not even mentioned at all. But when Scripture arrives at man, it dwells on him for a long time; it describes not only the fact but also the manner of his creation and returns in a very comprehensive manner in the second chapter of Genesis.[1] The special attention that is devoted to the origin of man is proof by itself that man is the end and the crown of the work of creation. But additional important detail is added to that.

There is, in the first place, the special counsel of God, which precedes the creation of man and in which particular emphasis is placed on the fact that man, in distinction from all other creatures, is created in God's image and likeness (Gen. 1:26). Furthermore, it should be noted that God did not create a single human being, but he created a pair of humans, male and female, who—not only each for themselves but together in covenant [90] with each other and therefore the parents of all of humanity—were created in God's image (Gen. 1:27–28). Finally, it is explicitly mandated that the man, who is created in God's image, must reign over all living beings and have dominion over the earth. Because the man is God's son, he is also king of the earth; being a child of God and inheriting the world belong together.

The story of the creation of humanity in Genesis 1 is explained in greater detail and further supplemented in Genesis 2:4–25; [in Genesis 1,] man is regarded as the pinnacle of creation; [in Genesis 2,] as the beginning of history. That is why [in Genesis 1] the first dwelling place of man is extensively discussed; namely, paradise, situated in the region of Eden, east of Palestine, either more to the north in Armenia or more to the south in Babylonia. Subsequently, in Genesis 2, the divine prohibition occurs: that

1. This portion of the paragraph matches a portion of one in *MD*, 166.

is, the freedom to eat from all the trees of the garden except from the one tree of the knowledge of good and evil, and thereby also the positive command to cultivate and guard the garden of Eden (to protect it against all evil power). Obedience to God and dominion over the earth, cult (*cultus*) and culture (*cultuur*) go together.

The third special feature in [Genesis 2] is the creation of the woman and the institution of marriage. Adam remains, therefore, the principal and head of the human race; the woman is not *beside* him but is created *from* him (1 Cor. 11:8), created out of him, in his (*zijn*) image, as a helper for man, not as a mistress, nor as beneath man as his servant, not inferior nor lower, but rather as her own free (*vrij*) and independent (*zelfstandig*) person distinct from the man.[2]

Therefore, Scripture narrates the origin of humanity, both of the man and the woman, and it introduces [91] the institution of marriage along with the beginning of the human race.[3] In our current time, each of these has been framed completely differently in the name of science with the concept of evolution (development) taking the place of creation. But it should be remembered that, first, man exists and therefore must come from somewhere; in rejecting creation, there is not much else left than having him gradually originate from the development of the animal; second, the scientist knows nothing of the origin of things with certainty, because if man originated from animals, this would have had to take place in prehistoric times, an area in which empiricism has failed us, leaving us only with guesses and opinions at most hypotheses; and third, just like the origin of matter, force, and movement, so also the origin of life, of consciousness, of reason and will, of religion and morality, and therefore all of culture, also according to the recognition of many men of science, belongs up to the present day to the unsolved riddles of the world.

32. The origin of man corresponds with his essence. For man, although his body was formed from the dust of the earth, received the breath of life from above and was fashioned by God himself; therefore, he has his own being; he has a nature of his own. That essence lies in the fact that he is the *image of God* and displays his *likeness*.[4] This distinguishes him from both

2. The previous two paragraphs are unique to *Handleiding*.

3. This sentence is identical to a sentence in *MD*, 172. The remainder of the paragraph is unique to *Handleiding*.

4. The first portion of this paragraph is identical to a portion of one in *MD*, 181. The remainder of this paragraph is an abridgement of *MD*, 181–88, drawing out the distinction between humans, angels, and animals.

animals and angels. He has similarities and differences from both with a nature of his own. Animals are not mechanisms but organisms; they are even called, like men, living souls (*zielen*) in the Scriptures (Gen. 1:20–21, 24); they are also maintained in their being by the Spirit of God, who is the origin of all life; but they do not have their [92] own free, independent spirit with reason and will and therefore no religion or morality, no proper culture; they are and remain natural beings (*natuurwezens*). Likewise, man is distinguished from the angels as the image of God; nonetheless, these were also created by God (Col. 1:16). They possess a reasonable and moral nature; they even surpass people in knowledge and power (Ps. 103:20; Matt. 18:10; 24:36), but they are mere spirits without a body (Heb. 1:14). They were all created at the same time, and thereby stand side by side as individuals; and though on account of their number and rank are divided into distinct classes (cherubim, seraphim, thrones, powers, etc.) (Gen. 3:24; Isa. 6:2; Eph. 1:21; 3:13; Col. 1:16; 2:10, etc.), they do not form an organic species. Ultimately, angels experience God's power, wisdom, and goodness, but humans share in his eternal mercies. God is their Lord, but he is not their Father; Christ is their head, but he is not their reconciler and Savior; the Holy Spirit is their sender and guide, but he never testifies with their spirits that they are children, heirs of God, and coheirs with Christ. That is why the eyes of the angels are cast toward the earth: for here, God's richest grace has appeared and God's manifold wisdom has been made manifest (Eph. 3:10; 1 Pet. 1:2).

The image of God, after which man was created, coincides with the whole of his human nature. Man is the image of God, on account of and insofar as he is man, in the full sense of this word; he is not an image-bearer but an image—a complete, totally corresponding image and likeness just as the words reinforce each other: *image* and *likeness*.[5] What man is in miniature, God is in greatness, in infinite greatness; as a creature, man is absolutely dependent on God, yet as a man he is related to him, like a son to his father. This image, [93] therefore, comes first in the spiritual (*geestelijke*), rational (*redelijke*), and moral (*zedelijke*) nature with all its faculties and powers; even the body is not utterly excluded from it; for though Scripture does explicitly say that God is Spirit (John 4:24) and nowhere writes of him as possessing a body, nonetheless insofar as the body serves man as the organ of his spirit (*geest*), it shows the only likeness of the way in which God works as Spirit, and by which Scripture also speaks analogically of God

5. Cf. *MD*, 188.

with his hands and feet, ears and eyes, etc. All this belongs to the image of God in a broader sense; and inasmuch as man, even after his fall in sin, has preserved this human nature and remained a man, he can even now still be called God's image and offspring (Gen. 9:6; Acts 17:28; James 3:9).[6]

But we all feel like we are not normal people; we are not who we ought to be; we are no longer spiritually and physically healthy people but have become sinners. That was not the case for the first man when he was first formed by God's hand. He was created in God's image, and this image included his spiritual and physical health, which was designated as knowledge, righteousness, and holiness or as original righteousness, and in Reformed theology as the image of God in a narrow sense, which is distinct from the above image in a broader sense (Eph. 4:24; Col. 3:10; Rom. 8:29; 2 Pet. 1:14).

The Reformed, contrary to Rome, held that this image of God in a narrow sense belonged to the essence of man—not as if it had existed in a substance that was lost by sin, for then the fallen man would no longer be truly human; but in this sense, original righteousness is a necessary property or quality of the normal man, just as health is such a property of the body. For if man loses this, he still will remain [94] a man but becomes an abnormal one, an ill one, a sick man. With this image in a full sense, therefore, the man was also bound to live in paradise, immortality, and to have dominion over the earth, but only if he remained obedient to God's command.[7]

33. Subjugation to the test command proves that the first man, despite how much he had, did not yet possess the highest, the heavenly blessedness, eternal life in the presence of God. He was indeed dependent on the changing of day and night, of waking and sleeping; while we are told of the heavenly Jerusalem that there will be no night there (Rev. 21:25; 22:5)[8] and the ones redeemed by the blood of the Lamb stand before the throne of God and serve him day and night in his temple (Rev. 7:15). The first man was bound by the division of the week into six days of work and one day of rest; but for the people of God an eternal, unshakable rest awaits (Heb. 4:9; Rev. 14:13). In the state of innocence, man needed food and drink daily; but in the future, God will abolish the stomach and food (1 Cor. 6:13). The first human couple consisted of a man and a woman, and they received the blessing to be fruitful and to multiply; but in the resurrection, they do not marry and are not given in marriage, but they will be like the angels

6. This paragraph is unique to *Handleiding*.

7. The previous two paragraphs are unique to *Handleiding*.

8. The remainder of the paragraph is identical to one in *MD*, 201–2.

of God in heaven (Matt. 22:30). The first man, Adam, was earthly; he was from the soil; he had a natural body (*natuurlijk lichaam*) that became a living soul, but believers will receive a spiritual body (*geestlijk lichaam*) in the resurrection and will then bear the image of the heavenly man, Christ, the Lord of heaven (1 Cor. 15:45–49). Adam was created in such a way that he could still err, sin, fall, and die; but believers are in principle already [95] above all that is here on earth: they can no longer sin, for "no one who is born of God makes a practice of sinning, for God's seed abides in him, and he cannot keep on sinning, because he has been born of God" (1 John 3:9); they can no longer fall away, for "they are by God's power being guarded through faith for a salvation ready to be revealed in the last time" (1 Pet. 1:5); they can no longer die either, for those who believe in Christ already have eternal, incorruptible life on earth; they never die, and they shall live even though they have died (John 11:25–26).

What Adam did not possess, he had to obtain by way of his works (hence the name of the covenant of works), according to free choice, through obedience to God's command. This commandment first of all included the moral law that the man created in God's image knew in his own heart, but also the *prohibition* to eat from the tree of the knowledge of good and evil, which was added as a test of the moral law. On this issue, it would and should become manifest whether man, in determining what is good and evil, would keep God's word unconditionally or would follow his own path. Though indeed Adam was able-to-not-sin (*kunnen-niet-zondigen*), he was not yet participating in the not-able-to-sin (*niet-kunnen-zondigen*); with all the riches that he possessed spiritually and physically, he lacked one important thing: *absolute certainty*.[9] As long as we are missing this, our rest and enjoyment will never be complete; what we possess, we can still lose again at any moment. So it was with the first man. His origin was divine, his nature was kindred with the divine, and his destiny was the vision of God. But whether or not he would reach that destiny was made by his own choice and made dependent (*afhankelijk*) on his own, free will.[10]

9. Cf. *MD*, 203.

10. These final two sentences are identical to the final two sentences of a paragraph in *MD*, 203.

10

Sin and Death

34. [96] Already by the third chapter of Genesis, we are told of the fall and of the disobedience of the first man. The fall was presumably only a short time after creation. But no matter how close creation and the fall were to each other in a time-based sense, they are essentially distinct: creation was God's work; the fall of man came about through the temptation of Satan.[1]

To be specific, sin was not first on the earth, but rather it broke out in heaven, in the immediate vicinity of God, at the foot of his throne. The thought, the desire (*wensch*), the will to resist God first arose in the heart of angels; perhaps pride (*hoogmoed*) was the first sin and therefore was the beginning and the foundation of their fall (1 Tim. 3:6).[2] This fall occurred after the completion of the creation work (Gen. 1:31) and before the disobedience of man, but is only briefly mentioned in Scripture (John 8:44; 1 John 3:8; 2 Pet. 2:4; Judg. 6). Yet that spiritual kingdom of wickedness stepped into being, with countless demons, evil spirits, unclean spirits, each one worse than the next (Matt. 12:45); they are the subjects of Satan the adversary (Job 1:6; 1 Chron 21:1; Zech. 3:1; Matt. 4:2; etc.), who is their head. The names by which Satan is referred to in Scripture are as follows: the devil (slanderer), the enemy, the evil one, the accuser, Belial [97] (wickedness), Beelzebul (originally the name of the flying god venerated in Ekron), chief of the devils, prince of the kingdom of the air, prince of the world, god of this age, great dragon, ancient serpent—all indicate that the realm of darkness, from the beginning to the end of the world, struggles against humanity and, more specifically, battles to overthrow the church of Christ if possible. This rupture already began in paradise; the serpent, who was more cunning (cleverer) than all the beasts of the field (Gen. 3:1; Matt. 10:16) served as an instrument of demonic power (John 8:44; 1 John 3:8;

1. Cf. *MD*, 203–4.
2. Cf. *MD*, 204. The remainder of this paragraph is original to *Handleiding*.

Rev. 12:9) and satanically approached the probationary command to tempt the man and lead him to disobedience.

First, therefore, the prohibition given by God is presented as an arbitrary, imposed burden, as an unnecessary restriction of man's freedom; thus in Eve's soul (*ziel*), the seed of doubt is sown concerning the divine origin and justification of the prohibition. Subsequently, that doubt developed into unbelief by the thought that God had given that prohibition only out of fear that man would become like him by knowing good and evil as [God] does. In turn, this unbelief stimulated the imagination and made the violation of the prohibition appear to be a path that leads not to death but to true life, to divinity. The imagination then influences the inclination and aspiration of man, so that the forbidden tree comes to be viewed in a different light: it becomes a delight for the eyes and a desire (*begeerlijkheid*) for the heart. Having taken hold, that desire (*begeerlijkheid*) drives the will (*wil*) and gives birth to the sinful deed; Eve "took of its fruit and ate, and she also gave some to her husband who was with her, and he ate" (Gen. 3:1–6).[3]

35. [98] In this simple but profoundly psychological (*diep-zielkundige*) way, Scripture tells the story of the fall and the origin of sin. Sin still arises this way; it begins with the darkening of the mind, continues in the excitement of the imagination, arouses desire (*begeerlijkheid*) in the heart, and ends in the act of the will.[4] Furthermore, Scripture makes no attempt to explain sin—that is, it derives sin from preexisting factors. In the dynamic (*veranderlijken*) state in which man was created, and in the probationary command that God gave him, lies the *possibility (mogelijkheid)* of sin, but the transition to *reality* (*werkelijkheid)* remains shrouded in darkness. Sin is there, but it should not be there; it was and is and remains in conflict with God's law and with the testimony of our conscience.

By connecting these two things with each other—that is, on the one hand to give a psychological (*zielkundige*) description of the origin of sin, whose truth is felt at every moment in our own lives; and on the other hand, through displaying sin fully in its irrational (*onredelijke*) and unlawful (*onwettelijke*) nature—the story of the fall in Genesis[5] rises high above all that the wisdom of men has devised in the course of the centuries concerning the origin of evil. Gradually, they attempted to explain sin from the

---

3. This paragraph is nearly identical to one in *MD*, 206.

4. The first portion of this paragraph is identical to a portion of a paragraph in *MD*, 206.

5. The first portion of this paragraph is identical to a portion of one in *MD*, 207.

circumstances in which man lives (the environment, the society), or from his sensual nature (the flesh, the carnal desires), or out of his animal origin, or from the eternality of matter as opposed to the spirit, or from an evil God, who eternally coexists next to a good God, the God of light, or out of a mysterious dark nature within God. But all these explanations reckon sin to God's account, rob sin of its ethical nature, and make it eternal and unconquerable, barring the road of the destruction of existence.

[99] With the distinction of creation and the fall, of God's work and man's voluntary (*vrijwillige*) and willful (*moedwillige*) disobedience, only the nature of sin remains. If sin does not have its origin in the will of the creature but in its being, which precedes the will, then it immediately loses its ethical character, its moral character, and becomes a physical, natural, existential, and an evil inseparable from the nature of things. Sin, however, is a phenomenon of moral nature; it is at home in the moral realm and exists as a deviation from the moral law, which God has given and established for the rational (*redelijk*) creature and his will.[6] The first sin consisted in the violation of the probationary command and therein the whole moral law, which rested with the probationary command in the same divine authority. The manifold names by which Holy Scripture identifies sin all point in the same direction: transgression, disobedience, iniquity, wickedness, and enmity against God, etc. Paul expressly states that we have knowledge of sin through the law (Rom. 3:20), and John (1 John 3:4) declares that all sin, the smallest as well as the greatest, is iniquity (*ongerechtigheid*), lawlessness (*wetteloosheid*), and unlawfulness (*onwettelijkheid*).

That is why evil can never come any other way than *after* good: first through and by the existence of good, and evil is also situated in nothing other than the corruption of good. Even the evil angels, though sin has corrupted their entire nature, are and remain good as creatures. Also the good, as far as it is in the essence and being of things, is not destroyed by sin but is steered in another direction and abused for another purpose. Man has not lost his essence or his human nature through sin; he still has a soul and a body, a mind and a will, and all kinds of affections (*aandoeningen*) and inclinations (*genegenheden*).[7]

All those gifts in themselves are good and descend [100] from the Father of lights, but are now used by men as weapons against God and put into the service of iniquity. Sin is therefore not merely an exposed absence,

6. The remainder of the paragraph is nearly identical to one in *MD*, 211.
7. Cf. *MD*, 211–12.

or solely a loss of what man originally possessed. For example, a man who was rich and became poor suffers a loss and greatly misses much of what he used to enjoy. But sin is a deprivation of that in which man must participate to be truly human; and it is at the same time, the introduction of a defect, a disfigurement, a deformity, which is contrary to God's law and his own nature.[8]

36. The first sin, which man himself was guilty of perpetrating, did not end in itself; it was not an act he could just shake off after committing; after that he could no longer behave as if nothing had happened. At the very moment when man gave a place to sin in his thought and imagination, in his desire and will, a terrible change took place within him. This is evident from the fact that immediately after the fall, Adam and Eve sought to hide themselves from God and each other. "Then the eyes of both were opened, and they knew that they were naked" (Gen. 3:7). They suddenly stood face to face in a completely different relationship: they saw each other as they had never seen each other before; they were afraid and could not see each other freely and open-mindedly; they felt guilty and unclean, and they stitched fig tree leaves together to conceal themselves from each other.[9] Shame and fear took hold of them because they had become sinners, lost God's image, and felt guilty and unclean before him.

But the terror of the first sin becomes even starker in this, that it spreads from the first human couple [101] to the whole of mankind. The first step in the wrong direction has been taken, and all of the descendants of Adam and Eve follow suit. The universality of sin is a fact that imposes itself on everyone's consciousness (*bewustzijn*), and which is unquestionably established according to both the testimony of experience and the teaching of Holy Scripture.[10] No one is exempt from it apart from Christ, the Righteous One, but no one else—not even Mary, as Rome claims: "for the intention of man's heart is evil from his youth" (Gen. 6:5; 8:21).

Such is the testimony before and after the flood, and this testimony is repeated again and again (1 Kings 8:46; Job 14:4; Pss. 14; 53; 103:3; 143:2; Eccl. 7:20; Prov. 20:9; Jer. 3:15; John 3:6; Rom. 3:9–20; etc.); the gospel is built on this supposition (Mark 1:15; 16:15–16; John 3:3): "the whole world

8. Apart from the final sentence, this is a nearly identical to a paragraph in *MD*, 212.

9. Apart from the final sentence, this is nearly identical to a paragraph in *MD*, 212–13.

10. The previous portion of the paragraph is identical to a section of a paragraph in *MD*, 213. The final sentence of the paragraph is unique to *Handleiding*.

lies in the power of the evil one" (1 John 5:19). This terrible state in which humanity and the world finds itself (*verkeeren*) automatically raises the question, "What is the origin of this?" Not only where did the first sin originate, but also where did the universality of wickedness originate and the guilt and depravity of all the human race? Is there any link between the first sin that was committed in paradise and the flood of iniquities that then poured out over all the earth? And if so, what kind of connection is this?[11]

There are those who, with Pelagius, completely deny that such a connection exists. According to them, each sin is its own individual deed, which is completely free in itself, bringing about no change in human nature and therefore in the very next moment can be replaced through a good deed. After Adam broke the commandment of God, he remained completely the same in his inner nature, his mind (*gezindheid*), and the inclination of his will. [102] Subsequently, all the children, who originated from the first human couple, are born in absolutely the same innocent and unaffected nature, which Adam had from his origin.[12] There is, then, no original sin; the universality of sin can only be explained by the poor example set by the elderly and followed by the youth. Indeed, the universality of sin then has its cause in the individual fall of each person separately either in this life, as Pelagius and his followers say, or before this life, as taught by some of the philosophers and especially by the theosophers.[13]

37. But this atomistic view of the human race is, especially as Augustine and the Reformed have recognized, diametrically opposed to the teaching of Scripture. According to Scripture, humanity does not consist of a mass of souls that from all sides are accidently flying into one another at any given place and who, for better or worse must now on account of their sundry

---

11. This paragraph is unique to *Handleiding.*

12. This portion of the paragraph matches one in *MD*, 217. The rest of the paragraph is specific to *Handleiding.*

13. The distinction between theologians and theosophers is rooted in the thirteenth-century work *Summa philosophiae*, originally attributed to Robert Grosseteste. The *Summa* makes a distinction between theologians and theosophers. In this work, theosophers were understood to be those inspired by the writings of Scripture. In the seventeenth century, this word took on a new gnostic-influenced meaning and was typically associated with the German mystic Jakob Boehme (1575–1624). In Bavinck's time, there was a revitalization of this mystical Gnosticism through the Theosophical Society, which was established in New York City in 1875. See Gordon J. Melton, "Theosophical Society," in *New Age Encyclopedia* (Farmington Hills, MI: Gale Research, 1990), 458–61.

contacts, find a way to get along. Rather it is a unity, a body with many members, a tree with many branches, a kingdom with many citizens. It is such a unity because of the unity of its origin and the unity of its nature. Physically, humanity is one on account of it being one in blood; legally and ethically, it is one on account of the foundation of natural unity; it is placed under the same divine law, the law of the covenant of works.[14] That is why it remains one also in its fall: "sin came into the world through one man, and death through sin" (Rom. 5:12). Guilt (the judgment God pronounces as judge) was from one who sinned, who condemned the whole of the human race to a judgment (Rom. 5:16, 18–19); all died in Adam (Rom. 5:17; 1 Cor. 5:22): "God has consigned all to disobedience" [103] (Rom. 11:32). Therefore, humanity, in its entirety and in all of its members, is *guilty* before God; it possesses a *morally corrupt* nature, and it is at all times subject to *corruption* and *death*. *Original sin*, then, first includes guilt: "For as one man's disobedience the many were made sinners"; those who emerged from him were made sinners by the righteous judgment of God (Rom. 5:19).[15] In addition to this, there is also *inherited sin*: all men are "brought forth in iniquity" and conceived in sin (Ps. 51:5) and are evil from their youth (Gen. 6:5; 8:21; Ps. 25:7); because from the unclean, the clean cannot be born, and from flesh, only flesh can be born (Job 14:4; John 3:6). This uncleanness extends not only to all men but it also extends into the entirety of man's nature, including his heart (Mark 7:22), intellect (Rom. 1:21; Eph. 2:18), will and affections (John 8:34; Rom. 8:7), conscience (Titus 1:15), and even his body with every member an instrument of iniquity (Rom. 3:13–17; 6:13).[16]

Nevertheless, one should keep in mind that Paul does not develop this doctrine of original sin independently, by and for itself, but rather in connection with and as a counterpart to the righteousness and life Christ obtained for his own. "God has consigned all to disobedience, that he may have mercy on all" (Rom. 11:32). There is, therefore, no reason for anyone to be proud and to hold themselves above others, but also no reason for anyone to despair or feel pity on themselves.

In the covenant of works, the same law is enacted in the covenant of grace. If we could not be held guilty and die in Adam, we could not be justified by God's grace through the redemption that is in Christ Jesus (Rom. 3:24). We, therefore, do not object to this law [104] when it comes to its rule

14. This sentence is identical to a sentence in *MD*, 223.

15. This sentence is identical to a sentence in *MD*, 226.

16. The final half of the paragraph is an abridgment of *MD*, 226–29.

in the inheritance of material goods and spiritual treasures that parents and ancestors have left us; but first, we come up against the solidarity of humanity (*menschheid*), people (*volk*), or generations when it imposes obligations and burdens. But then, would we only want to receive from God's hand what is good and not what is bad?

38. From this innate moral depravity springs forth all those sins that were formerly called by the name immediate (*actueele*) and includes all those transgressions of God's law that are executed by the individual themselves with lesser or greater conscience (*bewustheid*), with weaker or stronger will and intention (*opzet*).[17] Also, these sins are not disconnected (*los*) in themselves, or in the life of the individual person, or in the life of the family, descendants (*geslacht*), society, people (*volk*), humanity. Sin is a slippery slope: one sin gives birth to another (James 1:14–15). There is growth, expansion, and progression in the life of sin, albeit toward further corruption; there are individual sins, but also family, class, social, and national sins (*volkszonden*). Criminals do not constitute a special race of people, but they arise from within the same society in which we all live. One can rightly speak of a kingdom of sin in which all men are citizens. There is no one who does good; there is not even one. Every person is incapable of being true, perfect, and spiritually good; but on the contrary, in their hearts they are inclined to all evil.

In principle, then, just as virtues are one, sins are indivisible, so that whoever possesses one in principle possesses them all (James 2:10).[18] Nonetheless, not all sins are equal in degree, nor are all people equally guilty of all sins. One can divide sins in various ways, according to the seven [105] deadly sins (pride, greed, gluttony, lust, sloth, envy, and wrath); or according to the instrument with which they were made, sins of thoughts, words, and deeds, sins of the flesh and of the spirit; or according to the commandments that they oppose, sins against the first and second table, against God, our neighbor, and ourselves; or according to the form in which they occur, sins of omission or commission; or according to the degree in which they are distinguished, sins secret and public, silent and audible, human and devilish, (cf. Num. 15:27, 30; 1 Sam. 15:22; Prov. 6:30; Matt. 5:22; 11:21;

---

17. The word translated as "immediate" is *dadelijke*. Bavinck adds *actueele* to clarify his own writing.

18. In suggesting that the virtues are one, Bavinck is following in the footsteps of the classical articulation of the virtues put forth by figures such as Socrates, Plato, Augustine, and even Aquinas.

etc.). There is also a sin of hardening (*volharding*), of which Pharaoh is the typical example (Exod. 4:21f.), and this sin can lead to on to the unpardonable sin referred to in Scripture as blasphemy against the Holy Spirit (Matt. 12:31–32; cf. Heb. 6:4–8; 10:25–29; 12:15–17; 1 John 5:16).[19]

39. Indeed, if sin is now what Scripture says of it, then the worthiness of its punishment does not require any further explanation. Punishment is always an evil of suffering (in good, freedom, or living) imposed on a doer of evil. On sin as transgression of his command, before sin was committed, God already threatened the highest punishment, the penalty of death (Gen. 2:7). God, with all respect, cannot do otherwise, for he is the[20] Righteous and the Holy One who hates all ungodliness (Job 34:10; Pss. 5:5; 45:6–7), "who will by no means clear the guilty" (Exod. 34:7; Num. 14:18), who visits all ungodliness with his wrath (Rom. 1:18), curses (Deut. 27:26; Gal. 3:10), and vengeance (Nah. 1:2; 1 Thess. 4:6), and recompenses to every man according to his work (Ps. 62:12; Job 34:11; Prov. 24:12; Jer. 32:19; Ezek. 33:20; Matt. 16:27; Rom. 2:6; 2 Cor. 5:10; 1 Pet. 1:17; Rev. 22:12). The conscience bears [106] witness here in every man when it condemns him because of his evil thoughts, words, and deeds, and often persecutes him with a guilt-consciousness, repentance, remorse, and the fear of judgment. The administration of justice in every nation has been built upon the presupposition of the criminality of sin.

The punishment determined by God for sin consisted in death, physical death; yet this does not stand alone but is preceded by many other punishments—shame, fear, guilt (commitment to punishment), and a sense of guilt (moral uncleanness), work by the sweat of our brows, pain in childbearing, exile from paradise, a life of pain and grief, which then ends in death. But this death can occur at any moment: before, during, or shortly after birth. Man is dust and to dust he shall return (Gen. 3:19). In a sense, he was already dust before the fall; in his body, he was formed from the dust of the earth, by nature of the earth, an ensouled living creature (1 Cor. 15:45, 47). But this life of the first man was destined to be spiritualized and glorified without death. However, now on account of the transgression, the law came into effect: "You are dust and to dust you shall return."

At our present time, it is disputed by many in the name of science that death is a consequence and punishment of sin; but Scripture speaks of this

---

19. The previous four paragraphs are unique to *Handleiding*.

20. The first half of this paragraph is exclusive to *Handleiding*. The remainder of the paragraph is identical to a portion of a paragraph in *MD*, 237.

repeatedly and clearly (Gen. 2:17; Rom. 5:12; 6:23; 1 Cor. 15:21, 56; James 1:15). Our conscience places a seal upon it whenever someone says, "Death is unnatural." For science, death till this day remains a great and inexplicable mystery of life. The unnaturalness of death particularly appears when we understand the sense of Scripture. For in Scripture, death is not synonymous with destruction any more than life is nothing more than naked existence. [107] But according to the teaching of Scripture, life includes joy, abundance, and bliss; and death is sorrow, destitution, misery, and disintegration of what belongs together.

Now the man, who is created in God's image and lives in his fellowship, cannot die, for God is "not the God of the dead, but of the living" (Matt. 22:32). If, however, man breaks this fellowship, he dies the spiritual death (*geestelijken dood*) at that same moment; then his life on earth becomes a continual dying, death through sin and guilt (John 8:21, 24; Eph. 2:1) until it is subjected to physical death (*lichamelijken dood*). And thereafter death itself ends in the eternal death, which in the book of Revelation is called "the second death" (Rev. 2:11; 20:6, 14; 21:8).[21]

---

21. The previous three paragraphs are unique to *Handleiding*.

11

The Covenant of Grace

40. [108] The state of sin, misery, and death—in which humanity has now been for centuries—is one long, arduous punishment. Above [humanity's] head is written the word that Moses once uttered when he saw the generation of Israelites die in the desert before his eyes: "We are brought to an end by your anger; by your wrath we are dismayed" (Ps. 90:7). At the same time, this state of punishment in the hand of God serves as a means of awakening in humanity the thought and need for salvation. It is certainly true that there are always those on the one side who, like Pharaoh, harden themselves under God's judgments, and many on another side who flatter themselves with the imagination that there is no God or that he does not see evil (Pss. 10:11, 14; 14:1; 94:7; Mal. 2:7). Nevertheless, humanity bears witness as a whole to the fact that they harbor within them the hope that God himself planted within the soul; humanity has, at all times, lived with the hope of redemption.

Thus, on the one hand, however much we must maintain the gravity of sin and of its punishment, we may not, on the other hand, close our eyes to the blessing that, in spite of all this, God has poured out on the human race in its state of guilt and uncleanness. When Paul stated that God in past generations allowed all the nations to walk in their own ways (Acts 14:16), this should not be understood as if God had no interactions with [109] those peoples (*volkens*) and completely left them to their own fate. On the contrary, it was according to his counsel and will and under the governance of his providence that humanity survived after the fall, spread throughout the earth, and split into peoples (*volkens*), that those peoples (*volkens*) may receive a certain place, gift, and task and take a part in a rich and multifaceted development. In nature and history, according to God's order, there are not only degenerating but also regenerating, not only corrupting but also preserving and redeeming forces. Miraculously, in the history of humanity curse and blessing, wrath and mercy, justice and longsuffering are interwoven; and common grace, which immediately began to be at work alongside special grace after the disobedience of the first man, was established in a covenant after the flood and extended to all creatures, including nature and its ordering. God committed himself thereby to creation, in spite of its apostasy, to preserve it and makes its path straight. Even the punishment—which was pronounced upon the serpent, the woman, and the man, after the transgression—was mixed with blessing and grace.

This is especially seen in the religions of the nations. They each developed from and are continually nourished by that religious-moral consciousness (*godsdienstig-zedelijk besef*), which God himself preserved in the heart of man through his revelation (Acts 14:19; Rom. 1:19). And furthermore, they all contain the same concept of redemption: they want all religions to be redemptive. There exist many different opinions concerning evil, the path on which salvation is both to be sought and obtained, and about the highest good that is to be. Nonetheless, deliverance from evil and obtaining the highest good permeates all religions. The great question in religion is always: What must I do to be saved? [110]. That which cannot be obtained by civilization or development, or through subjugation and control of the earth, is precisely that which people seek in religion: enduring happiness, eternal peace, and perfect salvation. In religion, it is always what man does for God. In his sinful condition, he always imagines God entirely differently from who he really is; he seeks him with a wrong intention, along a wrong road and in a wrong place. Therefore, on further inspection, all the religions of the nations disappoint; they have all fallen into idolatry, image worship, to divination and sorcery. They no longer have knowledge of the holiness of God or knowledge of his grace. Nevertheless, they are a proof that man, having lost God, does not escape him and cannot live without him.

This desire for salvation, which is characteristic of the whole of humanity, is of great significance in itself and also for Christianity. For this need is continually awakened and kept alive by God himself in the heart of humanity. It indicates that God has not completely given over the fallen human race to itself. It is an ineradicable hope that sustains humanity in its life and work in the long and frightful journey through the world. And it is a guarantee and prophecy that there is such a salvation, and that this salvation is given by God out of pure mercy, which men seek in vain for themselves.[1]

41. There is a fundamental distinction between the self-willed religions of the nations (*volken*) and the religion that rests on the special revelation of Israel and in Christ. For in the case of self-willed religion, it is always man himself who tries to find to God but instead always forms a false image of

1. The previous four paragraphs are unique to *Handleiding*.

him and therefore never obtains true insight into the nature of sin and the way of redemption. But [111] in the religion of Holy Scripture, it is always God who seeks man, who unveils him to himself in his guilt and impurity but also makes himself known in his grace and mercy. There rises up out of the depths of the human heart the lamentation, "Oh that you would rend the heavens and come down" (Isa. 64:1)—here the heavens are opened and God himself descends on earth. In these [self-willed] religions, we always see man at work, whether it be through acquiring knowledge by keeping all sorts of commandments or by withdrawing from the world into the mystery of one's own mind to participate in redemption from evil and communion with God. Here all the work of man falls away, and it is God himself who acts, intervenes in history, and brings about the way of redemption in Christ, and by the power of his grace clears a path therein for man to walk. Special revelation is the answer that God himself provides in words and deeds to the questions that arise, through his own leading, within the human heart.[2]

Immediately after the fall, we see that God comes to man, seeks him, and guides him back into his fellowship (Gen. 3:7–15). Likewise, in the continuation of revelation, when seeking and calling, when speaking and acting occur, it is always God; the whole of redemption proceeds from him and returns to him. It is he who put forward Seth in the place of Abel (Gen. 4:25); who placed his favor on Noah (Gen. 6:8), and who preserved him in the judgment of the flood (Gen. 6:12f.); who called Abram and included him in his covenant (Gen. 12:1; 17:1); who chose to inherit the people of Israel out of sheer grace (Deut. 4:20; 7:6–8); who in the fullness of time sent his only begotten Son into the world (Gal. 4:4) and now at this present time is gathering out of the entire human race a congregation, which he has chosen [112] for eternal life and for the heavenly inheritance at the end (Eph. 1:10; 1 Pet. 1:5).[3]

If everything that is accomplished in time—the whole work of creation and providence—is based on God's counsel and the execution thereof, then this certainly applies, to an even greater extent, to the work of re-creation that is God's work par excellence. In the Scriptures, therefore, there is often talk of a counsel that precedes all things (Isa. 46:10), by which all things work (Eph. 1:11), and especially has the work of redemption as its content (Luke 7:30; Acts 20:27; Heb. 6:17). Furthermore, this counsel is not only from God's intellect but also from his omnipotent (Eph. 1:5, 11),

---

2. Cf. *MD*, 247–48.

3. This paragraph is a unique to *Handleiding*.

unbreakable (Isa. 14:27; 46:10), and unchangeable will (Heb. 6:17), which will stand forever (Ps. 33:11; Prov. 19:21).[4]

Other names illustrate this idea: we find mention not only of a counsel of God but also of a good pleasure toward men that God has revealed in Christ (Luke 2:14) and delights in providing for them and adopting them as his children (Matt. 11:26; Eph. 1:5, 9); of a plan, which proceeds the work of election (Rom. 9:11; Eph. 1:9), that is established in Christ (Eph. 3:11) and is realized in calling (Rom. 8:28); of an election and foreknowledge, which has its origin in grace (Rom. 11:5), Christ as its center (Eph. 1:4), particular persons as its object (Rom. 8:29), and their salvation as its end (Eph. 1:4); finally, of a predestination, which is by the means of the proclamation of the wisdom of God (1 Cor. 2:7), on the adoption of children, in conformity (*gelijkvormigheid*) to Christ, preserved unto eternal life (Acts 13:48; Rom. 8:29; Eph. 1:5).[5]

In this counsel, the whole work of redemption has been established from beginning to end, in breadth and in length. There is not the least room for arbitrariness or chance here; it is all determined [113] with unfathomable mercy and inscrutable wisdom. Both the application and the realization of salvation are included; both the goods and the partners; the Holy Spirit with all his gifts no less than Christ with all his benefits. It is a counsel that may be called an everlasting covenant ordered and secure in all its parts (2 Sam. 23:5), for it rests in the love of the Father, in the grace of the Son, and in the fellowship of the Holy Spirit.

With this counsel as the foundation of the work of redemption, believers are repeatedly exhorted in Scripture that they should not be frightened and in passivity lay down; far less, that they might abuse it and live in sin (Luke 7:30; Rom. 3:8), but on the contrary that they might assure themselves of the inscrutable grace of God and find complete rest in it. For that is precisely the difference between the covenant of work and the covenant of grace. In the covenant of works, it was up to the man who was created in the image of God: "Do this, and you will live." It might well have been a path to heaven for the fallen man, but it depended on his own free will, and this was precarious and unstable—the *certainty* was missing. But the covenant of grace is fixed in God alone since he stands, as it were, for both parties in Christ and through the Holy Spirit. Therefore, for fallen man—who has lost fellowship with God and can be no longer acquired in anyway—it is

4. This sentence is found in a paragraph in *MD*, 249.
5. This paragraph is found within a paragraph in *MD*, 249.

the path to heaven, but it can only be received again by grace, as a gift, through faith; yes, faith itself is received as a fruit of election (Acts 13:48; Rom. 9:15–16; Eph. 1:4; 2:8), and that faith is preserved unto the heavenly inheritance through the power of God (1 Pet. 1:5).

Therefore, here is an absolute certainty: a perfect love that excludes all fear, a covenant that knows no faltering [114] (Isa. 54:10). Adam was exchanged for Christ, who is the same yesterday, and today, and forever (Heb. 13:8).[6]

42. This covenant of grace is immediately made known to man after the fall.[7] Indeed, in the maternal promise (*moederbelofte*), not only is the serpent humiliated and condemned (Gen. 3:14–15) but also the evil power, whose instrument was the serpent. But it is also declared that from now on, enmity will prevail between the seed of the serpent and the seed of the woman; that it is God himself who creates and establishes this enmity in life. And therefore, this enmity and strife will emerge, so that the seed of the serpent shall bruise the heel of the seed of the woman; and conversely, the seed of the woman will crush the head of the seed of the serpent.

There lies here nothing less than the declaration and institution of the covenant of grace. It is true that the word *covenant* does not yet appear here; this is used first in later times with Noah, Abraham, etc., when men in their various struggles against nature, animals, and also among themselves, have learned of the necessity and usefulness of treatises and covenants through practical life experiences. But in principle and essence, everything is given in this maternal promise (*moederbelofte*), which constitutes the content of the covenant of grace. On account of his transgression, man has given up his obedience to God, abandoned his fellowship, and, on the contrary, sought a friendship with Satan and entered into an alliance with him. And now, between man and Satan, God in his grace comes to break this alliance and to substitute enmity in the place of friendship. By an almighty act of his gracious will, God brings back to his side the seed of the woman, which she had surrendered to Satan, and adds [115] the promise that—despite all kind of opposition and oppression—in the end, there will be an absolute victory over the seed of the serpent.[8] There is nothing conditional, and

6. The previous three paragraphs are unique to *Handleiding*.

7. The first sentence is unique to *Handleiding*. The remainder of the paragraph is identical to a portion of a paragraph in *MD*, 254–55.

8. In *The Sacrifice of Praise*, Bavinck similarly writes: "For before man entered into a covenant of friendship with Satan through his sin, God stepped between

nothing is uncertain here. God himself comes to man, he takes upon himself enmity, he opens the battle, he promises victory. Man has no choice other than to hear this and in childlike faith embrace it. Promise and faith are the contents of the covenant of grace, which is now being established with humanity, and for him—the fallen, the lost—and again opens the way to the Father's house and the entrance to eternal salvation.[9]

From its first announcement, this covenant has gone through various divisions in history, whereby especially those before, under, and after the law can be distinguished. But it always remains one in essence; it is always the covenant of grace; it continually flows forth from the grace of God; it always has as its contents, namely, the grace of the gospel (Rom. 1:2; Gal. 3:8), the same Christ, (John 14:6; Acts 4:12), the same faith (Acts 5:11; Rom. 4:11), the same benefits (Acts 10:43; Rom. 4:3), in substance; and it finds its purpose in the glorification of God's grace. Thereby, in all of its purposes, it proceeds in an organic and historical manner. While the doctrine of election calls our attention to the individual persons—foreknown by God and called, justified, and glorified by him in time—the covenant of grace considers them as the same people in connection with one another under Christ as the head. Never in history has it been established with a single, disjointed, self-standing individual, but always with a man and his family, with Adam, with Noah, with Abraham, with Israel, with the church and with their seed. Never does the promise apply to a single believer alone, but always to his house also.[10]

God does not realize his covenant of grace by [116] plucking a few people out of humanity and then putting them together outside of the world.[11] Rather, he carries it out within humanity, he makes it an element of the world, and now ensures that it is preserved within that world from the evil one. As the Recreator, he walks in the footsteps he laid as Creator, sustainer, and ruler of all things. Grace is something different from and higher than nature, but nevertheless it joins with nature and does not destroy it but restores it. It is not an inheritance which passes through natural birth, but it is a stream that flows in the bed that has been dug in the natural relations of the human race. The covenant of grace does not jump from one

---

them, substituting enmity for friendship, and through the seed of the woman bringing man back to his side," (7).

9. This paragraph is identical to one in *MD*, 254.

10. This paragraph is unique to *Handleiding*.

11. The first sentence is unique to *Handleiding*. The remainder of the paragraph is identical to a portion of a paragraph in *MD*, 260.

branch to another branch (*van den hak op den tak*), but proceeds in the family, offspring, and peoples (*volken*) in a historical and an organic way.

43. This particularity is in connection with this: that the covenant of grace is realized in a way that fully respects man's rational and moral nature. Of course, it rests on the counsel of God, and this must in no way be neglected. Behind the covenant of grace lies the sovereign and free will of God, which persists with divine energy and therefore ensures the triumph of the kingdom of God over all of the power of sin.

But this will is not a fate that falls down upon man from above but rather the will of the Creator of heaven and earth who does not deny his own work in creation and providence; the man, whom he has created as a rational and moral being, cannot be treated like a stick and a block. This will is more than that: it is the will of a merciful and kind-hearted Father who never forces us with crude power but always defeats our opposition through the spiritual power of his love. The will of God is not a blind, irrational force but a *will*—a wise [117], gracious, loving, and, at the same time, free and almighty *will*. That is why the covenant of grace, which in fact places no requirements or conditions upon us, is nevertheless given to us in the form of a commandment and exhorts us to faith and repentance (Mark 1:15).[12] Viewed in itself, the covenant of grace is only grace and excludes all work. It gives what it demands, and it fulfills what it prescribes. The gospel is simply a joyful message; not an obligation but a promise; not a duty but a gift. But in order that it may be realized in us as a promise and a gift, it takes the character of a moral exhortation in accordance with our nature. It does not force us but desires nothing other than for us to accept freely and willingly in faith what God gives to us. The will of God does not realize itself other than through our mind and will. That is why it is also correctly said that man receives through grace, and he himself believes and repents.

In this way, the covenant of grace thus enters historically and organically into the human race; it cannot present itself on earth in a form that fully corresponds to its essence. Much that accords with the claims of the covenant ("Walk before my face and be upright; be holy for I am holy; be upright in battle") remains in the life of true believers. But there may also be persons who, in our eyes, have been received into the covenant of grace; yet because of their unbelieving and unrepentant hearts, they are still deprived of all spiritual benefits of that covenant. That is not only the case

12. The first portion of this paragraph is unique to *Handleiding*. The remainder of the paragraph is in *MD*, 261.

today, but such a condition has existed for centuries. In the days of the Old Testament, not all of Israel were descendants of Israel (Rom. 9:6), for not the children of the flesh but the children of the promise were numbered as offspring (Rom. 2:29; 9:8). And in the New Testament [118] congregation, there is chaff among the wheat, there are bad branches on the vine, and there are not only golden but earthly vessels (Matt. 3:12; 13:29; John 15:2; 2 Tim. 2:20). There are men who have the appearance of godliness but deny its power (2 Tim. 3:5).

On account of this discrepancy between essence and appearance, there is surely a distinction and separation between an internal covenant, which was established exclusively with true believers, and an external covenant, which included those who only made a profession with their mouth. But such a separation cannot exist with the teaching of Scripture; what God unites, let no man separate. There must be no desertion of the demands that essence and appearance will correspond with each other; that confession of the mouth and the belief of the heart should be in harmony with each other (Rom. 10:9). But even if there are not two covenants that stand distinctly beside each other, there are nonetheless two sides to the one covenant of grace, of which one is only visible to us while the other is completely visible to God. We must adhere to the rule that we cannot judge the heart but only the outward walk, and even then only imperfectly. Those who walk before the eyes of men in the way of the covenant must, according to the judgment of love, be considered and treated by us as allies. But in the end, it is not us but God's judgment that decides. He is the knower of the heart and the tester of souls; with him there is no respect of persons: "Man looks on the outward appearance, but the Lord looks on the heart" (1 Sam. 16:7).

So, every man ought to examine himself to see whether he is in the faith, whether Jesus Christ is in him (2 Cor. 13:15).[13]

13. The final three paragraphs are identical to the final three paragraphs in *MD*, ch. 14 (261–62).

12

The Person of Christ

44. [119] The counsel of redemption is not a human design, the execution of which depends on all kinds of unforeseen circumstances and is therefore highly uncertain. But it is executed infallibly, because it is the decree of God's merciful and almighty will. As it has been established in eternity, so it is accomplished in time. Thus whatsoever the doctrine of faith has to treat further is a description of the manner in which the unchanging counsel of the Lord is worked out and applied concerning the salvation of his human children. This counsel is mainly about three great acts and, therefore, the teaching of the Christian faith in the future must also be occupied with these three acts concerning the mediator by whom salvation must be obtained, concerning the Holy Spirit by whom it must be applied, and concerning the people to whom it must be given.

First, it has to treat the person of Christ, who acquires salvation through his suffering and death. Second, it must demonstrate the way in which the person of the Holy Spirit makes the church partakers of the person of Christ and all his benefits. And third, attention has to be given to the people who participate in this salvation acquired by Christ and thus treat the church, or the congregation, as the body of Christ. This teaching naturally culminates [120] in the accomplishment of salvation, which hereafter awaits the believers. In the course of the discussion, it will become apparent that the counsel of redemption is properly ordered and secured in all its parts—and the unfathomable grace, the manifold wisdom, and the almighty power of God revealed in it.

Immediately in the person of Christ all these attributes appear in the brightest light. The belief in a mediator is not unique to Christianity. All people and nations (*volken*) not only live in the realization that they are not participants in salvation, but they also share the conviction that this salvation must, in one way or another, be designated and conferred upon them by a particular person. The thought is generally accepted that man, as he is, should not approach God nor can he dwell in his presence; he requires an intermediary who will open up the way to God for him. In all religions therefore there are mediators who, on the one hand, make divine revelations known to mankind and, on the other hand, offer the prayers and gifts of mankind to God.

Sometimes lower gods or spirits fill the role of mediators, but often they are also people who are endowed with supernatural knowledge and power and who stand in a special aroma (*reuk*) of holiness. They occupy a prominent place in the religious life of the peoples (*volken*) and are consulted in all important occasions in the special and public life, such as disasters, wars, illnesses, enterprise, etc. But whether they act as fortune tellers or magicians, as saints or priests, they show the path, in their opinion, on which man should walk in order to receive the favor of the divine, but they are not the path itself. The religions of the peoples (*volken*) are independent from their person.[1] This also applies to those religions that were [121] founded by particular people. Buddha, Confucius, Zarathustra, and Muhammad are indeed the professors of the religion founded by each of them, but they are not the content of that religion and, at the same time, are in an external and to some extent accidental connection. Their religion could remain exactly the same even if their name was forgotten or they were replaced by another person.

In Christianity, however, it is completely different. Now and then it is said that Christ never wanted to be the only mediator, and that he would have been completely satisfied with his name being forgotten if his principle and spirit survived in the church. But others, who have for themselves ruptured all their ties with Christianity, have opposed and refuted this idea in an indirect manner. Christianity has a completely different relationship to the person of Christ than the other religions of the people (*volken*) to the persons by whom they were founded. Jesus was not the first professor of the religion named after him. He was not the first and foremost Christian; rather, he occupies an entirely unique place in Christianity. He is not the founder of it in the ordinary sense, but he is the Christ, the Son sent from the Father, who established his kingdom on earth and now extends and

---

1. This is a somewhat wooden translation, but it conveys Bavinck's point. [Dutch: De godsdiensten der volken zijn van hun persoon onafhankelijk.] He is attempting to connect the practice of religion that is often disconnected from the "person" who embodies that religion. This can be made clearer by identifying the role of Christ. According to Bavinck, Christ is Christianity itself (see p. 105). Christ is then not the founder, or the teacher of Christianity, but the very essence of Christianity. In contrast, other religions have teachers, founders, etc., but those persons are not the religion itself. See also Bavinck, *What Is Christianity?*, 9.

preserves it until the end of the ages. Christ is Christianity itself; he is not on the periphery but at the center of it. Without his name, person, and work, there is no more Christianity. Christ is, in a word, not the signpost to salvation but the way itself. He is the only true and complete mediator between God and humanity. What other religions have suspected and hope for in the mediators of their faith is essentially and completely fulfilled in him.[2]

45. In order to see this entirely unique meaning of Christ [122], we must begin where Scripture does: that he did not exist first, as we did, at his conception and birth, but had existed eons before as the only begotten and beloved Son of the Father from all eternity. In the Old Testament, the Messiah is already referred to by the name of Everlasting Father, who is an eternal Father to his people (Isa. 9:6), and whose beginnings (origin and derivation) are from ancient times, from the days of eternity (Mic. 5:2). The New Testament is in harmony with this but expresses Christ's eternity even clearer.[3] After all, the whole earthly life of Christ is always presented as the completion of a work that was previously assigned to him by the Father to do, and to which he descended from heaven, entered the world, and was on earth to complete (Matt. 10:40; Mark 2:17; 10:45; 12:6; Luke 4:43; John 3:13; 5:24, 30, 36, 43; 6:38; 12:46; 13:3; etc.). He who is David's Son was already David's Lord (Mark 12:36), had already existed before Abraham (John 8:58), had already possessed glory with the Father before the world existed (John 17:5, 24), and was beyond all this was already in the form of God (Phil. 2:6; cf. 2 Cor. 8:9; Col. 1:15; Heb. 1:3–13; Rev. 1:11, 17; 22:13).

That is why he was already at work with the Father and the Spirit in the creation and preservation of all things (John 1:3; Col. 1:15; Heb. 1:2–3); even prior to his incarnation, he stood in an intimate relationship with the world (John 1:3), to the people whose life and light he was (John 1:4), and in particular to Israel who was his own (John 1:11). Among Israel, he dwelled and worked as the angel of the covenant or the angel of the Lord, who was the God of Bethel (Gen. 31:13), the God of the fathers (Exod. 3:2, 6), who led and redeemed the patriarchs (Gen. 48:15–16), who brought the [123] people out of Egypt to Canaan (Exod. 3:8; 14:21; 23:20; 33:14), and provided Israel the assurance that the Lord himself was in their midst as a God of redemption and of salvation (Isa. 63:9). This angel of the covenant is himself the one who will soon come to his temple in the future (Mal. 3:1),

2. The previous five paragraphs are identical to five paragraphs in *MD*, 262–64.

3. The first portion of this paragraph can be found within a paragraph in *MD*, 264; the remainder is unique to *Handleiding*.

and who therefore also prepares this coming through the prophecy in the so-called Messianic expectations (1 Pet. 1:10–11).[4]

From the outset, these expectations bear a universal character (Gen. 3:15), but then journey closer in the line of Seth (Gen. 4:26), in the tents of Shem (Gen. 9:26–27), in the seed of Abraham (Gen. 12:2–3), in the tribe of Judah (Gen. 29:35; 49:8–10), in the house of David (2 Sam. 7:9–16; Ps. 89:19–38; Amos 9:11; Hos. 3:5; Jer. 17:25; 22:4), until finally united altogether in the Son of David who, like the prophets (1 Kings 19:16; Ps. 105:15) and the priests (Lev. 8:12, 30; Ps. 133:2) and especially the kings (1 Sam. 10:1; 16:23; 2 Sam. 2:4; 5:3; etc.), was anointed to his office, would be called the Anointed One par excellence: *Messiah*, as a proper name and without an article (Dan. 9:25; John 4:25).

Of the Messiah, we are told in the Old Testament that he is indeed a man, yet he far exceeds all men in dignity and honor. He is a man, born of David's house, is a Son of David, and is called a Son of Man (2 Sam. 7:12f.; Isa. 7:14, 9:5; Mic. 5:1; Dan. 7:13). Yet he is more than a man; he sits in a place of honor at the right hand of God (Ps. 110:2), is David's Lord (Ps. 110:1), the Son of God in a unique sense (Ps. 2:7). He is Immanuel, God with us (Isa. 7:14), the Lord our righteousness (Jer. 23:6; 33:16), in whom the Lord himself comes to his people with his grace and makes his dwelling among them. It is the same prophecy whether the Lord or his Messiah rules over [124] his people; now it is said that the Lord and, then again, that his anointed king will appear, will judge the nations, and will save Israel (Isa. 40:10–11; Ezek. 34:23–24; Mic. 5:3). In the Messiah, God himself comes to his people (Isa. 7:14); his name is Wonderful, Counselor, Mighty God, Everlasting Father, Prince of Peace (Isa. 9:6). Nonetheless, however great the dignity and power of this Messiah may be, he will be born in humble circumstances and in times of trouble (Isa. 7:15–16), as a shoot from the stump of Jesse (Isa. 11:1; 53:2; Mic. 5:1), and as a branch from the house of David; not riding on a war horse but in peace mounted on a donkey (Jer. 23:5; 33:15; Zech. 3:8), a king indeed but also a priest (Ps. 110:4; Zech. 6:13), and as a priest he will atone for the sins of his people (Isa. 52:13; 53:12).[5]

46. Of all these prophecies, the New Testament presents itself as the fulfillment of the entire Old Testament. When Jesus says that the Scriptures bear witness of him (John 5:39; Luke 24:27), this is a concept that is the foundation for the whole of the New Testament and is always fulfilled. The

4. This paragraph is unique to *Handleiding.*

5. This paragraph is unique to *Handleiding.*

first disciples of Jesus recognized him as the Christ, because they found in him the one of whom Moses and the prophets had spoken (John 1:46). Paul testifies that Christ died, was buried, and was raised again according to the Scriptures (1 Cor. 15:3–4). Peter says that in the prophets, the Spirit of Christ testified beforehand of the suffering that would come upon Christ and the glory that would follow (1 Pet. 1:11). And all the books of the New Testament show, directly or indirectly, that the whole of the Old Testament has come to its fulfillment in Christ: the law with its moral, ceremonial, and civil commandments, with its temple and altar, priesthood and sacrifices, and the prophecy with its promises both with regard to the anointed king of David's house and [125] with regard to the suffering servant of the Lord. The whole kingdom of God was foreshadowed in the history and people (*volk*) of Israel, foretold in national forms under the law and announced by the prophecy in the Old Testament, came near in Christ and descended from heaven to earth, in him and his church.[6]

Thus Jesus is, in the first place, just like the Messiah in the Old Testament: a man, truly and completely a man to whom nothing human is foreign. For although he is the eternal Word, he became flesh in the fullness of time (John 1:14; Phil. 2:7; 1 John 4:2–3), bearing the likeness of sinful flesh (Rom. 8:3), sharing our flesh and blood, and being made like his brothers in every respect (Heb. 2:14, 17); as far as the flesh is concerned, he is from the patriarchs (Rom. 9:5), Abraham's seed (Gal. 3:16), out of Judah's tribe (Heb. 7:14), from David's line (Rom. 1:3), born of a woman (Gal. 4:4); a man in the full sense of the word, with a body (Matt. 26:26), of flesh and blood (Heb. 2:14), with a soul (Matt. 26:38), and a spirit (*geest*) (Matt. 27:50), with human development (Luke 2:40, 52), with human affections of joy and sadness, anger and compassion (Luke 10:21; Mark 3:15, etc.), placed under the law and all of its righteousness (Matt. 3:15; Gal. 4:4), and obedient unto death (Phil. 2:8). He has even been tempted in all things just as we have been but without sin (Heb. 4:15); in his days of his flesh, he offered prayers and supplications to God with a strong calling and tears, teaching obedience from what he suffered (Heb. 5:7–8); finally, he was crucified, died, and was buried.[7]

Among his contemporaries there was no doubt of his true and complete human nature; they typically referred to him with the simple, historical [126] name of *Jesus*. For although this name was given to him by an express

---

6. This paragraph is nearly identical to a paragraph in *MD*, 277–78.

7. This paragraph is unique to *Handleiding*.

command of the angels and with a particular meaning (Matt. 1:21), it was just a common name, which was also held by Moses' successor (Num. 13:16; Acts 7:45; Heb. 4:8) and others (Luke 3:29; Col. 4:11). For those acquainted with him, he was considered to be the man named Jesus (John 9:11); as the son of Joseph the carpenter, we know his father and mother, sisters and brothers (Matt. 13:55; Mark 6:3; John 6:42); the son of Joseph of Nazareth (John 1:45), Jesus the Nazarene (Matt. 2:23; Mark 10:47; John 18:5, 7; 19:19; Acts 22:8), Jesus the Galilean (Matt. 26:69), the prophet Jesus from Nazareth of Galilee (Matt. 21:11). The common title by which he was addressed was that of rabbi or *Rabboni*, "teacher," "master," or "my master" (John 1:39; 20:16)—this is also how the scribes and Pharisees were addressed at the time (Matt. 23:8). He not only accepted the title but also claimed it for himself (Matt. 23:8–10). Therefore, in these names and titles, it is not yet acknowledged that he is the Christ. Nor is it yet acknowledged when in general they called him Lord (Mark 7:28), Son of David (Mark 10:47), or a prophet (Mark 6:15; 8:28).[8]

47. But although truly and completely man, from the beginning, Jesus himself is conscious of being more than a man and recognized as such; this is confessed by all his disciples with greater awareness.[9] Therefore, in the first place, we observe that his coming was foretold centuries before in the aforementioned Old Testament prophecies and, in the fullness of time, was deliberately announced to Mary and Joseph by an angel of the Lord (Matt. 1:18f.; Luke 1:26f). In the second place, we are explicitly informed by Matthew and Luke and elsewhere more or less clearly (Mark 6:4; John 1:13; 7:41–42; [127] Rom. 1:3–4; 9:5; Phil. 2:7; Gal. 4:4) that he was not born of the will of the flesh but conceived in Mary's womb by the Holy Spirit (Matt. 1:20; Luke 1:35). The only begotten Son—who in the beginning was the Word, with God, and himself God—prepared himself a true human nature through this work of the Holy Spirit (Phil. 2:6–7), and also kept it free from the beginning of all guilt and blemish of sin.

In the midst of the whole human race, among all of its millions of members that are guilty before God, completely depraved and unclean, he is the only one (even Mary, his mother, the highly blessed one [Luke 1:42], does not share with him in this honor [John 2:4; Mark 3:31; Luke 1:42–43], as Rome erroneously claims) who dares to face his opponents with the statement: "Which one of you convicts me of sin?" (John 8:46). Yet Jesus, though

8. Cf. *MD*, 279–80.

9. This sentence is identical to a sentence in *MD*, 280.

the meekest and humblest of all men, in this respect distinguishes himself from all his disciples (Matt. 6:9, 12). He never, not even in the most terrifying hour in Gethsemane or on Golgotha, uttered a single word of confession of guilt from his lips. On the contrary, he is conscious (*bewust*) in all his words and works to do the will of his Father (John 4:34; 5:19–20, 30; 8:26, 28, 38; 12:50; 17:4, 6, 8). He has never committed any sin, and deception has never been in his mouth (2 Cor. 5:21; Heb. 7:26; 1 Pet. 1:11; 2:22; 1 John 3:5).[10]

Furthermore, he himself came to establish the kingdom of heaven on earth, and he assigns himself an entirely singular place.[11] Like John the Baptist, Jesus also preached that the kingdom of God was at hand and that citizenship in that kingdom was only available through faith and conversion (Matt. 1:15). But unlike John or one of the prophets, he places himself in a completely different relationship to that kingdom. [128] They all have prophesied of it (Matt. 11:11, 13), but Jesus is the owner and master. He received it from the Father, who ordained (decreed) it for him in his counsel (Luke 22:29). But that is precisely why it is *his* kingdom, in which he decrees freely for the benefit (*gunst*) of his disciples. It is the Father who prepares a wedding for his Son (Matt. 22:2), but the Son is the bridegroom (Matt. 22:2; Mark 2:19; John 3:29) who, in the future union with his bride, celebrates his own wedding (Matt. 25:1f). The Father is the owner of the vineyard, but the Son is nevertheless the heir (Matt. 21:33, 38). So, Jesus calls the kingdom of God at the same time *his* kingdom (Matt. 13:41; 20:21; Luke 22:30). He speaks of *his* church as being founded on the confession of his name (Matt. 16:18). He speaks of the mysteries of that kingdom not as the scribes but as one having authority (*machthebbende*) (Matt. 7:29). He casts out demons by the Spirit of God (Matt. 12:28; Luke 11:20). He even forgives sins (Matt. 9:6), and he distributes the kingdom, with all its benefits, according to his will (Matt. 11:27–30).[12]

In a word, in the kingdom of God, he is not just an ordinary or even a distinguished citizen, but he is the Messiah, the Christ, the king anointed by God himself. Already as a boy in the temple, he knew he must be about his Father's business (Luke 2:49). When he was baptized by John, he did not do this because he needed forgiveness of his sins, but only that he might be obedient to God's will in all things and, for his own sake, might be made suitable for his work by the Holy Spirit (Matt. 3:15–17). He was, therefore, already recognized as the Messiah by John the Baptist and by his first

10. This paragraph is unique to *Handleiding*.
11. This sentence is unique to *Handleiding*.
12. Cf. *MD*, 281–82.

disciple (John 1:29–52). Shortly afterwards, in the synagogue in Nazareth, he himself proclaimed that the prophecy of Isaiah was being fulfilled that day (Luke 4:16f.). When asked by [129] John the Baptist whether he was the promised Messiah, he answered affirmatively, pointing to his works (Matt. 11:3–6). He accepted and saw Peter's confession as a revelation of his Father (John 6:68–69): "You are the Christ, the Son of the Living God" (Matt. 16:16–17). The prayer of the mother of the sons of Zebedee was based on the belief that Jesus was the Messiah, and in this sense was understood and answered by Jesus (Matt. 20:20). His interpretation of Psalm 110 (Matt. 22:42), his entry into Jerusalem (Matt. 21:2f.), his appearance in the temple (Matt. 21:12f.), his institution of the Supper (Matt. 26:26f.) are all based on the assumption that he is the Messiah, David's Son, and David's Lord, and replaces the old covenant with the new one. What actually settles it all is nothing but the confession that he is the Christ, the Son of God, on account of which he was condemned and killed (Mark 14:62), and upon which the inscription above his cross "Jesus the Nazarene, King of the Jews" is affixed and sealed. In the apostolic letters, therefore, he is regularly called Jesus the Christ, Christ Jesus, our Lord Jesus Christ, etc., and by that name we are called Christians (Acts 11:26).[13]

48. With regard to the nature of the messiahship, there were all kinds of errors that were circulating among the people in Jesus' time. Even the disciples inadvertently thought that Jesus would be a Messiah as the Jewish people had generally imagined at the time: a king who would lead the battle against the pagan nations and elevate Israel to the head of the nations (Matt. 11:2f.; Acts 1:6). That is why Jesus had to be careful, so to speak, with that title; he *was* the Messiah, the Christ, but it was in a different sense than what was believed and hoped for at that time. Hence, he often spoken in parables (Matt. 13:13, 34). Likewise, [130] he often pointed to his works of mercy as proofs of his messianic dignity (Matt. 11:45); and on more than one occasion, forbade others to speak of his works and messiahship (Matt. 8:4; 9:30; 12:16; 16:20; etc.). Sometimes he especially avoided the title of Messiah, often designating himself and as a rule going by the peculiar name the *Son of Man*.[14]

This name is undoubtedly borrowed from Daniel 7:13, where the other empires of the world are represented by the image of animals, but the reign of God over his people is under the likeness of a son of man.[15] The situation

---

13. This paragraph is unique to *Handleiding*.

14. This paragraph is unique to *Handleiding*.

15. This first and last sentence of this paragraph is unique to *Handleiding*. The middle portion is in *MD*, 286.

was also explained in some Jewish circles in the messianic sense, and so the name was known by some as a title for the Messiah (John 12:34); yet it does not seem to have been a common name or to have had a fixed meaning. Such worldly expectations could not be associated with this name, as for example with the name Son of David, King of Israel. That is why this name was most suitable for Jesus: for on the one hand, it expressed that he was the Messiah promised by the prophets; and on the other hand, he was *not* [the Messiah] in the opinion or thought of the Jewish people (*volk*). Thus he identifies himself with this name, especially in two sets of places: namely, in places where he speaks of his poverty, suffering, and humiliation; and in others wherein he speaks of his power, loftiness, and exaltation.

Thus, for example, he says in the first case: "The Son of Man came not to be served but to serve, and to give his life as a ransom for many" (Matt. 20:28). In another case, he declares before the high council that he is indeed the Messiah and then adds: "But I tell you, from now on you will see the Son of Man seated at the right hand [131] of power and coming on the clouds of heaven" (Matt. 26:64). Thus Jesus identifies himself with this title in its full messianic meaning, just as the Old Testament prophecies had described it: as a king anointed by God but also as a suffering servant of the Lord, as king who is not only just and powerful but who is also meek and humble and links lordship with priesthood. The name of the Son of Man denotes Jesus in his humiliation and in his exaltation, in his grace and his power, in his suffering and in his glory, as Savior and as Judge.[16]

Still a higher—indeed the highest honor—is attributed to this Christ when the Scriptures call him the Son of God, the Word of God, the Image of God, yes, even God. He is not the son of God in the creaturely, ethical, or theocratic sense, like the angels (Job 38:7), the people of Israel (Exod. 4:22; Deut. 14:1; Isa. 63:6; Hos. 11:1), the judges (Ps. 82:6, cf. John 10:34f.), the kings (2 Sam. 7:11–14), Adam (Luke 3:38), or the believers (2 Cor. 6:18)—and Christ himself is occasionally called the son of God (Matt. 4:3; 26:63; John 1:34, 50, etc.). But he is and is often called the Son of God in an entirely metaphysical sense because he is the only begotten Son of the Father (John 1:18; 3:16, 18; 1 John 4:9), the beloved Son with whom the Father is well pleased (Matt. 3:17; 7:15; Eph. 1:6; Col. 1:13), the only Son and heir (Mark 12:6–7), *the* Son (Mark 13:32) whom no one knows but the Father, and to whom the Father gave all things (Matt. 11:27), who called God his Father (John 5:18) and is the Father's own Son (Rom. 8:32).

---

16. Cf. *MD*, 286.

Therefore, this name also points to a unity between God and Christ that is unlike any link between the Creator and his creation. He and the Father are one (John 10:30); he is in the Father, and the Father is in him (John 10:38). Even though Christ has taken on a human [132] nature that is finite and limited, which began to exist in time; as a person, as an individual (*Ikheid*), Christ stands in Scripture not on the side of the creature but on the side of God, and he shares his attributes of eternity (John 1:1; 1 John 1:1; Rev. 22:13), omnipresence (John 1:18; 3:13; Matt. 28:20; Eph. 1:23; 4:10), immutability (Heb. 13:8), omniscience (Acts 1:24; 7:59–60; Rom. 10:12–13), omnipotence (Matt. 28:18; 1 Cor. 15:27; Eph. 1:22; Rev. 1:4; 19:16), and yes, the divine life itself (John 5:26).[17]

While in the possession of all of these divine perfections, he also participates in all divine works. He is the Creator and Sustainer of all things with the Father and the Spirit[18] (John 1:3; Col. 1:15, 17; Heb. 1:3; Rev. 3:14), just as the Father is presently the savior of the world (1 Tim. 1:1; 2:3; Titus 1:3, etc.), so the Son is also named (2 Tim. 1:10; Titus 1:4; 2 Pet. 1:11; etc.), the Lord, King, and Judge of the universe (John 5:21, 27; 17:2; Acts 2:36; 5:31; 10:36, 42; 17:31; etc.). He is the Word of God in whom the Father is fully proclaimed, made known, and gives himself (John 1:1, 14; 1 John 1:1; Rev. 19:13); the image of God in whom the invisible God has become visible, and the fullness of the Godhead dwells physically (John 14:9; 2 Cor. 4:4; Col. 1:15; 2:9; Heb. 1:3); yes, God above all to praise for eternity (John 1:1; 20:28; Rom. 9:5; Heb. 1:8–9; 2 Pet. 1:1). In the baptismal command of Jesus (Matt. 28:19) and in the blessings of the apostles (2 Cor. 13:13; 1 Pet. 1:2; Rev. 1:4–6), Christ the Son stands on equal footing with the Father and the Spirit.

49. Jesus the Christ, the Son of the Living God—on this rock the church is built. From the outset, the significance of Christ was established for believers. He was confessed by all as the [133] Lord who through his teaching and life obtained salvation, the forgiveness of sins, and immortality. He was then exalted by the Father to his right hand and will return to judge the living and the dead.[19]

---

17. The previous two paragraphs are unique to *Handleiding*.

18. The previous section of the paragraph is identical to a section in *MD*, 299. The remainder of the paragraph is unique to *Handleiding*.

19. This is an allusion to the Apostles' Creed: "He is seated at the right hand of the Father, and he will come to judge the living and the dead." This paragraph is identical to a portion of a paragraph in *MD*, 300.

But as soon as people began to think about the content of this confession, all kinds of differences of opinion arose. Already during the apostles' lives, we learn about the various erroneous teachers who entered the church and tried to tear it away from the steadfastness of its faith. In Colossae, for example, there was a party that had a deficient view of the person and work of Christ, and the gospel turned into a new law (Col. 2:3f., 16f.). In Corinth, libertines arose who were abusing Christian freedom, who did not want to bind themselves to any rule (1 Cor. 6:12f.; 8:1f.). In his first letter, the apostle John fights against the later so-called Docetists, who denied the coming of Christ in the flesh and thus also neglected to do justice to the truth of his human nature.[20]

In the postapostolic time, these errors increased in power and influence. There were those who believed in the true human nature of Christ, his supernatural birth, his resurrection, and ascension; but who did not see him as divine in any way other than in an extraordinary measure of gifts and powers of the Spirit, which were imparted to him by God at his birth or baptism, and which made him capable of his religious-moral work. Those who followed this thought were under the influence of the deistic Jewish idea concerning the relationship of God and the world. They could not think of a more intimate fellowship between God and man than that which existed in a conveyance of gifts. Jesus was therefore a richly gifted man, a religious genius, [134] but he was and nevertheless still remains a man.[21] On the other hand, others, who had been previously raised in paganism and felt more attracted to polytheism, thought they could understand very well that Christ was one of many, or perhaps the highest of all divine beings, in his inner nature; but they could not believe that such a pure, divine being would have assumed a human, a material, and a fleshly nature. That is why they gave up the true humanity of Christ, saying that he had only walked around on earth temporarily in a false form, just as the Old Testament angels had done so many times.

Both of the above trajectories lived on in the centuries that followed and live on to this day. At times, the divine nature in Christ is sacrificed to the human; and at other times, vice versa. Thus, for example, in the fourth century, Arius taught that the Son preceded the whole world in time and rank, was created before the world by God for the creation of the world, and was endowed with divine power and honor, but nevertheless he was a

20. Cf. *MD*, 300–1.

21. Cf. *MD*, 301. The remainder is identical to a paragraph on the same page.

creature; there was a time when he was not and when he was created, like all other creatures; he was not generated from the essence of God but by his will. On the other hand, it was also already taught by Sabellius in the third century that the three persons in the Divine Being were not one eternal subsistence, but only forms and manifestations that the Divine Being successively revealed himself as—in the Old Testament—in the person of Christ and since the Day of Pentecost as the dispensation of the Spirit.[22]

Faced with these errors, the church at the Council of Nicaea (AD 325) expressed its faith in the one God, the Father, the Almighty Creator of all things, visible and invisible, and in the Lord Jesus, the Son of God, [135] who was eternally generated from the Father as the only begotten Son—that is, from the essence of the Father, God from God, light from light, true God from true God, generated and not created, at one with the being of the Father, through whom all things in heaven and earth were created and in the Holy Spirit.[23]

But even though this council had determined the relationship of Christ to the essence of God, to the world, and to humanity, the question remained of how the relationship of the two natures could be thought of in a single person. And here, too, there was a difference of opinion. Nestorius, for instance, taught in the fifth century that if there were two natures in Christ, then there must be two persons, two selves, in him, who only through an ethical bond—such as, for example, in marriage between husband and wife—could be united. Eutyches, starting from the same identification of nature and person, concluded that if there was only one person, one self in Christ, then the two natures must have mixed and fused together so that there was only one mixed divine-human nature that emerged. There the distinction of the natures was maintained at the cost of the unity of the person, while here the unity of the person was preserved it was at the expense of the two-ness of natures.[24]

After a long, fierce struggle, the church also overcame these disputes. At the Council of Chalcedon in 451, it stated that the one person of Christ existed in two natures, which existed side by side, unaltered and unmixed (against Eutyches), and unseparated and undivided (against Nestorius), but had their unity in the one person.[25] This decision was approved in the East

22. This paragraph is unique to *Handleiding*.

23. Cf. *MD*, 303.

24. The description of Nestorius is identical to *MD*, 303.

25. This paragraph is identical to a portion of a paragraph in *MD*, 303. The remainder of the paragraph is unique to *Handleiding*.

and the West, by the Greek and Roman churches, and later by all Protestantism, including Lutheran and Reformed people. The confession of the first four great councils (Nicaea 325, Constantinople 381, Ephesus 431, and Chalcedon 451) [136] forms the universal foundation of the official Christian churches.

50. Of course, this confession is not infallible; to speak of two natures in one person is just as deficient as in the doctrine of the Trinity when speaking of three persons in one being. Yet it is of excellent value, for it cuts off the errors of left and right and leads the church and theology down the right path.

Remaining what he was, the eternal Word and only begotten Son, Christ became what he was not. He did not discard the divine attributes—as the so-called Kenotics (derived from the Greek word that means "emptiness"; Phil. 2:7) teach—but humbled (*vernietigde*) himself, according to the word of the apostle, in the sense that he who was in the form of God assumed the form of a man and the form of a servant (Phil. 2:7–8). He did this so completely that he did not bring human nature down from heaven, as is the feeling of the Anabaptists, but formed it and took it from Mary's own flesh and blood (Matt. 1:20; Luke 1:52; Gal. 4:4) and wholly incorporated it, placing it in service to his person. For it is always the same Christ, the same I, who speaks and works; he, who is according to the same flesh as the fathers, is to be praised as God above all forever (Rom. 9:5). The same one who has descended has also ascended far above all heavens (Eph. 4:10).

In this unity of person, however, he is also in the possession of the use of all the attributes and powers that are inherent to both natures. He does not communicate the divine attributes to human nature itself, as the Lutherans teach, in order to be able to hold Christ's physical presence in the Lord's Supper; but he is always, as the one subject, both [137] natures and all of their attributes are shared (the communication of attributes). He thereby maintains human nature so completely in his own nature that he submits to the laws of its development; and according to the gifts of the Spirit not all at once, but successively, to an ever-greater extent (the communication of gifts) (Luke 2:40, 52; Mark 13:32). He makes use of the fullness of the Godhead that dwells in him physically in such a manner that he brings about that one great work of redemption the Father commanded him to do (the communication of works). That is why Christ may and can be the object of our faith and trust (*vertrouwen*) (John 14:1; 17:3; etc.), of our honor and worship (John 14:13; Acts 7:59; 9:13; 22:16; Rom. 10:12–13; Phil. 2:9; Heb. 1:6; Rev. 22:20).

The confession that Christ is God and man in unity of person is, therefore, not a product of pagan philosophy but grounded in the apostolic witness. It defines and maintains the mystery of godliness: that he, who was the Word in the beginning, was with God and was himself God (John 1:1); who was in the form of God and did not count equality with God a thing to be grasped (Phil. 2:6); who is the radiance of the glory of God and the exact imprint of his nature (Heb. 1:3); who in the fullness of time took on flesh (John 1:14), born of a woman (Gal. 4:4), but humbled (*vernietigde*) himself, having taken the form of a servant, and become like man (Phil. 2:7).[26]

26.The previous four paragraphs are unique to *Handleiding*.

13

The Work of Christ

51. [138] The incarnation is indeed the commencement and introduction of the work of Christ on earth, but it is neither the whole nor the most important content of his work. For Scripture teaches us that the Son of God not only became man, like us in every way apart from sin, but that he also took the form of a servant, humbled himself, and became obedient to death, even to the death of the cross (Phil. 2:7–8).[1] It was fitting for him to fulfill all the righteousness of the law (Matt. 3:15) and to be sanctified through suffering (Heb. 2:10). And it was not only appropriate and fitting, but it *had* to be that way. It is written that the Christ would suffer and rise from the dead on the third day (Luke 24:46; 1 Cor. 15:3–4). The Father sent him to accomplish his work on earth (John 4:34) and gave him a command to lay down his life and take it back up again (John 10:18).

Therefore, what happened to Christ was the execution of what God's hand and counsel had predetermined to occur (Acts 2:23; 4:28). Only on the cross could Christ say that everything was finished and that he had completed the work that the Father had given him to do (John 17:4; 19:30). While the life of Jesus is sketched with relative brevity in the Gospels, his final passion and death are amply recorded; likewise, rarely does the apostolic preaching [139] go back to the conception and birth of Jesus, but they all emphasize the cross, the death, and blood of Christ. We are not reconciled to God through the birth but by the death of his Son (Rom. 5:10).

That is why Christ obtained a human nature from Mary that was holy yet *weak*; he became not only human but flesh (John 1:14), was sent in the likeness of sinful flesh (Rom. 8:3), taking the form of a servant (Phil. 2:7), and became like us in every respect yet without sin [2] (Heb. 2:17; 4:15). Such a weak human nature was necessary for Christ to take on in order that

1. Cf. *MD*, 311–12; The remainder of the next two paragraphs are identical to one in *MD*, 313.

2. The first portion of the paragraph is unique to *Handleiding*. The remainder is identical to a portion of a paragraph in *MD*, 318–19.

he be tempted, to learn obedience through suffering, to fight and sanctify himself in battle, to feel empathy for our weaknesses, and to be a merciful and faithful high priest—in a word, to suffer and die. Although he was like Adam before the fall in that he was sinless, yet he was different from him in other respects. For Adam was created as an adult, but Christ was conceived in Mary's womb and born as a helpless babe. At Adam's advent everything was prepared for him, but at Christ's advent on earth, nobody had seen him coming and there was not even a place for him in the inn. Adam came to rule and to subjugate the whole earth; Christ came not to be served but to serve and to give his soul as a ransom for many.

Therefore, the incarnation of the Son of God was not only an act of condescending goodness, just as it presently remains in the state of exaltation; but it was, at the same time, an act of deep humiliation. This humiliation, commenced at conception, continued throughout his life, even to death and to the grave [140]. Along various steps, as it were, such as a humble birth, circumcision, the persecution of Herod and the flight to Egypt, the private life and the carpenter's business in Nazareth, [Jesus'] baptism by John, and his temptation in the desert, the opposition, denial, and hatred to which he was exposed in his public activity, his imprisonment and condemnation, his crucifixion and death, his funeral and descent to hell—upon these stairs, he descended deeper and deeper, always farther from the Father's house, always closer to us in the community our sin and death, until finally on the bottom step, he let out a frightened complaint of his own abandonment by God, but here the victory cry could also be heard: It is finished![3]

52. That "finished" meant the work he came to earth to do in obedience to his Father, which, especially in Calvin's case, many have treated under the doctrine of the three offices. This treatment offers various advantages. It immediately confronts us with the work of Christ, for it makes us see this not as the exercise of some business or profession chosen by him, but as an obedience to the command of the Father (John 4:34; 5:20, 30; 6:38; 7:16; 8:28; 10:18; 12:49–50; 14:10, 24; 17:4), as a function of the offices for which he was appointed by the Father (Heb. 3:2, 5–6; 5:5; 1 Pet. 1:20).

Furthermore, in these three offices lies a reference to the original calling and destiny of man, who was created in God's image in true knowledge, righteousness, and holiness, as a prophet to proclaim God's glory, as a king to rule under him over everything created, and as a priest with his whole self devoted to him (1 Pet. 2:9; Rev. 1:6; 5:10). [141] Moreover,

3. This paragraph is identical to one in *MD*, 319.

this doctrine of the three offices is directly in line with the revelation in the Old Testament, which gave the people of Israel throughout history a prophetic, priestly, and royal task (Exod. 19:6), called special individuals to these three offices, and they all acknowledged that these three would be perfectly united in the Anointed One par excellence (Isa. 61:1). And finally, the work of Christ is only given its full accord when it is treated under the three offices, for it makes us know Christ as a perfect Savior who redeems us completely and restores us in the image of God.[4]

Nevertheless, it should be kept in mind that the three offices in the life and work of Christ cannot be separated and are, therefore, not to be split up or placed in a temporal succession one after the other. It is the case that sometimes one and then another office comes to the fore such that, for example, Christ's public preaching is more prophetic, his final suffering and dying more priestly, and in his exaltation to the right hand of the Father, we are reminded of his royal office; but in essence, Jesus has filled his three offices, always and everywhere simultaneously.[5]

When he spoke, he proclaimed the words of God as a prophet, but he also displayed his priestly mercy and his royal power, for by his word he healed the sick, he forgave sins, he calmed the storm; he is the king of truth. His miracles were signs of his divine mission and the truth of his word simultaneously a revelation of his compassion for all kinds of wretched people and proof of his reign over sickness, death, and the violence of Satan. His death was a seal of his life but also a sacrifice of perfect obedience and a willing act of power to lay down his life. In a word, his whole appearance, word, and work always [142] bears a prophetic, priestly, and royal character at the same time.[6]

53. He already announced himself as a prophet in the synagogue in Nazareth when he prophesied that Isaiah [61:1][7] was fulfilled in him (Luke 4:6), and soon, as a prophet, he was honored by all the people for his words and works (Luke 7:16; 9:1; 24:19; John 4:19). Yet it was in a deeper and more elevated sense than the Jews had recognized. For he not only explained the law and the gospel (Matt. 5–7), etc., he not only in his preaching unfolded the origin and nature, development, and completion of the kingdom of God (Matt. 13), but he is also greater than Solomon and Jonah, than John

---

4. The previous two paragraphs are unique to *Handleiding*.

5. The first sentence of this paragraph is unique to *Handleiding*; the remainder is identical to a portion of a paragraph in *MD*, 314.

6. This paragraph is identical to a portion of a paragraph in *MD*, 314.

7. Here Bavinck incorrectly provides Isa. 11:1, which we have corrected to 61:1.

the Baptist, or any of the prophets (Matt. 11:11; 12:41–42). He is the only teacher (Matt. 23:8, 10; John 13:13–14), the only Son, through whom God has spoken to us in these latter days (Heb. 1:1), the Eternal Word through whom God has revealed and given himself to us (John 1:1, 14). While the law was given by Moses and the gospel was also proclaimed by the prophets, grace and truth have become in him and his person inseparable (John 1:17). His preaching was a self-proclamation and therein a declaration of the Father and revelation of his name (John 1:18; 17:6).

He sealed this proclamation with his works that, especially as miracles, were signs of his divine mission and power (John 2:11, 24; 3:2; 4:54, etc.), but also a demonstration of his priestly mercy (Matt. 8:17). This priestly activity came throughout his life of service, but especially in his giving his life as a ransom for many (Matt. 20:28), in his obedience unto death (Phil. 2:8), and in the sacrifice of his body on the cross (Eph. 5:2; Heb. 10:10; 1 Pet. 2:24). That is why, [143] in the letter to the Hebrews, he is specifically mentioned as our high priest, but not according to the order of Aaron; for Christ, who had sprung from Judah, had no claim to the priesthood (Heb. 7:14) but rather according to the order of Melchizedek (Ps. 110:4), and thus in the spiritual, true sense, imperishable and eternal (Heb. 7:17, 21, 24).

With this priesthood, which is also closely related to his royal office (Zech. 6:13), we have such a high priest, who is also a king and is seated at the right hand of the throne of majesty in heaven (Heb. 8:1). The king's name does not belong to Christ figuratively or symbolically, but actually, legally, and rightfully (Luke 1:32–33; 23:38, 42). But this is precisely why his kingship is of a different nature than the Jews had imagined (Matt. 4:8–10; 14:23; 20:25–28). It proceeded out of the power with which he bore to the truth, established the kingdom of heaven on earth, distributed the goods thereof, subdued nature to himself, caused sickness and death to depart, laid down his life on the cross and took it up again, and rules at the Father's right hand until his congregation is gathered together and all his enemies are laid under his feet (Ps. 2:7; Zech. 9:9–10; John 10:18; 18:36–37; 1 Cor. 15:25).

54. The whole of Christ's life—in his prophetic, royal, and priestly work—ends in death; in the narrow sense, for him this is the purpose and consummation of his work. It was established thus in God's counsel (Acts 2:2; 4:28); so it was also foretold by the suffering servant of the Lord, and so it was established from the beginning in Jesus' consciousness (Luke 4:16f.; John 1:29; 2:19; 3:14; 12:24), even though he did not [144] first begin to speak clearly of it to his disciples until much later (Matt. 16:21). This death is therefore at the center (*middelpunt*) of apostolic preaching, not only later

but from the very beginning (Acts 2:23f.; 3:14f.; 4:10f.), and not only for Paul but for all the apostles. In the suffering and death of Christ, they saw a fulfillment of his prophetic (1 Tim. 6:13; 1 Pet. 2:21) and of his royal work (John 10:17–18), but above all of his priestly work.

In connection with the sacrificial cult, which has existed since the oldest of times (Gen. 4:3f.) and occurs in all nations and in all religions, this is in close connection especially with the Old Testament worship, which gave such a large place to the sacrifice, so that Israel might understand that the benefits of the forgiveness of sins could only be obtained by way of atonement through blood (Lev. 17:11; Heb. 9:22). With this in view, the New Testament presents the death of Christ as a sacrifice; as the genuine, true sacrifice; as the complete fulfillment of all sacrifices.

That death, after all, is a ransom—a ransom whereby many are redeemed from the bondage of sin (Matt. 20:28); the fulfillment of the covenant sacrifice with which the old covenant was inaugurated (Exod. 24:8) and the foundation of the new covenant was in his blood (Matt. 26:28); a fragrant offering and a sacrifice (Eph. 5:2; Heb. 9:14, 26); the true Passover sacrifice (John 1:29; 19:36; 1 Cor. 5:7; 1 Pet. 1:19; Rev. 5:6, 9); the veritable sin and guilt offering (Rom. 8:3; 2 Cor. 5:21; Heb. 13:11; 1 Pet. 3:18); and the sacrifice of the great day of atonement par excellence (Heb. 2:17; 9:12f.).

Just as in the Old Testament cult, the blood, as the place of life, by its outpouring in death and its sprinkling on the altar was actually the means of atonement (*zoenmiddel*), so it is also under the new covenant that the blood of Christ is the operative [145] cause of the atonement, forgiveness, and purification of our sins (Matt. 26:28; Acts 20:28; Rom. 3:25; 5:9; 1 Cor. 11:25; Eph. 1:7; Col. 1:20; Heb. 9:12, 14; 12:24; 1 Pet. 1:2, 19; 1 John 1:7; 5:6; Rev. 1:5; 5:9; etc.).[8]

When the New Testament speaks of Christ's suffering and death in this way as a sacrifice, then it employs an image. But one must not forget that the Scriptures always began with this thought: that the sacrifices in the Old Testament were actually types and shadows, and they first received their fulfillment in the sacrifice on the cross. Just as Christ is not a prophet, a priest, and king by way of comparison but in a true sense, so too his surrender to death is not a sacrifice in a figurative way but in the most essential and true meaning of the word. After all, that sacrifice consisted of a complete surrender to the will of the Father that commenced with the incarnation, continued through his life, and was completed in his death. Coming into

8. The previous seven paragraphs are distinct to *Handleiding*.

the world, he said, "Behold I have come to do your will, O God" (Heb. 10:5–9). He descended from heaven not to do his own will but the will of the one who sent him (John 4:34; 6:38), and he remained obedient unto death—even till death on a cross (Matt. 26:39; Phil. 2:8). This obedience falls together, as it were, with his person and with his life; it is one whole, one piece of work, like the robe he was wearing without seam; it was fully woven from above and included both his deeds and his sufferings. For his work, his completion of God's law was a suffering; and his suffering, undergoing God's punishment, was a work (Luke 12:50; John 10:18).[9]

He accomplished this whole "passive" (*lijedelijk*) and "active" (*dadelijke*) obedience, according to Scripture, only for our sake [146] and in our place; it bore a substitutionary character.[10] As early as the Old Testament, we read that Abraham offered a ram in his son's place as a burnt offering (Gen. 22:13), that the Israelites offered a sacrificial animal in their place by the laying on of hands (Lev. 16:21), and that the servant of the Lord is "pierced for our transgressions and crushed for our iniquities" (Isa. 53:5). In the same way, the New Testament establishes the closest connection between Christ's sacrifice and our sin. The Son of Man came into the world to give his soul (his life) a ransom in the place of man (Matt. 20:28; 1 Tim. 2:6). He was delivered for our sake, or for the sake of our sins (Rom. 4:25); he died on account of our sins (Rom. 8:3; Heb. 10:6, 18; 1 Pet. 3:18; 1 John 2:2; 4:10) or, as it is most commonly expressed, for us or for our sins (Luke 22:19–20; John 10:15; Rom. 5:8; 8:32; 1 Cor. 15:3; 2 Cor. 5:14–15, 21; Gal. 3:13; 1 Thess. 5:10; Heb. 2:9; 1 Pet. 2:21; 1 John 3:16; etc.).

55. The benefits Christ obtained for us through his perfect obedience are so rich that they seem almost impossible to enumerate and are never fully appreciated.[11] They include no less than the whole and complete work of salvation; they consist in redemption from the greatest evil—sin—with all its consequences of misery and death, and include the gift of the highest good—communion with God and all his blessings.[12] Among all these

9. Cf. *MD*, 331–32.

10. The first sentence is unique to *Handleiding*. The remainder of the paragraph is in *MD*, 336–37.

11. Throughout this section, Bavinck uses *verzoening*, which could mean "propitiation," "atonement," or "reconciliation." To provide clarity, we indicate in this section when the word is used.

12. The first two sentences are identical to the start of *MD*, ch. 18 (338), "Het Werk van Christus in Zijne Verhooging." It also signals the start of a new division in this chapter.

benefits, atonement is at the top. This is expressed in the New Testament by two words, which unfortunately have been translated as the same word in our translation. The one word (or rather different words but from the same stem) appears in Romans 3:25, Hebrews 2:17, 1 John 2:2 and 4:10: it is the [147] translation of a Hebrew word that originally means "to cover" and then indicates the propitiation (*verzoening*) brought about by the sacrifice to God. Just like now, in the Old Testament worship the sacrificial blood was an actual means for atoning for (Lev. 11:17; Heb. 9:12) the sin (guilt, impurity) of the sacrificer before God, and so deprived sin of its power to provoke God to anger. Likewise in the New Testament, Christ is the high priest who through his sacrificial blood, through his perfect obedience unto death, covers our sins before God, turns away his wrath, and makes us partakers of his grace and favor. He is the means of propitiation (Rom. 3:25), the atonement (*de verzoening*) (1 John 2:2; 4:10), the high priest, who is working with God to atone for the sins of the people.[13]

Distinct from this objective atonement (*verzoening*), which Christ has brought about on our behalf before God, is now another kind [of atonement], which in the New Testament is indicated by a second, specific word. This word appears in Romans 5:10–11 and 2 Corinthians 5:18–20; it originally has the meaning of reversal, exchanging, reckoning, settling, and denoting—in the places where it occurs—that new, gracious disposition God has toward the world on the basis of the sacrifice made by Christ. As Christ covers our sin by his death and has averted God's wrath, God sets himself in another reconciled relationship to the world and says this to us in his gospel, which is thus called the word of *reconciliation* (*verzoening*).[14]

This reconciliation (*verzoening*) is also an object; it is not something that comes about first through our faith and our conversion, but it rests on the atonement (satisfaction) that Christ has already made, consists of the reconciled, merciful relationship of God to us, and is received and accepted by us in faith (Rom. 5:11). Since God has cast off his hostile [148] disposition on the basis of the death of Christ, we are exhorted to also put off our enmity and to be reconciled to God and to enter into the new, reconciled relationship God himself sets before us. Everything is finished; there is nothing left for us to do. We may rest with all our soul and for all of time in the perfect work of redemption that Christ has accomplished; we may accept by faith that God has renounced his wrath and we have been

13. Cf. *MD*, 338–39. The remainder of this paragraph is distinct to *Handleiding*.
14. This paragraph is identical to one in *MD*, 340.

reconciled (*verzoend*) in Christ to God, and that he is God and Father to guilty and unholy sinners.[15]

Whoever wholeheartedly believes this gospel of reconciliation immediately receives all the other benefits acquired by Christ. For in the relationship of peace in which God places himself to the world in Christ, all other goods of the covenant of grace are contained. Christ is one and cannot be divided nor accepted in part; the chain of salvation is unbreakable. "Those whom God has predestined, these he has called, and those whom he called, these he has also justified, and those whom he has justified, these he has also glorified" (Rom. 8:30). Thus all who are reconciled to God through the death of his Son receive the forgiveness of sins, adoption as his children, peace with God, the right to eternal life, and the heavenly inheritance (Rom. 5:1; 8:17; Gal. 4:5). They are in union with Christ, having been crucified with him, buried, and raised, seated in heaven, and are increasingly conformed to his image (Rom. 6:3f.; 8:29; Gal. 2:20; Eph. 4:22–24). They receive the Holy Spirit who renews them, guides them into the truth, testifies of their sonship, and seals them until the day of redemption (John 3:6; 16:13; Rom. 8:15; 1 Cor. 6:11; Eph. 4:30). In this fellowship of the Father, the Son, and the Holy Spirit, believers are free from the [149] law (Rom. 7:1f.; Gal. 2:19; 3:13, 25; 4:5; 5:1), and they are exalted above all power of the world and death, hell and Satan (John 16:33; Rom. 8:38; 1 Cor. 15:55; 1 John 3:8; Rev. 12:10). God is for them, so who then will be against them (Rom. 8:31)?[16]

56. Since the work of salvation is God's work and his alone, the benefits of Christ could not have come to us if he had not been raised from the dead and exalted at God's right hand. A dead Jesus would be enough for us and for our salvation, no more [than a dead Jesus] would be needed if Christianity were just a teaching we had to set in our minds or a moral precept and an example we had to follow. But the Christian religion is something else entirely and much more than that; it is the complete redemption of all humanity, of the whole organism of humanity, and of the whole world. And Christ came to redeem the world in this full sense. He did not come to obtain only the possibility of salvation for us and then leave it to our free will whether we should make use of that possibility. But he humbled himself and became obedient to the death of the cross, to make us truly, completely, eternally saved.[17]

15. This paragraph is identical to one in *MD*, 340.

16. This paragraph is identical to a paragraph in *MD*, 340–41.

17. This paragraph is identical to a paragraph in *MD*, page 344.

That is why his work did not end with his death and burial but continued in another way—in his exaltation. The acquisition of salvation is completed and fully accomplished (John 17:4; 19:30; Heb. 9:28, 10:10, 12, 14), but what would it benefit us if it were not also applied and communicated to us? So, Christ must rise and live again that he might rule over both the living and the dead (Rom. 14:9; Rev. 1:19). By [150] the resurrection he was made Lord and Christ, Prince and Savior, so that he might grant Israel repentance and forgiveness of sins and put all enemies under his feet (Acts 2:36; 5:31; 1 Cor. 15:25; Eph. 1:20–23; 4:9–10; Phil. 2:9–10).[18]

This exaltation was not completed at once but, like his humiliation, took place along various "steps" (*trappen*). It did not begin with the literal sense of a descent to hell or the underworld—like Greek, Roman, and Lutheran Christians teach for different purposes—for there is no mention anywhere in Scripture of a *particular (plaatselijke)* descent; but it began with the *resurrection*, the vivification and resurrection from the grave, to prove that he really is the Son of God, the Lord and Christ, the prince and savior (Acts 2:36; 5:31; Rom. 1:3–4), that he completely conquered death (John 11:25; 1 Cor. 15:21; Heb. 2:14), making known righteousness, life, and immortality (Rom. 4:25; 2 Tim. 1:10).

Forty days later, his resurrection was followed by the *ascension* (Mark 16:19; Luke 24:51; Acts 1:1–12), which existed not in a kind of spiritualization but in a particular change of place that made Christ known as the victor over all hostile power (Eph. 4:8; Col. 2:15; 1 Pet. 3:20, 22) and entitled heaven to himself and to all his own in the place of honor at God's right hand. The ascension, therefore, immediately ties *to sitting at the right hand* of God, which in an earthly image (1 Kings 2:19; cf. Ps. 45:10; Matt. 20:21; Rev. 3:21) denotes the highest dignity and honor to which Christ is exalted by virtue of his mediatorial work—namely, to that of absolute sovereign of heaven and earth (Matt. 28:18; 1 Cor. 15:24–28; Eph. 1:20–23; Phil. 2:9–11; Heb. 2:8–9). Even though we do not yet see all things [151] as subdued to him, yet he will reign as king until he has completed his kingdom and subdued all his enemies (1 Cor. 15:25), and then his exaltation will reach its pinnacle in his *return to judgement* (Matt. 25:31–46). In this state of exaltation, Christ continues the work he began on earth in the sense that he is now applying and distributing the fullness of his acquired benefits to his church. After he himself first was exalted to the head of the church through his suffering and death, he must shape the church into his body

18. This paragraph is unique to *Handleiding*. Cf. *MD*, 345.

and fill it into the fullness of God in his resurrection and ascension (Eph. 1:23; 3:19). That is why he continues to work in heaven today as its prophet, priest, and king.[19]

57. That he continued his work as a prophet even after his resurrection is immediately apparent from the significant teaching Jesus provided to his disciples in the forty days of his appearances, which shed new light to them concerning his person and work and about their own future, calling, and task, and about the foundation, confirmation, and propagation of Christ's church on earth (Matt. 28:18–20; Mark 16:15–20; Luke 24:13f., John 20–21; Acts 1:3–9). He also continued his prophetic work through his Spirit in the hearts of the apostles.[20] By the Spirit of truth, he led them into all truth, for that Spirit did not testify about himself but testified of Christ, causing them to remember what he had told them; [the Spirit] also proclaimed to them the things to come (John 14:26; 15:26; 16:13). Thus the apostles possessed the capacity to produce the Scripture of the New Testament, which, in connection with the books of the old covenant, is a lamp to our feet, and a light on our path for centuries. It is Christ [152] himself who gave this word to his church and through that word constantly carries out his prophetic ministry on earth. He preserves and spreads it; he applies and explains it. That word is the instrument by which he makes the nations his disciples, incorporates them into the fellowship of the Triune God, and causes them to walk in his commandments. Through his word and Spirit, Christ is still with us until the end of the world.

In this way, in his exaltation Christ also continues to work as a priest; he is, after all, a priest of the order of Melchizedek forever (Ps. 110:4; Heb. 7:17, 24). His priesthood did not end with his death on earth, but he continues in his priestly service in the heavenly, true sanctuary (Heb. 8:2). His whole earthly life and work can even be seen as a preparation and qualification for his high priestly activity in heaven on behalf of his people. This work consists in the fact that he, having entered by his blood into the heavenly sanctuary (Heb. 9:12), appears before God on our behalf (Heb. 9:24) to atone for the sins of the people; in all these works that are performed before God to atone for the sins of the people, he proves himself to be a merciful and faithful high priest (Hebrews 2:17) who comes to the aid of those who are tempted (Heb. 2:18; 4:15), always acts as their faithful intercessor before the Father (Rom. 8:34; Heb. 7:25; 1 John 2:1), prepares for them a

19. This paragraph is unique to *Handleiding*.

20. Cf. *MD*, 357.

place in the Father's house (John 14:2–3), keeps an inheritance for them and has them as an inheritance (1 Pet. 1:4), and so leads many children to glory (Heb. 2:10).[21]

Even the royal office remains Christ's in his exaltation. There may be less difference of opinion on this point, because Christ has been exalted through his resurrection and ascension to Lord and Christ, to Prince (leader) and Savior, set by the Father at [153] his right hand on the throne, and received a name that is above all other names (Acts 2:36; 5:31; Phil. 2:9–11; Heb. 1:3–4). The kingship of Christ, therefore, becomes much brighter in the light of his exaltation than in his humiliation.[22]

But in this kingship, the Holy Scripture makes a clear distinction. There is a kingship of Christ over Zion, over his people, over the church (Pss. 2:6; 72:2–7; Isa. 9:5; 11:1–5; Luke 1:33; John 18:33),[23] but the relationship between the king and his subjects in the realm of grace is so close and tender that the name of king in the New Testament often alternates with other names.[24] Christ is so close to the church that he bought with his blood that a single name is not enough to give us a conception of its content. And so Scripture uses all sorts of images to make us understand what Christ is to his church: what the bridegroom is to his bride (John 3:29; Rev. 21:2), the husband to his wife (Eph. 5:25; Rev. 21:9), the firstborn for his brothers (Rom. 8:29; Heb. 2:11), the foundation stone for the building (Matt. 21:42; Acts 4:11; 1 Pet. 2:4–8), the vine for the branches (John 15:1–2), the head for the body (Eph. 1:22; 4:15; 5:23; Col. 1:18, 2:19)—that much more is Christ for his church.

In addition, and in connection with that, he exercises a kingship of power over all creatures that do not willingly submit to him (Pss. 2:8–9; 72:8; 110:1–2; Matt. 28:18; 1 Cor. 15:25–27; Rev. 1:5; etc.). He is not a head and bridegroom to them, etc., but the King of kings, the Lord of lords, the ruler of all kings of the earth; and he will prove to be in this: He will one day overcome all his enemies and crush them under his feet (1 Cor. 15:25; 1 Tim. 6:15; Rev. 17:14; 19:16).[25]

---

21. This paragraph is unique to *Handleiding*.

22. This paragraph is identical to a paragraph in *MD*, 364.

23. Cf. *MD*, 364.

24. This sentence is unique to *Handleiding*; the remainder of the paragraph is identical to a portion of one in *MD*, 364.

25. This paragraph is unique to *Handleiding*.

14

The Outpouring of the Holy Spirit

58. [154] The first work that Christ performs after his ascension on behalf of his church on earth is the sending of the Holy Spirit on the day of Pentecost in Jerusalem (Acts 2). This event is an entirely unique fact in history, alongside creation and the incarnation; just as Christ accepted human nature in his conception, never to lay it down again, so the Holy Spirit on the day of Pentecost chose the church as his temple to dwell in it forever. Therefore, Scripture speaks of this sending (*zending*) of the Spirit also as the mission (*uitstorting*) or outpouring (*uitgieting*) of the Holy Spirit (Acts 2:17–18, 33; 10:45; Titus 3:6) and sees within it the fulfillment of the centuries-old prophecy of the Old Testament (Isa. 32:15; 44:3; Jer. 31:31f.; Ezek. 36:26–27; Joel 2:28f.; Zech. 12:10; Acts 2:16f.), and the fulfillment of Jesus' own promise (John 14:16; 15:26; 16:7; Acts 1:4; 2:33).

Yet this does not mean that the Holy Spirit did not exist or was not active on earth and in the church before then. For Scripture clearly teaches that with the Father and the Son, he is Creator and sustainer of all things (Gen. 1:2; Pss. 33:6; 104:30), the worker (*Werkmeester*) of all life and salvation, of all gifts and ability (Exod. 28:3; Num. 11:17, 25; Judg. 14:6; Job 32:8; 33:4; Pss. 51:13; 143:10; Isa. 63:9–12; etc.); even Simeon is said to have been led to the temple by the Holy Spirit [155] (Luke 2:26–27), and even more so of John, who was later called "the Baptist," and of Elizabeth—that they were filled with the Holy Spirit (Luke 1:15, 41, cf. Exod. 31:3; Mic. 3:8).

Yet the Old Testament teaches that in the future the Holy Spirit will rest in an extraordinary way on the Messiah (Isa. 11:2), and the New Testament confirms this by saying that God gave him the Spirit without measure (John 3:34). Indeed, Jesus was conceived by the Spirit (Matt. 1:35), is anointed with the Spirit (Matt. 3:16), and, like no other man before or after him, in all his words and deeds was led and trained by that Spirit (Luke 4:1, 14, 18–19; Heb. 9:14; Rom. 1:3; Acts 1:2; 1 Pet. 3:22). Certainly, he received the Holy Spirit in all his fullness and with all his gifts at his exaltation (Eph. 4:8–10), so that he now possesses the seven Spirits as exalted mediator (that is precisely the Holy Spirit in his fullness), just as he has the seven stars (Rev. 3:1) and has become a life-giving Spirit (1 Cor. 15:45; 2 Cor. 3:17).[1]

For Christ possesses the Spirit as a glorified mediator in a way no other creature was or could partake of him before. Yes, Christ possesses him in his exaltation to an even greater extent than in the state of humiliation. Therefore, John can say that the Holy Spirit was not yet there at first, since Christ was not yet glorified (John 7:39). But when Christ was glorified and had made the Spirit of God wholly his Spirit, the Spirit of Christ, then he could also, just like the Father, make this Spirit proceed from himself, with him give all his gifts to the church, letting him live in it (John 15:26). This happened on the day of Pentecost in Jerusalem.

While the Holy Spirit in the past was given to a few independent individuals temporarily and for a specific purpose [156], he has now descended upon all members of the church and from now on continues living and working in them all. Just as the Son of God appeared on earth more than once in the days of the Old Testament, but it was only through the conception in Mary's womb that he chose human nature as his permanent home, so there was also in the past all sorts of activity and gifts of the Holy Spirit, but only on the day of Pentecost did he make the church his temple, which he continually sanctifies, builds ups, and will never leave.[2]

This indwelling of the Holy Spirit gives the church of Christ an independent existence; it is no longer enclosed in the national life of Israel, within the borders of Palestine, but lives independently by the Spirit who lives in it and spreads itself all over the earth. From the temple on Zion, God by his Spirit is now going to live in the body of Christ, the church; thereby, born on this very day was the mission church and the global church. The ascension of Christ is essential and proves its truthfulness in the descent of the Holy Spirit. Just as he first sanctified, perfected, and exalted Christ to the highest heights through his suffering, so now in the same way he forms the body of Christ until it obtains its full maturity, the fulfillment, the *plērōma*,[3] coming to an end in him, who fills all in all.[4]

59. In the first days, this outpouring of the Holy Spirit was accompanied by all kinds of extraordinary powers and workings, such as speaking

1. The previous three paragraphs are unique to *Handleiding*.

2. This paragraph is identical to a portion of one in *MD*, 372.

3. *Plērōma* is a transliteration of the Greek word πλήρωμα meaning "a filling up, fullness."

4. This paragraph is nearly identical to a portion of a paragraph in *MD*, 372.

in different or new languages (Acts 2:4f.; Mark 16:17), speaking in tongues (*glōssolalia*)[5] (Acts 10:46; 15:8; 19:6), prophecy (Acts 11:28; 20:23; 21:11), visions and revelation (Acts 7:55; 8:39; 10:19; 13:2; 15:28; 16:6; 20:22), miraculous healings [157] (Acts 3:6; 5:5, 12, 15–16; 8:7, 13; etc.). All these wonderful works lasted for quite some time, not only with a man like Paul (Acts 16:6–9; Rom. 15:18; 1 Cor. 14:6, 18; 2 Cor. 12:1–7, 12; Gal. 2:2), but also with many ordinary members of the congregation (Rom. 12:6–8; 1 Cor. 12:8–10).[6]

But these miraculous gifts were not the only or the most important gifts. The most significant, and of an enduring nature, was the boldness given by the Spirit to the disciples to speak the word (Acts 4:8, 31), the strength of faith (Acts 6:5; 11:24), the comfort and joy (Acts 9:31; 13:52), knowledge and wisdom (Act 6:3, 10), and above all love, without which all gifts are worthless (1 Cor. 13). The extraordinary work of the Spirit was temporary and served a special purpose—namely, to promote the foundation of the church in the world; but they stand behind and are subordinate to that lasting work of the Holy Spirit, whereby he, after first constituting Christ as the head of the church, now forms the church into the body of Christ.[7]

The Old Testament already contains indications of this activity of the Holy Spirit. All kinds of extraordinary gifts and powers were, indeed, attributed to the Holy Spirit in those days; but as the prophets and psalmists were more deeply introduced to the hostility of the people of Israel and to the cunningness and wickedness of the human heart, they also spoke with greater strength and clarity that only a renewal by the Holy Spirit could make the people of Israel a people of God in a real sense. A Moor [*Statenvertaling*] cannot change his skin,[8] a leopard his spots; so neither can they do good who have been taught to do evil (Jer. 13:23). God must change the heart of the people by his Spirit if they are to walk in his ways and keep his commands. The Spirit of the Lord [158] alone is the Master of the true, spiritual, and moral life (Pss. 3:10; 51:13–14; Isa. 32:15; Ezek. 36:27).[9]

This aligns with the preaching of Jesus in the Gospel of John. For in the conversation with Nicodemus, Christ explains that there is no access to

5. *Glossolalia* is a transliteration of the Greek word γλωσσολαλία, meaning "speaking in tongues."

6. This paragraph is unique to *Handleiding*. The first sentence, however, is nearly identical to a sentence in *MD*, 372.

7. This paragraph is unique to *Handleiding*.

8. *Statenvertaling* translates to "Moorman"; in Jer. 13:23, the ESV translates this as "Ethiopian."

9. Cf. *MD*, 377.

and no fellowship with the kingdom of heaven except by being born again, and that this birth can only be accomplished by the Holy Spirit (John 3:3, 5). In the farewell addresses (*afscheidsredenen*) (John 14–16), he develops broadly that the Spirit, whom he will send after his glorification by the Father, will replace his presence among the disciples. It is, therefore, beneficial for them that Christ departs, for otherwise the Comforter would not come to them; but if [Jesus] ascends to the Father, he can and will send the Spirit to them.[10] Through that Spirit, Christ himself will come again to them and unite with them in such an intimate way as had not occurred and could not have occurred before during his bodily presence on earth.[11] In Christ, the Father himself comes to them again; both Father and Son come to make their home with them in the Spirit. So that is what the Holy Spirit will bring about in the first place: a communion between the Father and the Son on the one hand and with the disciples on the other, just as it never existed before.[12] And the ultimate goal is for all believers to be one, just as Christ himself says in his own words, "Just as you, Father, are in me and I in you, that they also may be in us, so that the world may believe that you have sent me" (John 17:21–22).[13]

In harmony with the aforementioned is the writing of the apostle Paul in particular, who describes the church as one body whose members need one another and must serve one another (Rom. 12:4; 1 Cor. 12:12f.), but that itself has its root, its unity, its head in Christ (Rom. 12:5; Eph. 1:23; Col. 1:24), who by his Spirit [159] dwells in them. Believers are one Spirit with him (1 Cor. 6:7); they are temples of the Holy Spirit by whom God himself dwells in them (1 Cor. 3:16–17; 6:19). They live, they confess, they walk, they pray, they rejoice in the Spirit (Rom. 8:4, 9, 15; 14:17; 1 Cor. 12:3); they are spiritual people who understand and consider the things of the Spirit (Rom. 8:2; 1 Cor. 2:14); they are continually led by the Spirit and sealed until the day of redemption (Rom. 8:15–16; 2 Cor. 1:22; Eph. 1:13; 4:20); through that Spirit, they all have access to the Father and are built together on the foundation of the apostles and prophets into a dwelling place for God (Eph. 2:18, 22).[14]

---

10. The previous section of the paragraph is identical to a portion of one in *MD*, 377–78.

11. This sentence is unique to *Handleiding*.

12. The previous two sentences are pulled from a paragraph in *MD*, 378.

13. This sentence is pulled from a paragraph in *MD*, 378.

14. Cf. *MD*, 379–80.

60. This fellowship of believers in the person of Christ, which is established and sustained by the Holy Spirit, now also brings together the community in all his goods and benefits.[15] There is no partaking in the benefits of Christ without our sharing in his person, for the benefits are inseparable from his person. That would be conceivable, at least to a certain extent, if the goods Christ gave were of a material nature; after all, someone can give us his money and goods without giving himself to us. But the goods Christ bestows are of a spiritual nature; they exist before everything in his grace, in his love, and these are thoroughly personal and cannot be detached from Christ. The "treasure of merit" ("*schat van verdiensten*") is therefore not deposited by Christ anywhere on earth, not in the hands of a pope or a priest, not in a church or a sacrament; but the treasure of merit lies solely with and in Christ himself. He is that treasure himself; in him the Father turns to us his kind and merciful face, and that is our salvation.

[160] Thus conversely there is also no fellowship with the person of Christ without at the same time taking part in all his treasures and goods. Just as the Father gave life and all things to his Son (Matt. 11:27; John 3:35; 16:15; 17:10), Christ in turn shares of himself and all that is his to the church through the Holy Spirit, who for his part also takes everything from Christ (John 16:13–15). He keeps nothing for himself. As the fullness of the Godhead dwells in him bodily (Col. 1:19; 2:9), so he also fills the church until it reaches the measure of the magnitude of his fullness and is filled to all the fullness of God (Eph. 1:23; 3:19; 4:13, 16).[16]

All the benefits that Christ by his Spirit gives to the church and to every believer can be summarized under one word: *grace* (John 1:16). But this one word implies a wealth of blessings. The Holy Scripture mentions a multitude of words: calling, rebirth, faith, repentance, justification, forgiveness of sins, adoption as children, deliverance from the law, spiritual freedom, faith, hope, love, peace, joy, gladness, comfort, sanctification, preservation, endurance, glorification, and so on. No complete list or treatment of it is possible.[17]

Essentially, three groups of benefits can be clearly distinguished. There is, in the first place, a group of benefits that prepares and initiates man into the covenant of grace and gives him the ability to receive and accept the

---

15. The first sentence is unique to *Handleiding*. The remainder of the paragraph is identical to one in *MD*, 451.

16. This paragraph is composed of portions of a paragraph in *MD*, 382.

17. Cf. *MD*, 383.

blessing of that covenant with a willing heart; they are the benefits of the calling, being born again (in the narrow sense), faith, and conversion. A second group includes those blessings that change the state of man in relation to God, release him from guilt, and thus renew his consciousness; these are especially [161] the benefits of justification, forgiveness of sins, adoption as children, the testimony of the Holy Spirit with our spirit, deliverance from the law, spiritual freedom, peace, and joy. And, finally, there is a third group of benefits that changes the condition of man, delivers him from the stain of sin and renews him in the image of God; this includes in particular the rebirth (in a broader sense), the dying and rising up with Christ, the ongoing conversion, the walking in the Spirit, and the perseverance to the end.[18]

All of these benefits are perfected and completed in the heavenly glory and salvation which God, hereafter, prepares for his own and which will be discussed separately later.[19]

---

18. This paragraph is composed of a portion of a paragraph in *MD*, 383–84.
19. This sentence is nearly identical to a sentence in *MD*, 384.

15

Calling

61. [162] In order to bestow upon us this union with Christ's person and benefits, Christ employs not only the Spirit he has poured out on the church but also the word he has given according to the same Spirit of teaching and correction (2 Tim. 3:16). He has made such a connection between the two that together they serve the operations of his prophetic, priestly, and royal office.

Concerning that connection, there are a variety of ideas. The followers of Pelagius regarded Christianity solely as a teaching, seeing in Jesus nothing more than a lofty example. They made the gospel a new law and denied it its regenerative effect, as well as the personality of the Holy Spirit. On the other hand, the so-called spiritists (antinomians, enthusiasts, mystics) underestimate the significance of the word in the conversion of man and often incorrectly appeal to Scripture, sometimes with an incorrect quotation of Paul (2 Cor. 3:6), calling it a dead letter and not just the new life, but also of all true knowledge derived from the internal illumination of the Holy Spirit.[1]

Both extremes were avoided by Roman, Lutheran, and Reformed churches. But while Rome binds the operation of the Spirit to the church in such a manner that it only distributes the supernatural grace to the faithful through the priest and through the sacraments, [163] and the Lutherans do not know of any operation of the Spirit other than as proceeding through the word as though through a canal, the Reformed tried to maintain both the connection and distinction between the word and Spirit and taught[2] that the Spirit can sometimes work alone, but that as a rule, according to his good pleasure, he binds himself to the word and thus works salvifically where the word is proclaimed—that is, within the circle of the covenant of grace, in the community of the church.

Now in a certain sense, word and Spirit proceed together with all the works of God; but the word does not always work in the same way, and

1. The previous two paragraphs are unique to *Handleiding*.

2. Cf. *MD*, 387–88.

accordingly, the Spirit does not always work in the same way. They work together in creation and bring all things into existence (Ps. 33:6, 9); in the work of preservation, they cause all things to continue to exist (Ps. 104:30; Heb. 1:3); and similarly, they work together in calling but not always with the same result. In the calling itself, there is a distinction according to the content of the word that God sends and the working of the Spirit he connects with it.[3]

62. There is in the first place a "material" (*zakelijke*) calling that goes out to all people from God; it does not come to them deliberately through the preached word but through "affairs" (*zaken*), events, promptings, and experiences, etc.[4] Even after the fall, God continues to reveal himself to his children in his eternal power and divinity; he does not leave them without a witness. He appoints their times and determines their dwellings, so that they might seek the Lord and perhaps feel their way toward him and find him (Acts 14:17; 17:26–27; Rom. 1:20).[5] Thus the Gentiles do not share in the calling of the word of the gospel, but they are absolutely not deprived of a calling. God also speaks to them through nature [164] (Rom. 1:20), through history (Acts 17:26), through reason (John 1:9), and through their conscience (Rom. 2:14–15).[6] This calling is not sufficient for salvation, for it does not reveal Christ who is the only way to the Father and the only name under heaven to salvation (John 14:16; Acts 4:12); it is, nevertheless, of great value and its significance cannot be underestimated. Through it, God maintains, in man, the consciousness (*bewustzijn*) of his dependence and the sense (*besef*) of his accountability. He causes him to strive for a religious, moral life, and after committing a transgression, accuses and condemns him according to his own conscience. It is not an external coercion, but it is an internal, moral bondage that fixes man to God and his revelation. It is a testimony of the Spirit of God, which even in fallen man still makes itself heard and exhorts him to do good.

It makes a human society and a civil justice possible, which in turn paves the way for a higher civilization, for a richer culture, for the flourishing of arts and sciences. Truly, the earth is still full of the goodness of God. The Lord is good to all, and his mercies are over all of his works. He makes

---

3. This paragraph is unique to *Handleiding*.

4. This sentence is unique to *Handleiding*.

5. This section of the paragraph is nearly identical to a section in *MD*, 389.

6. This section of the paragraph is nearly identical to a section in *MD*, 389. Regarding the remainder of the paragraph, cf. *MD*, 390.

his sun rise on the evil and on the good and sends rain on the just and on the unjust. He has not left himself without a witness but does good from heaven, gives rain and fruitful times, and fills our hearts with food and joy (Pss. 104:24; 145:7; Matt. 5:45; Acts 14:17).[7]

This "material" calling is distinguished from the other second calling, which is contained in the word of the gospel and comes to all who live within the boundaries of Christianity. This special calling also incorporates the content of the general calling, the calling that occurs through nature and history, through reason and conscience, especially also [165] through the revelation of God declared and restored in the moral law; but this is joined by the gospel, which gives it a special character distinct from the general calling. Law and gospel are, therefore, the two components of the word of God, distinct but never separate; they accompany each other throughout Scripture, from the beginning to the end of revelation.[8]

This distinction between the law and the gospel is, therefore, quite different from that of the Old and New Testaments. For these terms indicate two successive dispensations in one and the same covenant of grace, and accordingly also the two groups of biblical books, each of which has its content a dispensation of this covenant of grace. But the names "law" and "gospel" represent two very different covenants. The law actually belongs to the so-called covenant of works, which was established with the first man and promised him eternal life in the path of perfect obedience. But the gospel is the proclamation of the covenant of grace, which was first made known to man after the fall and bestows on him eternal life by grace through faith in Christ.

Law and gospel are not distinguished by degree but in essence; they differ as demand and gift, as command and promise. The law, as well as the gospel, contains God's holy, wise, good, and spiritual will (Rom. 2:18, 20; 7:12, 14; 12:10). Yet the law has become powerless on account of sin; it does not justify but increases sin, arouses wrath, condemnation, and death (Rom. 3:20; 4:15; 5:20; 7:5; 8:9, 13; 2 Cor. 3:6f.; Gal. 3:10, 13, 19). On the other hand, there is the gospel that has Christ as its content (Rom. 1:3; Eph. 3:6) and brings nothing but grace, reconciliation, forgiveness, justice, peace, and eternal life (Acts 2:38; 20:24; Rom. 3:21–26; [166] 4:3–8; 5:1–2; etc.). What the law demands of us is given to us for free in the gospel.[9]

---

7. This paragraph is identical to a portion of paragraph in *MD*, 390.
8. This paragraph is unique to *Handleiding*.
9. Cf. *MD*, 391, regarding previous two paragraphs.

63. The calling that comes to Christians through the word is, therefore, high above that which the Gentiles participate in through nature and history. But Scripture and experience force us also to distinguish also between those who hear the gospel and receive it and others who reject it. This distinction has existed throughout the centuries.[10] In the household of Adam, Cain and Abel were already separated; the human race before the flood was distinct within the line of Seth and Cain, and after the flood this separation continued in the family of Shem and his brothers. The family of the patriarchs saw the opposition of Isaac and Ishmael, and of Jacob and Esau, and soon between Israel and the nations. Even among the people of the covenant, not all of Israel who descended from the flesh of Abraham were children of the promise or counted as offspring (Rom. 9:6–8).

In the days of the New Testament, we are faced with the same fact. Many are called but few are chosen (Matt. 22:14). There is not only a sharp contrast between the church and the world, but in the church itself there are thousands who are hearers but who are not doers of the word (James 1:22). Even if one were to reject the whole of Christianity, one does not get rid of this contradiction. For there are and remain everywhere the good and evil, the righteous and the unrighteous. Among people, there is not only a difference in rank and status, in gift and strength, in wealth and honor, but there is also a much deeper spiritual and moral difference among them.[11]

This inequality is so general and goes so deep that it cannot be explained in any area, but especially not in that of [167] religion, by people's own free choice, and thus to a distinction in the calling itself, which can be traced back to the good pleasure of God. In the Reformed confession, a distinction was therefore made between and internal and external calling.[12] The external calling of the word is serious and well founded; in the word preached is the power of God for salvation to everyone who believes (Rom. 1:16; 1 Cor. 15:2)—not a word of men but a word of God (1 Thess. 2:13), living and powerful, sharper than any double-edged sword (John 6:33; Heb. 4:12; 1 Pet. 1:25). In a certain sense, it always doing its work, for if it is not a smell of life to life, it is a smell of death to death (Isa. 55:11; 2 Cor. 2:16); those who reject it are therefore not to blame the gospel, nor

10. The first part of the paragraph is unique to *Handleiding*. The remainder of the paragraph is in *MD*, 394–95.

11. This paragraph is identical to a portion of one in *MD*, 395.

12. *Canons of Dort*, Third and Fourth Heading, Articles 9 and 10.

Christ who is offered to them in the gospel, but to search themselves in their unrepentant hearts.[13]

Nevertheless, the external calling—that is, the purely advisory, moral operation of the gospel—is not enough to renew the heart of mankind. Indeed, Scripture bears witness and experience confirms every day that man is darkened in his mind (Eph. 4:18; 5:8), bound in his will by sins (John 8:34; Rom. 6:20), and dead in sins and trespasses (Eph. 2:2–3). He cannot, therefore, see the kingdom of God (John 8:3), does not understand the things of the Spirit of God (1 Cor. 2:14), does not submit to the law of God (Rom. 8:7), and does nothing good on his own (John 15:5; 2 Cor. 3:5). The gospel may be on behalf of man, but it is not *from* man—not in accordance with his wishes and thoughts (Gal. 1:11); therefore, it is always rejected and resisted by him when he is left to himself.[14]

[168] But herein lies the riches of the grace of God: that nevertheless with those whom he has chosen for eternal life, he binds together with the calling through the word the working of his Spirit.

Already in the Old Testament, the Spirit of the Lord was master and guide of the spiritual life (Pss. 51:12; 143:10), but above all he promised there as the one who in the days of the new covenant teaches all, who gives a new heart and writes the law of the Lord on the heart (Isa. 32:15; Jer. 31:33; 33:39; Ezek. 11:19; 36:26; Joel 2:28). To this end, he was poured out on the day of Pentecost. He was to bear witness to Christ with and through the apostles and then continue to dwell in the congregation, to regenerate it (John 3:5), to bring it to the confession of Jesus as its Lord (1 Cor. 12:3), to comfort and lead the church, and to remain with it forever (John 14:16; Rom. 8:14; Eph. 4:30; etc.); and likewise, to permeate from the congregation into the world and convince it of sin, righteousness, and judgment (John 16:8–11).[15]

The work of God's redemption is both objectively and subjectively his alone. It is not of those who will, nor of those who run, but of the mercy of God (Rom. 9:16). There is an external calling that comes to many (Matt. 22:14); but there is also an internal effective calling that is the result of election (Rom. 8:28–30). God not only gives the gospel but also preaches it in power and in the Holy Spirit (1 Cor. 2:4; 1 Thess. 1:5–6), and he himself provides growth (1 Cor. 3:6–9). He opens the heart (Rev. 16:14), enlightens

13. This paragraph is unique to *Handleiding*.

14. Although the first sentence is unique to *Handleiding*, the remainder is in *MD*, 400.

15. The previous two paragraphs are one paragraph in *MD*, 400.

the mind (Luke 24:45; 2 Cor. 4:6; Eph. 1:18, 3:9; Col. 1: 9–11), bends the will, (Rev. 9:6), and works both the willing and the working according to his good will (Phil. 2:13).[16] Jesus himself points back to a revelation [169] of the Father for us to have knowledge of his name (Matt. 11:25; 16:17; cf. Gal. 1:16).

64. The change of heart, which the internal calling brings about in man, is called the circumcision of the heart in Scripture (Deut. 10:16; 30:6), the giving of a new heart of flesh (Jer. 24:7; 31:31–34; 32:39; Ezek. 11:19; 36:26–28; Joel 2:28–32), and above all, rebirth or, better, birth from above (John 3:3–8). For in the teaching given by Jesus to Nicodemus on this subject, he does not emphasize that a second birth is necessary for entrance into the kingdom (although of course, rebirth can be so called), but Jesus wants to make it clear to Nicodemus that only a birth from above (v. 3), from water and Spirit (v. 5), and from the Spirit (v. 8) will open the entrance to the kingdom.[17]

This birth is different from the birth of the flesh, for what is born of the flesh is flesh (John 3:6); it is not out of the blood, not of the will of the flesh, nor of the will of man, but of God (John 1:13). Therefore, it is as incomprehensible in its origin and direction as the wind, but it is nevertheless possible, for it is the birth of the Spirit (v. 8). After Jesus first described generally that it is a birth of water and Spirit (both without an article) (v. 5), he spoke in verses 7 and 8 specifically of *the* Spirit (with the article) to indicate that this Spirit, as the Spirit of God, can accomplish this great work of the birth from above. In the case of water (v. 5), Jesus did not think of baptism, but he described the nature of birth with it; it is a birth that bears the character of a renewal and purification—of which the water is an image (Ezek. 36:25; cf. the connection of the Spirit and fire in Matt. 3:11)—and that gives birth to a new spiritual life. That forms this birth from [170] above, because it is birth of *the* Spirit, from God himself (vv. 6–8).[18]

By virtue of this birth from God, the faithful are his children (John 1:13; 1 John 3:1; James 1:18) created in Christ (Eph. 2:10), his handiwork and construction (1 Cor. 3:9), and a new creature (2 Cor. 5:17). Regeneration, therefore, is not a work of human strength, not a product of slow, gradual development of natural life, but a break with the old existence and the creative beginning of a new, spiritual life; the death of the old and the resurrection of the new man (Rom. 6:3f.).[19]

---

16. This first portion of the paragraph is identical to one in *MD*, 400–1. The final sentence is unique to *Handleiding*.

17. This paragraph is unique to *Handleiding*.

18. This paragraph is identical to a portion of one in *MD*, 407.

19. This paragraph is identical to a portion of one in *MD*, 407–8.

On the other hand, it is not a second creation entirely out of nothing, but a re-creation of the human being, who was born to his parents and had an existence. In regeneration, he remains essentially the same man, the same I, the same personality. Paul says of himself that he was crucified with Christ and, therefore, he himself no longer lives but Christ in him, but then he immediately continues like this: "The life I now live in the flesh, I live by faith in the Son of God" (Gal. 2:20). [As Paul argues,] I have been crucified with Christ and died, but it was also I who was resurrected immediately with Christ; I was not destroyed and replaced by another, but I was reborn and renewed. He also says of some believers in Corinth that they were formerly fornicators, idolaters, and adulterers, etc., but they have been washed, sanctified, and justified in the name of the Lord Jesus and by the Spirit of our God (1 Cor. 6:10–11). The continuity, unity, and coherence of the human being are not broken through rebirth, but it nevertheless makes a significant change in [the human being].[20]

This change is of a spiritual nature: what is born of the Spirit is spirit (John 3:6) who lives from and walks [171] according to the Spirit. Rebirth deposits a principle of new life (*beginsel van nieuw leven*), which the Holy Spirit creates in connection with the resurrection of Christ from whom he takes everything (1 Pet. 1:3). Rebirth plants a seed in the heart (1 Pet. 1:23; 1 John 3:9) from which a whole new man emerges. It begins in a mysterious and hidden way and has its center at the heart of man's personality, in his own self (Gal. 2:20); but from there it extends to all man's faculties, to his mind (Rom. 12:2; 1 Cor. 2:12; Eph. 4:22) and heart (Heb. 8:10; 10:16; 1 Pet. 3:4), to his will (Rom. 7:7) and affections, to his mind, soul, and body (1 Thess. 5:23; Rom. 6:19). A whole person is born, who—although not fully mature and still fighting against all kinds of sins of the flesh—nevertheless wishes to walk in the newness of the Spirit (Gal. 5:17; Rom. 6:4; 7:6).[21]

65. This new life proves its truth and genuineness in the fruits it produces; this is primarily in faith on the side of understanding, and in repentance on the side of the will.[22]

Believing, in general, as we speak of it in our daily lives, is the acceptance of a testimony. We believe something when we have not seen or observed it ourselves but are, nevertheless, assured of it because other reliable persons, either orally or in writing, in the past or in the present, have told

20. This paragraph is identical to one in *MD*, 408.

21. This paragraph is identical to one in *MD*, 408.

22. This sentence is unique to *Handleiding.*

us about it. This basic meaning of the word is preserved when it is utilized in the religious sphere, and it must retain this meaning, for we know nothing of the entire contents of the gospel, or of the whole person and work of Christ, except through the testimony of the apostles; only through [172] their word can we believe in Christ (John 17:20); through fellowship with the apostles, we come into fellowship with the Father and with his Son, Jesus Christ (1 John 1:3).[23]

But nevertheless, when it comes to the religious sphere, and as it is specifically presented in Holy Scripture as the way into the kingdom of heaven, belief is modified very significantly in accordance with this special use. One can also accept the gospel in the same way, if one believes the testimony concerning a historical person or fact, but then one does not accept the gospel as the gospel and the faith by which one accepts it is not true faith. Like Jesus in the parable of the sower, there are very different attitudes that hearers may adopt toward the gospel.[24]

There are those, like Pilate, who are indifferent and with a proud and contemptuous smile turn away from the gospel. There are also those who, like the proud Pharisees and the wise Greeks, see in the cross of Christ an offense and foolishness and depart from it in extreme hostility and hatred (Matt. 12:24; John 8:22; 1 Cor. 1:23). There are others who believe but do not come to a confession: who love the honor of men more than the one God (John 12:42–43); who remain hearers of the word until their death but never become doers of the word (Matt. 7:26; John 13:17; Rom. 2:13; James 1:23); who, like Simon of Samaria, accept the gospel for the sake of the signs and great powers it brings about (Rev. 8:13f.); or, like Agrippa, at some point in their life are almost moved to become a Christian (Acts 26:27–28); or, like Demas, serve the gospel for many years and then love the present world again (2 Tim. 4:10).[25]

There are all kinds of belief—historical, temporary and miraculous faith [173]—which bears the name of faith but does not possess the content; which shows a form of godliness but denies its power (2 Tim. 3:5).[26]

True, saving faith is distinguished from all the aforementioned forms of belief in three respects. First, it has a different origin. Historical, temporal,

---

23. This paragraph is in *MD*, 409.

24. Although the last sentence in this paragraph is unique to *Handleiding*, the remainder of it is in *MD*, 409–10.

25. Cf. *MD*, 411.

26. The previous two paragraphs are largely identical to one in *MD*, 411.

and miraculous beliefs are not in themselves wrong; they are better than total unbelief and bitter enmity; they even have a temporary use; but they are, nevertheless, only gifts of God's common grace and are also given to natural people. But the saving faith is a gift of God's special grace (Phil. 1:29), a result of election (Rev. 13:48; Rom. 8:30; Eph. 1:5), a work of the Holy Spirit (1 Cor. 12:3), a fruit of regeneration (John 1:12–13).[27]

Second, saving faith is essentially distinct from all other faiths. It includes knowledge and stands against all doubts, but this knowing (*kennen*) is of a special kind, entirely distinct from the knowledge (*kennis*) we gain in everyday life through observation and thinking. The knowledge (*kennis*) of faith is a practical knowledge (*kennis*), a knowledge (*kennis*) of the heart rather than the head, a knowledge (*kennis*) with the deepest personal interest, because it concerns a matter that involves people's life, soul, and salvation. It is, in a word, a knowledge (*kennis*) of the only true God in the face of Jesus Christ, whom he has sent, and it is joined with eternal life (John 17:3).

Third, saving faith differs from all other faith in its object. For historical faith remains with the report and does not penetrate any deeper; historic faith (*tijd-geloof*) sees in this message some beauty and rejoices in it but ignores its actual content; and faith in miracles attaches itself to the signs and powers, but it is fundamentally indifferent [174] to the one who works them. However, saving faith does not stop at words and deeds but penetrates to the person from whom they proceed. Believing is an acceptance of Christ—not merely an acceptance of the testimony of the apostles concerning him, but an acceptance of Christ himself (John 1:12); it includes a putting on of Christ as a garment (Gal. 3:27), a dying and rising with Christ (Rom. 6:4), a life in his fellowship (Gal. 2:20), an abiding in him as the vine (John 15:4), etc. Through and in Christ, God is their Father, and they are his sons and daughters (2 Cor. 6:18).[28]

66. Just as faith is the fruit of regeneration with regard to the conscience, so in conversion new life manifests itself with regard to the will. This is already mentioned repeatedly in the books of the Old Testament, for Israel was guilty of unfaithfulness and disobedience; and God, through his prophets, preached repentance to them (2 Kings 17:13). All prophets have been preachers of repentance and conversion, but they have also been preachers of the forgiveness of sins and of perfect salvation. Thus they are also heralds and forerunners of John the Baptist and of Christ, who both began

27. This paragraph is identical to one in *MD*, 411–12.

28. The previous two paragraphs are distinct to *Handleiding*. Cf. *MD*, 412–14.

their public ministry with the message: the kingdom of heaven is at hand—repent and believe the gospel (Mark 1:4, 15).[29]

To indicate this conversion, the Greek New Testament uses two words:[30] the first one appears as noun or verb [to repent, repentance] in Matthew 3:2, 8, 11; 9:13; 11:20; Acts 2:38; 2 Cor. 7:9–10, and indicates an internal, spiritual change, to experience (*te kennen*) a change in moral disposition; the other [to turn back] we find, for example, in Mark 13:16;[31] [175] Luke 1:16–17; 22:32; Acts 9:35; 11:21; 14:15; 15:19; 26:18, 20. It is more concerned with the external change, the change in the direction of life, which is a manifestation and consequence of the internal change. In Acts 3:19 and 26:20, both words are connected: "repent, therefore, and turn back"—that is, change your mind and your heart and your walk, repent and return.[32]

As long as the Christian church had to expand into the world of the Jews and Gentiles, conversion was not only an internal change but also an external change, an abandonment of the service of the mute idols (1 Cor. 12:2; 1 Thess. 1:9), of poor and weak principles (Gal. 4:3, 9; Col. 2:8, 20), of dead works (Heb. 9:14; 1 Thess. 1:9), of public sins and trespasses (1 Cor. 6:10; Eph. 2:2–3; Col. 3:5, 7; Titus 3:3), to serve from now on the living and true God (Heb. 9:14; 1 Thess. 1:9) and to cleave to the Lord (1 Cor. 6:15–20). Such conversion received its sign and seal in holy baptism (Acts 2:38).[33]

But when this sending period (*zendingsperiode*) was over and the church was reproducing itself in the family, from parents to children, the essence of conversion did not change, but it took on a different form with the children of the faithful, who had been included in the covenant of grace from birth and were baptized as a sign of it. At times, it was even completely deprived of its inner spiritual meaning, and Rome turned it into a sacrament of penance, in which one can be sure of repentance and regret over the consequences of sin. The Reformation resisted this and restored conversion it is original, spiritual sense. As such, it is from a repentance for the consequences of sin, as occurred in Cain, Esau, and Judas, and of the sorrow of the world (2 Cor. 7:10), and also of a superficial, external conver-

29. Cf. *MD*, 414–15.

30. Bavinck has in mind: (1) "repent" (μετανοέω) and (2) "to turn back" (ἐπιστρέφω).

31. Although Bavinck lists Matt. 13:16 here as an example of "to turn back," that term does not appear in this verse, so we have replaced it with Mark 13:16.

32. This paragraph is identical to a portion of one in *MD*, 416.

33. Although the final sentence in the paragraph is unique to *Handleiding*, the remainder of it is identical to a portion of a paragraph in *MD*, 417.

sion [176]; and although no one can determine the degree and extent of it, it exists essentially in a breaking of the heart (Ps. 51:19; John 2:37), in a sorrow for sin, as God wills and works, in a return to the Father, with the confession: "Father, I have sinned against heaven and before you" (Luke 15:18).[34]

This true conversion is therefore the fruit of regeneration; it stands in the closest connection with saving faith, continues throughout life, and therefore it is discussed in the Heidelberg Catechism—not in the section on the doctrine of misery or redemption but in that of gratitude.[35]

---

34. This paragraph is unique to *Handleiding*.

35. This paragraph is unique to *Handleiding*. The Heidelberg Catechism is split into three parts: 1. Our sin and misery (Lord's Day 1–4); 2. Our deliverance (Lord's Day 5–31); and 3. Our Gratitude (Lord's Day 32–52). Conversion is discussed on Lord's Day 33.

16

JUSTIFICATION

67. [177] Regeneration, which manifests itself in the fruits of faith and repentance, unlocks the door to the kingdom of God. And whoever is a citizen of this kingdom will immediately receive all the benefits that are its contents and that can be gathered together under three headings: righteousness, holiness, and salvation. The first of these glorious benefits is mentioned here.[1]

Righteousness is ordinarily defined as the steadfast and constant will of a rational being who gives to each his own. It includes, in the first place, a moral character (quality, condition) of the person to whom it is granted, and, second, an attitude (*houding*) toward and treatment of other persons resulting from this attitude (*houding*), recognizing them in the rights to which they are entitled. Righteousness (*gerechtigheid*) is justice (*rechtvaardigheid*) that a person possesses himself and justice (*rechtvaardige*) he gives to others: the first is called "righteousness" (*gerechtigheid*); the latter "justice" (*rechtvaardigheid*).[2] In this sense, Scripture repeatedly ascribes to God righteousness (*gerechtigheid*) (Deut. 32:4); he is righteous (*rechtvaardig*) as a legislator who proclaims his judgments (Deut. 4:8), as a king who upholds them (Exod. 19:5; Mic. 6:8; Amos 5:14–15; Isa. 1:16–17), and as a judge who acquits the innocent and condemns the guilty (Deut. 10:17; 16:19; 25:1; Pss. 7:10; 11:7; 33:5; 96:13, etc.).

However, since no human being can stand before [178] God by this standard (Pss. 130:3, 143:2), the righteousness of the revelation of the grace of God within his covenant gradually takes on a different, deeper meaning. Righteousness is more and more often (not in opposition but) in connection with God's mercy, truth, and faithfulness (Pss. 40:11; 89:15; 103:17; 116:5) and becomes the principle of salvation and redemption upon which the pious plead (Pss. 4:1, 143:1)[3] because God, as the righteous God who

1. This paragraph is identical to the first paragraph in *MD*, ch. 21 (see 420).

2. The first half of the paragraph is nearly identical to a portion of a paragraph in *MD*, 420. The remainder of the paragraph is unique to *Handleiding*.

3. Cf. *MD*, 423–24.

tests the minds and hearts, will confirm (Ps. 7:9), deliver (Ps. 31:2), acquit (Ps. 34:23), vindicate (Ps. 35:23), forgive (Ps. 51:16), answer (Ps. 65:6), give life (Ps. 139:40), hear (Ps. 143:1), and bring them out of trouble (Ps. 143:11).

This most important change surrounding the concept of God's righteousness is not due to the fact that they consider themselves saints entitled to God's exoneration, for the faithful confess their iniquities before the Lord in the humblest way. It is explained from this: God—in his covenant, by promise and oath—has committed himself to do justice to his people against their enemies and to lead them to salvation. When he forgives their sins and gives them his salvation, he does so not for their sake but for his name, his covenant, his glory, his honor (Pss. 25:11; 31:4; 79:9; 105:8; 109:21; 143:11; Isa. 48:9, 11; Jer. 14:7, 21; Ezek. 20:9, 14, 22, 44; Dan. 9:19). Even if the people are unfaithful and disloyal, he remembers his covenant and makes it stand forever (Pss. 105:8; 111:5; Isa. 54:10).[4]

The righteousness (*gerechtigheid*) of God, which pious Israel advocates, does not conflict with this but is related to his lovingkindness and salvation and is closely related to his truth and faithfulness; it commits God by his own word and promise and obliges him to save his people [179], by grace alone, from all their afflictions.[5]

This is how God acted in former days when he delivered Israel from all their enemies time and time again (Exod. 2:24; Judg. 2:1; Isa. 37:20); but he will do so much more gloriously in the future when, for his great name's sake, he will blot out their transgression, provide them with righteousness, make a new covenant with them, and pour out his Spirit upon them. Then they will be called by a new name: the Lord is our righteousness (Isa. 43:25; 45:24–25; 46:13; 54:17; 62:2; Jer. 23:6; 33:16; 31:31–34, etc.). This prophecy is fulfilled in Christ in whom God reveals righteousness apart from the law and seemingly despite it (Rom. 1:17; 3:21), through whom God has made reconciliation through faith in his blood (Rom. 3:25), who became to us righteousness from God (1 Cor. 1:30; 2 Cor. 5:21; Phil. 3:9). The righteousness of God becomes in Christ the righteousness of his people. Thus God is able (as it were, contrary to the law, which commands to condemn the wicked) to acquit the wicked, to justify those who possess faith in Jesus, while remaining completely righteous himself (Rom. 3:26; 4:5).[6]

---

4. Apart from the final sentence (which is also in *MD*, 427), this paragraph is unique to *Handleiding*.

5. This paragraph is identical to a portion of a paragraph in *MD*, 427–28.

6. This paragraph is unique to *Handleiding*.

68. The term "vindication" (*rechtvaardiging*) or "justification" (*rechtvaardigmaking*) is to be understood as that abundantly gracious but also judicial act of God, by which he acquits sinners from guilt and punishment and gives them the right to eternal life.[7] According to Rome, and all those who seek the ground of human justification wholly or partly in man himself (in his faith, in his good works, in Christ in us, in the new principle of life (*nieuwe levensbeginsel*), etc., and thus confuse this benefit with that of sanctification, this judicial declaration of righteousness is always objected to with the objection that such a legal declaration [180] is false and unworthy of God. For if the basis of our justification, they say, lies entirely outside of us and faith and good works do not in any way contribute as a part of our righteousness before God, then the person who is justified is not really righteous, and then God makes an untrue, unjust judgment on such a man, for he *is* not what he is *declared* to be.

It is sufficient to note that Holy Scripture always understands justification as a judicial act. It repeatedly speaks of the righteousness of sinners before God and then uses a word derived from legal language that always has a legal meaning. God commanded the judges of Israel to speak righteously to the just and to condemn the unjust (Deut. 25:1; Ps. 82:2–3; Prov. 17:15; 24:24; Isa. 5:23), and he himself shows his righteousness in that he neither justifies the wicked nor kills the righteous (Gen. 18:25; Exod. 23:7; 2 Chron. 6:23).[8]

When this word is communicated in the spiritual realm, it retains its legal meaning, such as Matthew 11:19 and Luke 7:29 clearly teach, where the moral meaning of "making righteous" or "sanctifying" is altogether excluded. The same is true when the word is used, especially by Paul, in the salvation of sinners: for he says not only that God, who justifies (*rechtvaardigende*) him by faith in Jesus, remains righteous (*rechtvaardig*) himself (Rom. 3:26), but he also uses "to justify" (*rechtvaardigen*) and to impute righteousness (*gerechtigheid*) interchangeably (Rom. 4:3, 5–6, 11); he sets the righteous against the damned—that is, the condemned (Rom. 8:33–34). In Romans 5:18, Paul speaks of a justification (of life, that involves life) through [181] one judgment of righteousness (concerning Christ), just as all men were condemned by the one transgression (of Adam). He expresses himself even more strongly in the following verse when he says that just as

---

7. The remainder of this paragraph is identical to a paragraph in *MD*, 438.

8. This paragraph is identical to a portion of one in *MD*, 438.

many have been made sinners by Adam's disobedience, so also have many been made righteous by Christ's obedience.[9]

Furthermore, those who disagree forget that there are two ways in which one thing or another may be given to us:[10] we can acquire ownership of it by a court decision; and we can, on the basis of such a court decision, take possession of it sooner or later. Anyone who is appointed heir in a legal will has already received a right to the bequeathed goods in the future, but it may happen that he can only act as the owner years later. Even when law and reality coincide in the same moment, there is still in fact a great difference between the two. Property is legal; possession is the actual power over a thing.

This is also the case in the spiritual domain: for we stand before God in a legal relationship but not exclusively; he is our Creator and therefore also our Lawgiver, King, and Judge (Gen. 18:25; Ps. 47:3; Isa. 33:22; Heb. 4:12; James 4:12). This legal relationship is not abolished in the gospel but restored and fulfilled, for God has revealed his righteousness in the gospel, apart from the law (Rom. 1:17; 3:21–26). Therefore, if salvation is to be given to us in full for Christ's sake, then it should first be properly imputed to us and then actually communicated to us (Isa. 1:27).

Thus justification and sanctification belong together; they are inseparably linked with each other. Both [182] are equally necessary in order to make mankind partakers of the whole of redemption, but they are still distinct. This distinction, as the Reformation has brought to light again in connection with Paul, is of such great importance that he, who neglects it or erases it and seeks to establish his own righteousness, denies the perfection and sufficiency of God's righteousness in Christ, transforms the gospel into a new law, takes away the comfort of souls, and makes salvation depend upon the merits of man.

69. In order to maintain justification in this comforting sense, it must be emphasized that the ground on which it rests lies entirely outside of us: in Christ and his righteousness. It has its origin in God's grace, but its foundation in the redemption is wrought by Christ (Rom. 3:24). Grace and justice, forgiveness and reconciliation do not therefore conflict; it is precisely in the path of the righteous, of the righteousness given to man in

---

9. This paragraph is unique to *Handleiding,* but it does have similarities to paragraphs in *MD*, 438–39.

10. Although the first sentence is unique to *Handleiding*, the remainder of the paragraph is identical to a portion of one in *MD*, 436.

Christ, that God glorifies his grace. We owe everything to the love of the Father and to the grace of the Son (John 3:16; Rom. 5:8; 2 Cor. 8:9) that Christ became our righteousness and a propitiation for our sins (Rom. 3:25; 1 Cor. 1:30; 2 Cor. 5:21; Gal. 3:13). This righteousness is so perfect and sufficient, it does not need the slightest supplement on our part.[11]

Besides, as a sinner, man has no righteousness with which to appear before God or on the basis of which to demand forgiveness of sins in eternal life. No flesh can be justified by the works of the law (Rev. 13:39; Rom. 3:20, 28; 8:3, 8; Gal. 2:16; 3:11). On the contrary, the law condemns him and subjects him to its punishment (Rom. 1:18; 3:19–20; 4:15; [183] Gal. 3:10). The good works the regenerate person performs out of faith cannot be considered as grounds for his justification either; for, first of all, all these works are still very imperfect and contaminated with sin; if the believer wants to do good, he always finds himself in the presence of evil (Rom. 7:21).[12] On the other hand, all these good works are already based on the righteousness given by Christ and accepted in faith; the believer walks only in good works that God has prepared, and for which he, as God's workmanship, was created in Christ (Eph. 2:10).

But the confession of justification (*rechtvaardigmaking*) means that God no longer demands the righteousness (*gerechtigheid*) of the law from us, but that he himself, apart from the law, has revealed in Christ another righteousness that, with its passive (*lijdelijke*) and active (*dadelijke*) obedience, is wholly sufficient before God to forgive us all our sins (Matt. 20:28; 26:28; Acts 2:36, 38; 5:30–31; Rom. 3:25; 1 John 2:2) and to give to us, at the same time, a family or adoption as children and the right to the heavenly inheritance of eternal life (Rom. 8:14–17; Gal. 4:5–7). The righteousness (*gerechtigheid*) by which God acquits us and grants to us the right to live forever is therefore a righteousness from God; it is neither wholly nor in part of our works, but it is the gift of God, a free gift of grace (Phil. 3:9; 2 Tim. 1:9; Titus 3:5). Christ himself—not something of him but himself, the crucified and glorified Christ—is this righteousness (*gerechtigheid*) (1 Cor. 1:30).

That is why this righteousness (*gerechtigheid*), given to us by God in Christ, can only be accepted by our faith. This faith, therefore, appears in righteousness as a receiving organ, as the hand that accepts a gift, as the soul's confidence [*vertrouwen*] in Christ and in his righteousness alone. It

---

11. The previous three paragraphs are unique to *Handleiding*.

12. The first part of the paragraph is unique to *Handleiding*, although the final section is also in *MD*, 435.

is true, however, that [184] Holy Scripture repeatedly expresses that by faith righteousness is imputed to us (Gen. 15:6; Rom. 4:3, 5, 9, 22; Gal. 3:6; James 2:23), but by this it does not in any way intend to express that faith justifies in itself, by virtue of its inner quality, as a good moral act.

For first of all, justification (*rechtvaardigmaking*) by or through (never because of) faith is always diametrically opposed to justification (*rechtvaardigmaking*) by the works of the law (Rom. 3:20, 28; 4:4f.; Gal. 2:16; 3:11f). This contrast alternates with the other: that justification (*rechtvaardigmaking*) through faith is a justification (*rechtvaardigmaking*) by grace, and as such excludes all boasting and all merit (Rom. 3:24, 4:4f.; Titus 3:5). In Romans 4:16, the apostle explicitly states that the inheritance is of faith, precisely so that it may be out of grace; but this could not be said if faith itself, on account of its inner worth and strength, was what justified a person. Finally, if faith performed this service, then Christ would lose all significance in justification (*rechtvaardigmaking*); the only thing that would matter would be what someone believed. According to Scripture, however, it is precisely the content and the object of justifying faith that is important. Faith can replace the righteousness (*gerechtigheid*) created by the law and be imputed as righteousness (*gerechtigheid*), because it is faith in Christ Jesus, whom God presented as an atonement through the power of his blood (Rom. 3:25), who bore our curse (Gal. 3:13), became sin for us (2 Cor. 5:21), who died and was resurrected, who is God's right hand, who prays for us (Rom. 8:34), and who has therefore become God's righteousness for us (1 Cor. 1:30) in whom we become the righteousness of God (2 Cor. 5:21).[13]

In a word, faith justifies because it shares in [185] the righteousness of Christ that is as perfect and sufficient as that which is required by the law but is now given in the gospel by God by grace in Christ (Phil. 3:9); it justifies, not by its inner dignity but by its content—namely, the righteousness of Christ.[14]

70. The benefit of the justification (*rechtvaardigmaking*) by faith alone is that it contains a rich comfort for the Christian. The forgiveness of sins, hope for the future, and assurance of eternal salvation do not depend on the degree of holiness one has attained in this life but are fixed in the grace of God and in the redemption that is in Christ Jesus.[15] Indeed, if they had

---

13. The previous three paragraphs are unique to *Handleiding*. Cf. *MD*, 440–41.

14. This paragraph is identical to one in *MD*, 441–42.

15. Although the first part of the paragraph is identical to a portion of one in *MD*, 446, the remainder it is unique to *Handleiding*.

to derive their firmness from the good works of the Christian, they would remain insecure at all times; but now they are fixed in Christ and his righteousness and his salvation can never be shaken. His house is built on a rock and can endure the violence of the torrential rain, of the waves, and of the winds.

Furthermore, that faith, which rests on God's grace alone and is certain of the forgiveness of sins, first makes one capable of doing good works. For as long as we allow our salvation to depend on the good works we do, we remain more or less in anxiety and fear, and we are still servants who work for wages. But if we are certain, through the faith, of our salvation in Christ, we can devote all our attention to doing good works to glorify the Father. We, therefore, died through the law that we might live in God (Gal. 2:19).[16]

Released from the law, the Christian is then, finally, in the freedom with which Christ has set him free. The believer is not released from the law in the sense that he can live according to the discretion [186] of his heart; that he, as long as it is called today, may indulge himself according to the inclination and direction of his sinful nature. On the contrary, the believer is much more firmly bound by the law than was previously the case, for faith does not destroy the law but affirms it (Rom. 3:31); its law (*recht*) is fulfilled in those who walk not according to the flesh but according to the Spirit (Rom. 8:4). For those who have died to sin, how can they still live in it (Rom. 6:2)?[17]

But the relationship between the believer and the law is very different from how he used to stand before it. He remains bound to the law here as a rule of gratitude, but he is free from its requirement and curse.[18] He is no longer a servant or an immature (*onmondige*) son, as Israel in the days of the Old Testament (Gal. 3:23–24; 4:1–2), but he participates in the adoption as children (Gal. 4:5): no longer under the law but under grace (Rom. 6:5) and free over all creatures (Matt. 6:25f.; Rom. 8:35, 39; 1 Cor. 7:20–24; 1 Tim. 4:4). All things belong to the believers because they are Christ's (1 Cor. 3:21–23), and all things must come together for their good because they love God and are called according to his purpose (Rom. 8:28).

16. This paragraph is unique to *Handleiding*.

17. The first sentence of this paragraph is unique to *Handleiding*. Cf. *MD*, 448.

18. This portion of the paragraph is in *MD*, 448. For the remainder of the paragraph, see *MD*, 449.

17

Sanctification

71. [187] If the image of God existed not only in knowledge and righteousness but also in holiness, then the re-creation must restore man to a right relationship with God and also renew him inwardly according to the demands of his holy law. Sin is guilt but also a blemish (*smet*). Justification (*rechtvaardigmaking*) frees him from guilt; sanctification frees him from the stain (*smet*) of sin. Through the former one, his consciousness (*bewustzijn*) is changed; through the latter one, his being is changed. Through the first, man becomes good again; by the latter, he becomes good again and able to do good again.[1]

The word *holy* in Hebrew probably derived from a stem meaning "to cut off/to isolate" and appears on almost every page of the Holy Scriptures. In the first place, holiness is attributed to God, who is distinct from and exalted above all creatures, especially in this respect: that he has no communion with sin (Exod. 15:11; 1 Sam. 2:2; Isa. 5:16; 6:3); for all things that proceed from God are holy, his name (Lev. 20:3), his arm (Ps. 98:1), his covenant (Dan. 11:28), his word (Ps. 105:42), his Spirit (Ps. 51:11; Isa. 63:10, 17); furthermore, all of this is separated from the world, placed in relationship to God, and is made his own [is holy]: his people (Exod. 19:6; 29:43–46; Lev. 11:44; 19:2), the priest and Levites who administer the holy things and are solemnly consecrated to their ministry (Exod. 29), and the places, times, sacrifices, tools, [188] priestly garments, temple, altar, etc., that are consecrated to and intended for the Lord's service.[2]

God is holy in all of his revelation; that is why he is especially so in Christ, who is the Holy One (Luke 1:35; Mark 1:24; John 6:69; Acts 4:27;

1. This paragraph is identical to the first paragraph of *MD*, ch. 22 (450), "De Heiligmaking."

2. "§20. Liturgiek" (no date), Box 346, Folder 227, Archive of Herman Bavinck, Vrije Universiteit of Amsterdam, Amsterdam, Netherlands. In this theological encyclopedia, Bavinck has a short section on liturgy. In harmony with this paragraph, he suggests that all liturgies possess a holy place, a holy time, holy persons, and holy actions.

Rev. 3:90) and who also could sanctify himself and sanctify his people. He not only took their sin upon himself and bore their punishment, but he also submitted to the law of God for them, fulfilled all righteousness, learned obedience, even obedience unto death on the cross (Matt. 3:15; Phil. 2:8; Gal. 4:4; Heb. 5:8). Thus he sanctified himself completely and unconditionally; in spite of all temptation, he committed himself to God (John 17:19) and also through suffering completed this (Heb. 2:4; 5:9) so that he might be our sanctification and we too might be sanctified in truth (John 17:19; 1 Cor. 1:30).

In order to understand the benefit of sanctification, it is therefore necessary to understand clearly that Christ is our holiness in the same sense as he is our righteousness. The holiness in which we must participate has been acquired by Christ and lies in him, completely ready for his own. Sanctification, like justification, is a blessing, a gift of God's grace. He first imputes to us Christ with all his blessings and then communicates him to us in all his fullness.[3]

Therefore, already in the Old Testament it is said that God circumcises the heart (Deut. 30:6), replaces the heart of stone with a heart of flesh (Ezek. 12:19), gives a new heart and a new spirit (Ps. 51:12; Ezek. 12:19; 36:26), writes the law on their hearts, and makes them to walk in his ways (Jer. 31:33; 33:38; Ezek. 36:27–28; etc.).[4] If possible, even more strongly, the New Testament says that believers are God's workmanship, created in Christ Jesus for good works (Eph. 2:10), a new [189] creation (2 Cor. 5:17; Gal. 6:15), God's work (Rom. 14:20), God's field and building (1 Cor. 3:9; Eph. 2:20; Col. 2:7; 1 Pet. 2:5); it is all from God (2 Cor. 5:18). When they died and were raised up with Christ, they were also washed and sanctified in him (1 Cor. 1:2; 6:11; Titus 3:5); and they are continually sanctified (John 17:17; 2 Cor. 3:18; 1 Thess. 5:23; Eph. 5:26; Titus 2:14; Heb. 13:20–21) until they are conformed to the image of the Son (Rom. 8:28; 1 Cor. 15:49; Phil. 3:21). The chain of salvation is unbreakable, because it is the work of God from beginning to end. Those whom he foreknew he has called and justified and also glorifies (Rom. 8:30).

On the basis of this work of sanctification, which God accomplishes in the church through the Spirit of Christ, believers are always mentioned in the Scripture by the name of saints. Israel was already called this in ancient

3. The previous three paragraphs are unique to *Handleiding*.

4. This first section of the paragraph is unique to *Handleiding*. The remainder is identical to a portion of one in *MD*, 457.

times (Exod. 19:6); it was separated from the nations that it might be the property of the Lord (Lev. 20:26) and might walk in his ways (Exod. 19:5). In the future, when God establishes his new covenant, [Israel] will still more rightly and profoundly be called the holy people, the redeemed of the Lord (Isa. 62:12; Joel 3:17; Obad. 17; Zech. 8:3; 14:20). In the days of the New Testament, the high priest sanctified himself for his people, so that they too might be sanctified in truth (John 17:19); the believers also immediately receive the name of saints (Acts 9:13, 32, 41; 26:10; Rom. 1:7; 1 Cor. 1:2, etc.).

It does not imply that they are free from and above all sins in the moral sense, but it expresses the fact that the New Testament congregation has now taken the place of ancient Israel and become the possession of the Lord (2 Cor. 6:16; Gal. 6:16; 1 Pet. 2:5), because it is sanctified in Christ [190] and is a temple of the Holy Spirit (John 17:19; 1 Cor. 1:30, 3:16; 6:11, 19).[5]

72. But this holiness, which was given to the church in Christ and was first communicated to it by the Holy Spirit, lays on the believer a costly obligation. Sanctification is a work of God, but it is intended to become a work in which the believers themselves work together in the power of God.

In the Old Testament, it is said that the Lord himself sanctifies his people (Exod. 31:13; Lev. 20:8, 21:8), and then again that the people must sanctify themselves (Lev. 11:44; 20:7; Num. 11:18). Sometimes it is said that the Lord circumcises the heart (Deut. 30:6), and other times it is said that Israel itself is called to circumcise the foreskin of the heart (Deut. 10:16; Jer. 4:4). Conversion (*bekeering*) is at once a work of God (Jer. 31:18; Lam. 5:21) and a duty of man (Jer. 3:12–13).

Likewise, in the New Testament, sanctification occurs as a gift of God in Christ and as a work of the Holy Spirit through whom believers are sanctified (John 17:17, 19; 1 Cor. 1:2; 1 Thess. 5:23); yet they are repeatedly admonished to be perfect as their Father in heaven is perfect (Matt. 5:48) to produce good works that glorify the Father (Matt. 5:16; John 15:8), to make their members serve the righteousness of sanctification (Rom. 6:19), to become holy in their entire walk (1 Pet. 1:15; 2 Pet. 3:11), to pursue sanctification, and complete it in the fear of God (2 Cor. 7:1; 1 Thess. 3:13, 4:3), for without it no one will see the Lord (Heb. 12:14).[6]

The one does not contradict the other at all. Rather, the work of believers in their own sanctification is only possible because of this: it is the work of God he accomplishes in them [191]. Grace does not destroy nature but

5. The previous two paragraphs are one paragraph in *MD*, 458–59.

6. The previous three paragraphs combine into one in *MD*, 458.

restores it. While humanity, through sin, lacked the desire and strength to walk in the ways of the Lord, in re-creation it again receives the disposition (*gezindheid*) and the ability (*bekwaamheid*), at least in principle, in order to live in sincerity not according to some of but according to *all* the commandments of God.[7]

Faith, which in justification (*rechtvaardigmaking*) accepts Christ with all his benefits, thereby becomes an effective force precisely in sanctification; in both respects, it is rightly compared to a hand: with one hand we accept something and at the same time desire to carry out our own work.[8] The faith, which justifies and saves, is not a dead one but a living one; it bears fruit of the good works of its own nature; it works in love (Gal. 5:6). One does not become righteous through love, but the faith that justifies shows its vitality and its active (*werkzame*) power in love. Without love, faith is not the true, saving faith (1 Cor. 13:1); and true faith is always accompanied by the work of love (1 Thess. 1:3), for the end of the commandment (of all the apostolic preaching) is love, out of a pure heart, a good conscience, and an unfeigned faith (1 Tim. 1:5). This love, as the fruit of faith, is a perfect love that casts out all fear (1 John 4:18); it is also the perfect fulfillment of the law (Matt. 22:37–40; Rom. 13:8–10; Gal. 5:14; James 2:8).

Therefore, the gospel does not nullify the law but restores and endorses it. Its demand and curse have ended because Christ placed himself under the law, fulfilled its demand, and bore its curse.[9] For the believer, however, it still retains its authority and validity as a rule of gratitude; faith obliges far more than any threat of law to be [192] imitators of God, to walk in the Spirit, to flee all sins, and to glorify God with the body and that spirit that are God's (Matt. 4:48; Rom. 6:1f.; 8:4f.; 1 Cor. 6:15f.; etc.). In the Old and New Testaments, the moral law is one and the same; it is included in the commandment of love (Matt. 22:37–40; Rom. 13:8–10; Gal. 5:14; James 2:28).

It was for this reason that it gradually became the habit of explaining Christian morality, virtues and duties of humanity, by means of the Ten Commandments. This custom was especially adopted by the Reformers, because they thought one of the characteristics of good works is that

---

7. This paragraph is identical to a portion of one in *MD*, 458–59.

8. The first part of this paragraph is distinct to *Handleiding*. The remainder of the paragraph, however, can be found in *MD*, 464–65.

9. These first two sentences are in *MD*, 459, while the remainder of the paragraph is unique to *Handleiding*.

they are done according to God's will. They thus took a stand against the Roman Church, which considers among the good works such acts as those based on human institutions. Rome namely distinguishes between commandments and advice (counsels); it considers the former mandatory for all Christians but sets the latter's continuation in man's own choice, including among them the so-called chaste or unmarried state, on the basis of Matthew 19:11–12 and 1 Corinthians 7:7f.; the poverty or the renunciation of all earthly possessions with appeals to Matthew 19:21 and 1 Corinthians 9:14; and total obedience to authority, under whose leadership one has placed oneself, following the example of Matthew 16:24, Luke 14:26–27; and also all kinds of abstinence, chastisement, and self-affliction with reference to Matthew 5:29, 39, 42, etc.[10]

It goes without saying that the Reformation did not agree with this distinction. Deeply convinced of the corruption of human nature, it observed that the born again could not even fully observe the law, that their best works were still tainted with sin, and that the most holy could not go any further than a small principle of absolute obedience.[11] The believer [193] can never be expected to follow counsel because he already has enough to do to fulfill the commandments. But God also demands in the moral law that we love him with all our mind and with all our strength, and our neighbor as ourselves (Matt. 22:37; Luke 10:27)[12]; how can there be any additional counsel to such a commandment, of which it would be up to us whether or not we would follow it? And so, in that deep, spiritual sense, the law of the Ten

10. Cf. *MD*, 466–67. Bavinck cites the Heidelberg Catechism answer 91 in *MD* in this paragraph. Heidelberg Catechism Lord's Day 33, Question 91: "What are good works?" Answer: "Only those which are done out of true faith, conform to God's law, and are done for God's glory; and not those based on our own opinion or human tradition."

11. Cf. *MD*, 467. In this paragraph in *MD*, Bavinck cites the Heidelberg Catechism questions 62 and 114. Heidelberg Catechism, Lord's Day 24, Question 62: "Why can't our good works be our righteousness before God, or at least a part of our righteousness? Answer: "Because the righteousness which can pass God's judgment must be entirely perfect and must in every way measure up to the divine law. But even our best works in this life are imperfect and stained with sin." Lord's Day 44, Question 114: "But can those converted to God obey these commandments perfectly?" Answer: "No. In this life even the holiest have a small beginning of this obedience. Nevertheless, with all seriousness of purpose, they do begin to live according to all, not only some, of God's commandments."

12. This part of the paragraph is nearly identical to one in *MD*, 467, but the remainder is unique to *Handleiding*.

Commandments must, according to Jesus' own statement and according to its extension and application given in all of Scripture, be understood and explained. It is spiritual (Rom. 7:14) and governs, in principle, all the relationships in which man finds himself in relationship to God, his neighbor, himself, and the whole of nature. The believer loves it precisely because it is holy and righteous and good; he has a delight in it according to the inner man. "Oh, how I love your law! It is my mediation all the day!" (Ps. 119:97).

73. Even though the believers in regeneration immediately receive an inner desire and love to live according to the will of God in all good works, they are not all at once perfect and even in this life never reach perfection. Sanctification is different from justification. The latter exists in a divine acquittal, which is completed in one act; the former is repeated time and again and applied to the consciences, but it is not augmented or multiplied. Yet the life of sanctification, like all of life for creatures, is subject to the law of development; sanctification has its beginning in regeneration; it needs nourishment to be strengthened and to grow, and it only reaches its highpoint when it is revealed in full with Christ.[13]

That is why Scripture always distinguishes between lambs and nursing infants (Isa. 40:11; cf. Isa. 61:1–3; [194] Ezek. 34:16), the lesser and the greater, the first and the last (Matt. 11:11; 20:16), the weak and the strong (Rom. 14:1f.; 1 Cor. 8:7f.), the fleshly and the spiritual (1 Cor. 3:1–3; Gal. 6:1), children and adults (1 Cor. 3:2; Heb. 5:12; 1 Pet. 2:7), and the young men and the fathers (1 John 2:12–14). In the spiritual world, as in the natural world, man is born small and weak and must constantly grow (*opwassen*) in the grace and knowledge of Christ (2 Pet. 3:18).

But there are many other obstacles to this normal development. The life of the Christian is not a quiet growth but a constant struggle against external enemies such as spiritual malice (Eph. 6:12) and the world with its passions (1 John 2:15–17), and no less against the enemy who lives within his own bosom, and who as flesh stands against the Spirit as the old man against the new man (Rom. 7:14f.; Gal. 5:17–22; Eph. 4:22–24; Col. 3:9–10). The gravity of this battle immediately leads one to believe that perfect moral victory will not be fully achieved on this side of the grave either for the church as a whole or for the individual believer.[14]

In the face of all of those who sooner or later consider perfection to be attainable through all its saints, Holy Scripture clearly testifies that they all

13. This paragraph is identical to one in *MD*, 470.
14. The previous two paragraphs are unique to *Handleiding*.

stumble and many like David and Peter can fall into serious sins. Whoever we listen to, we will never hear them say, as is sometimes heard from the lips of Christians, "I have or no longer sin." On the contrary, all the pious who speak in Scripture—Abraham (Gen. 12:12), Isaac (Gen. 26:5), Jacob (Gen. 26:35), Moses (Num. 20:7–12; Ps. 106:33), David (Ps. 51), Solomon (1 Kings 8:46), Isaiah (Isa. 6:5), Daniel (9:4f.), Paul (Rom. 7:7–8; Gal. 5:17; Phil. 3:12), John (1 John 1:8–10), [195] etc.—they all confess their sins and their errors; they pursue perfection, but they have not obtained it. Moses and the prophets of the people of Israel, Christ and his disciples as well as the apostles of the church bear witness to this (Rom. 6:19; 1 Cor. 3:1–4; Gal. 3:1; Phil. 1:6; James 3:3; 1 John 1:8), not to mention what the glorified Christ testifies through the mouth of John to the seven churches in Asia Minor (Rev. 2:3).[15]

74. But in the face of this disheartening experience, believers may be assured of their present as well as their future salvation. Out of fear that such certainty would create a false assurance and a sense of frivolousness to life, many have denied it and have also opposed the perseverance of the saints. But here, too, Scripture gives an unambiguous testimony.[16] All the saints who go before us in the Old and New Testaments share this assurance of salvation. Not only Abraham (Gen. 15:6; Rom. 4:18f.), Jacob (Gen. 49:18), David (2 Sam. 22:2f.), and Habakkuk (Hab. 3:17–19), but also all the believers whose situations are described through the psalmist, proverbs, and prophets. They often find themselves in deep misery, oppressed, persecuted, mocked by their enemies: Where is your God now? You relied upon the Lord, that he may now deliver you (Pss. 22:8; 42:3; 71:11)! Sometimes doubt takes hold of their souls, whether God has forgotten them and has exchanged his mercies for anger (Pss. 1; 11; 13:2; 28:1; 44:10f.; 77:8f.). They also acknowledge the right of God's judgment, confessing their sins (Ps. 51:6; Nah. 9:33; Dan. 9:14).

Nevertheless, God is their Father and they are his people, the sheep of his pasture (Pss. 95:7; 100:3; Isa. 63:16; [196] 64:8); for the sake of his covenant, he will never leave them or forsake them (Ps. 79:8–9). "For his anger is but for a moment, and his favor is for a lifetime" (Ps. 30:6). "He does not deal with us according to our sins, nor repay us according to our iniquities" (Ps. 103:10). He forgives their trespasses and forgives their sins (Ps. 32:1).

---

15. Cf. *MD*, 479–80.

16. While the first part of the paragraph is unique to *Handleiding*, the remainder of it is in *MD*, 487.

The Lord is their rock and fortress, their tower and high room, their shield and the horn of their salvation, their light and their joy, their one and their all (Pss. 18:3; 73:25).[17]

Equally as certain is the tone in which the apostles and believers of the New Testament speak of their salvation. There is no doubt: they know that God has not spared his own Son but gave him up for all of them and will now, with him, give them all things (Rom. 8:32); that they are justified by faith, have peace with God, and can no longer be accused by anyone (Rom. 5:1; 8:33); that they have been born again to a living hope and have passed from death to life (1 Pet. 1:3; James 1:18; 1 John 3:14); that they have received the Spirit of adoption as children, and that this Spirit bears witness with their spirit that they are children of God (Rom. 8:15–16).

This knowledge of theirs not only relates to the present, to who they are, but it also extends to the future, to who they will be. For the Father chose them in Christ before the foundation of the world (Eph. 1:4), predestined them to eternal life (Acts 13:48) to be conformed to the image of his Son (Rom. 8:29); this election is immutable (Rom. 9:11; Heb. 6:17) and brings with it a calling, justification, and glorification in its time (Rom. 8:30). Christ, in whom all the promises of God are yes and amen (2 Cor. 1:20), died for those who were given to him by the Father [197] (John 17:6, 12) that he might give them eternal life and not lose any of them (John 6:39–40; 10:28; 17:2). The Holy Spirit, who resurrected them, remains with them forever (John 14:16) and seals them until the day of redemption (Eph. 2:13; 4:30).[18]

The covenant of grace is established and confirmed by an oath (Heb. 6:16–18; 13:20), as unbreakable as a marriage (Eph. 5:31–32) or a will (Heb. 9:17). By virtue of that covenant, God calls his chosen ones, writes the law within them, and places his fear in their hearts (Heb. 8:10; 10:14f.), does not allow them to be tempted beyond their strength (1 Cor. 10:13), establishes and finishes the good work he has begun in them (1 Cor. 1:9; Phil. 1:6), keeps them for the future of Christ, and makes them partakers of the heavenly inheritance (1 Thess. 5:23; 2 Thess. 3:13; 1 Pet. 1:4–5). Through his intercession with the Father, Christ is always working on their behalf, so that their faith does not cease (Luke 22:32), that they may be kept in the world from the evil one (John 17:11, 20), be completely saved (Heb. 7:25),

17. This paragraph is identical to a portion of one in *MD*, 487.

18. The previous two paragraphs are identical to two paragraphs in *MD*, 487–88.

receive forgiveness of sins (1 John 2:1), and one day all be with him and behold his glory (John 17:24). The benefits of Christ at last, of which the Holy Spirit makes them partakers, are all unimaginable (Rom. 11:29) and inextricably linked; he who is called is justified and glorified (Rom. 8:30); he who is adopted as a child of God is an heir of eternal life (Rom. 8:17; Gal. 4:7); he who believes—even now, here, right away—has eternal life (John 3:16). And that life itself, while eternal, is also immovable; it can neither sin (1 John 3:9) nor perish (John 11:25–26).[19]

The certainty of salvation, based on God's promises of keeping the saints and planted in the hearts of the believers by the testimony of the [198] Spirit, is a powerful means of making believers pursue sanctification, without which no one will see God. God does not compel them but acts with man in a reasonable manner. He does not make them passive in a false sense; but through his promises and exhortations, he stirs them to walk in the good deeds he has prepared for them. He sanctifies them through the truth (John 17:17; 15:3).[20]

Far be it, then, that faith in the preservation of God would make true believers prideful and worldly carefree; rather, it is a root of true humility, childlike fear, true godliness, patience in all strife, ardent prayers, steadfastness in the cross and the confession of truth, as well as steadfast joy in God. The contemplation of this benefit is an incentive to them for serious and the constant practice of gratitude and good works, as the testimonies of Scripture and the examples of the saints demonstrate.[21]

---

19. This paragraph is nearly identical to a portion of one in *MD*, 484.

20. This paragraph is unique to *Handleiding*. Cf. *MD*, 484–85.

21. Cf. *MD*, 487. This paragraph is nearly identical. What is missing in *Handleiding* is a reference to the Canons of Dordt Chapter 5, Article 12: "This assurance of perseverance, however, so far from making true believers proud and carnally self-assured, is rather the true root of humility, of childlike respect, of genuine godliness, of endurance in every conflict, of fervent prayers, of steadfastness in cross-bearing and in confessing the truth, and of well-founded joy in God. Reflecting on this benefit provides an incentive to a serious and continual practice of thanksgiving and good works, as is evident from the testimonies of Scripture and the examples of the saints."

18

The Church of Christ[1]

75. [199] Christ gives to his believers on earth his rich blessings, and they receive their perfection and crown in the glory that awaits them after death but only fully after the day of judgment.[2] Before we can discuss this benefit, however, we have to consider the way in which Christ establishes, maintains, and strengthens the benefits of calling and regeneration, faith and conversion, justification and adoption, renewal and sanctification in the faithful on earth. We have already seen, when we dealt with calling [see ch. 15], that he gives all these blessings by means of his word and Spirit. We must now draw our attention to the fact that he also gives these only in the fellowship that unites believers together. He does not hand [these blessings] out to a few isolated individuals but to a large number of people, who from the beginning forms a historical continuity, an organic whole.

In the covenant of grace, which God establishes with man immediately after the fall, he does not receive a single person apart from all others, but he calls, in that one person, his family and lineage at the same time. He did so with Adam, with Noah, with Abraham, and with the people of Israel. Under the Old Testament, there was a close connection between ethnic unity (*volkseenheid*) and the religious community [200]; even when, as a result of much unfaithfulness and apostasy, there were schism and divisions, the pious remained united and strengthened in one another's fellowship (Pss. 1:1; 16:3; 22:23; 26:4–12; 35:18; 40:16; 66:16; 122:1f.; 133:1f.).[3]

This division continued by the preaching of John the Baptist and Jesus; but simultaneously, Christ gathers his disciples around him and unites them in the confession of his name.[4] This confession bound them so closely that,

1. Cf. *MD*, 492. *MD*, ch. 23, is titled slightly different from *Handleiding*; rather than "The Church [*Kerk*] of Christ," it is "The Congregation [*Gemeente*] of Christ."

2. This sentence is identical to one in *MD*, 492. The remainder of the paragraph is unique to *Handleiding*.

3. This paragraph is distinct to *Handleiding*. Cf. *MD*, 494.

4. In *Handleiding*, it is somewhat opaque what division Bavinck is referencing; but if one returns to Bavinck's expansion in *MD*, 494, the division becomes

even after the Messiah left them, they remained united to one another and persisted in prayer and supplication (Acts 1:14).[5] On the day of Pentecost, they were girded with power from on high and received in the Holy Spirit an independent life principle (*zelfstandig levensbeginsel*), which freed them from every national bond and organized them into their own community, independent from nation (*volk*) and country (*land*) in the midst of the world.[6] The outpouring of the Holy Spirit gave the congregation of Christ its independent existence.[7]

From the beginning, the assembly of the faithful, who professed Jesus Christ as their Lord, was called by the name of congregation (*gemeente*) or church (*kerk*).[8] The Hebrew Old Testament already had two words for the assembly of the people of Israel: one that was translated into Greek as *synagoge* [synagogue] and other as *ekklesia*.[9] When Jews and Christians in the time of the apostles separated for good, it gradually became customary to refer to the assembly of the Jews with the name of *synagoge* and the assembly of the Christians with the name *ekklesia* (congregation or church), although this distinction was not originally in any way enclosed in the two words (cf. James 2:2; Heb. 2:12; 10:25; Acts 7:38; 19:32, 39–40), and this practice has continued to this day.

In the Dutch translation of the Bible, the word [201] *ekklesia* was translated as "congregation"; the word *church*, probably derived from the Greek word that means (house) "of the Lord," only occurs in connection with

---

abundantly clear. The division is between the people of God and the ungodly. "While these faithful ones separated themselves from the wicked ones, they also draw closer together and strengthen themselves in each other's fellowship [Dutch: "Terwijl deze vromen van de goddeloozen zich afzonderden, sluiten zij zich onderling aaneen en sterken zich in elkanders gemeenschap."]

5. See Bavinck, *The Sacrifice of Praise*, 85.

6. Bavinck writes of the activity of the Holy Spirit as imparting a subjective life principle (*levensbeginsel*) (see pp. 140, 147). This living force within man is regeneration. It is crucial component to the organism of humanity which is animated by the Holy Spirit. See Bruce Pass, *The Heart of Dogmatics: Christology and Christocentrism in Herman Bavinck* (Göttingen: Vandenhoek & Ruprecht, 2020), 29–35, 70, 74fn98.

7. Cf. *MD*, 495.

8. This sentence is identical to one in *MD*, 495. The remainder of this paragraph is also in *MD*, 495.

9. The Dutch word *synagoge* and the transliteration of "synagogue" are the same. It is possible that Bavinck is utilizing the Dutch word here; but with the consistent references to *ekklesia*, it is more likely that Bavinck is utilizing the transliteration of "synagogue" as well.

the church-keeper (*kerkbewaarster*) and church-robber (*kerkroover*) (Acts 19:35, 37). The translators (*statenoverzetters*) undoubtedly preferred the word *congregation*, because this name indicates the assembly of believers in their mutual community, while the word *church* makes it more known as an organized institution. Both words are still used interchangeably; in the confessional writings, there is constant reference to the church (Belgic Confession, Art. 27–32; Heidelberg Catechism, Lord's Day 7, 23).[10] They are not opposed to each other, but both see the assembly of believers from a different perspective and complement each other in a beautiful way.[11]

The word *congregation* was first used by Christ himself (Matt. 16:18; 18:17). There is nothing strange about it when we consider that the Hebrew word used by Jesus appears in the Old Testament time and time again and was well known. The novelty lies only in the fact that Christ applies this word to the circle of his disciples, thus already indicating that this, his congregation, will supersede that of the people of Israel. Furthermore, with this word, Jesus does not indicate a local assembly of believers but rather all those who would one day believe in him through the word of the apostles; he employs it as generally as possible. Later, in accordance with the development of the church, the word took on more specific meanings.[12]

In Acts 2:47; 5:11; 8:1; 11:22, the name of congregation for the local assembly of believers is used, which was in Jerusalem and which at first existed practically alone. Then, through the preaching of the disciples, assemblies of believers were formed elsewhere, and the name of congregation was also applied to each of the [202] local congregations. The congregation of Jerusalem was not a society that caused divisions elsewhere, but it had meetings of believers next to them who formed their own congregation as well.[13]

There is the congregation of Antioch (Acts 11:26; 13:1), the congregation of Lystra, Derbe, and the surrounding country (Acts 14:20–21), in Syria and Cilicia (Acts 15:41). Paul consistently gives to every local assembly of believers, in Rome, Corinth, Ephesus, Philippi, Colossae, etc., the name of congregation and speaks accordingly also in the plural of the

---

10. Bavinck references Day 7, 21 of the Heidelberg Catechism, but there is not a reference to the church in this question. There is a reference in question 23.

11. The final sentence in this paragraph is unique to *Handleiding*. The remainder of the paragraph is nearly identical to one in *MD*, 497. This paragraph is missing from the English translation of the first edition of *MD*.

12. This paragraph is identical to one in *MD*, 498.

13. This paragraph is identical to one in *MD*, 498.

congregations that are in Galatia (Gal. 1:2) or Judea (Gal. 1:22).[14] Even the name of congregations is given to the house churches—that is, to those assemblies of believers who because of the large number of individuals could not gather together in one place and, therefore, joined together in the houses of different brothers and sisters (Acts 2:46; 5:42; Rom. 16:5; 1 Cor. 16:19; Col. 4:15; Philem. 2).

Nevertheless, all these congregations were one, and so they could all bear the name of congregation together; yes, this name often includes all believers together, whether they have already been taken up to heaven (the church triumphant; cf. Heb. 12:23) or whether they still live or will live as the church militant on earth today. The congregation in its entirety is the body of Christ (Eph. 1:22–23, 4:15–16; Col. 1:18, 24), the bride of the Lamb (Eph. 5:32; 2 Cor. 11:2; Rev. 21:2), the house and temple of God (1 Cor. 3:10–16; Eph. 2:20–22; 1 Tim. 3:15; 1 Pet. 2:5; Rev. 21:3), "a chosen people, a royal priesthood, a holy nation, God's special possession, that you may declare the praises of him who called you out of darkness into his wonderful light" (1 Pet. 2:9).[15]

76. This congregation has all sorts of wonderful attributes. In the first place, that of *unity*. There is [203] in it a great variety of gifts, ministries, workings—which should be the case, because the church is a body with many members and each member has to serve the other with his gifts (Rom. 12:6; 1 Cor. 12:4f.; 14:12, 25; Eph. 4:7; 1 Pet. 4:10), yet it forms a *unity*.[16]

This not only means that there has been and always is only one church, but also that it is always and everywhere the same church, with the same benefits, privileges, and goods. It is not a unity that comes from the outside that is imposed by force or created by a contract temporarily entered into against a common enemy. It does not even emerge from the social instincts of religious life; but it is spiritual in nature; it rests and has its foundations and its example in the unity between the Father and Christ as the Mediator (John 17:21–23); it rises from Christ as the vine, who produces and nourishes all the branches from himself (John 15:5) as the head from whom the whole body grows (Eph. 4:16)[17]; and it is accomplished by the one Holy

14. The first part of the paragraph is identical to a portion of one in *MD*, 498. The remainder of the paragraph is unique to *Handleiding*.

15. This paragraph is nearly identical to one in the first edition of *MD* (see *MD*, 1e, 592).

16. This paragraph is unique to *Handleiding*. Cf. *MD*, 499–501.

17. This portion of the paragraph is identical to a portion of one in *MD*, 501. For the remainder of the paragraph, cf. *MD*, 501–2.

Spirit by whom we are all led to one Father (1 Cor. 12:13; Eph. 2:18; 4:4). Although this unity in its present reality is highly imperfect and flawed and has been torn apart in the most miserable way, yet it comes to such an extent that all the Christian churches are separated from the world by one and the same baptism, holding on to the confession of the twelve articles in the doctrine of the apostles, and observing the breaking of the bread and the prayers in a variety of forms. The unity of the congregation is an object of faith; although we do not see it—not as clearly as we would like—it does exist and will one day come into its fullness (John 17:21; Eph. 4:13).

In the same way, the second attribute [204] that belongs to the congregation is also present: namely, that of *holiness.*[18] The congregation is holy—a holy people, and the believers are saints (Rom. 1:7; 1 Cor. 1:2, etc.), for they are together and each one [individually] themselves the temple of the Holy Spirit (1 Cor. 3:16–17; 6:19); they are washed by that Spirit and sanctified in Christ Jesus (John 17:17, 19; 1 Cor. 1:2; 6:11; Eph. 5:26–27), and thus all sin, all work according to the flesh, all worldly passions, are to be avoided and fought to the point of shedding blood (Gal. 5:19; Col. 3:5; Heb. 12:1, 4). On the other hand, they are to practice all virtues and to promote all good works (Gal. 5:22; Phil. 4:8; Col. 3:12; Titus 2:14; etc.). It is a life of love that Christians must lead (Eph. 5:2), for it is the greatest of all the virtues (1 Cor. 13:13), the bond of perfection (Col. 3:14), and the fulfillment of the law (Rom. 13:10).[19] However, much of this holiness was left to be desired in the apostolic time, so the letters teach us, and later centuries have often seen a profound religious and moral decay of the congregation.

Each time there was a collapse, however, revival and renewal came about through the Spirit of Christ. The holiness of the congregation is also a quality Christ acquired for and works out in the congregation,[20] which will therefore one day be completely the church's (John 17:19; Rev. 21:2).

Finally, the congregation has the attribute of catholicity or *universality.* The name first appears in postapostolic writing and, in the face of all kinds of heresies and schisms, indicated that the true church is the one that abides by the bishop and remains with the whole, for the universal catholic church where Christ is. Later, all kinds of explanations of the name were given. It was understood that the church is spread out all over the world, that it

---

18. This sentence is unique to *Handleiding.*

19. This portion of the paragraph is identical to a portion of one in *MD*, 504.

20. This section is identical to a portion of a separate paragraph in *MD*, 504. The remainder is unique to *Handleiding.*

encompasses all the [205] believers from the beginning to the present day, that it shares all truth and grace, and that it is therefore an adequate means of salvation for all. These explanations are not incorrect, provided that in the church one does not mean only one denomination—for example, the Roman Catholic Church—but also the Christian congregation in which all churches together, in different degrees of purity, come to revelation.[21] For this church is indeed catholic. It was from the beginning (Gen. 3:15) and remained in its temporal limitation under Israel for all the nations of the earth (Gen. 12:2; Joel 2:32; Mic. 4:1–2; Zeph. 2:11; Isa. 25:6–10). Jesus bound the entrance into the kingdom of heaven solely to the spiritual qualities of regeneration, faith, and conversion (Mark 1:15; John 3:3); and after the resurrection, he gave his disciples the charge to preach the gospel to all creatures and to make disciples of all nations (Matt. 28:19; Mark 16:15).

Thus while the goods that the congregation possesses are all of a spiritual nature—not in gold or silver, in power or force, but in righteousness, peace, and joy through the Holy Spirit—the congregation is therefore entitled to the quality of universality. It is not bound to a land and people (*volk*), to time and place, to race and age, to money and goods; it is independent of all earthly distinctions and contradictions; it brings the gospel to all creatures, and that gospel is always and only the gospel, a glad tiding, which is suitable and necessary for all people, in all times, in all circumstances, for all situations. The kingdom of God is hostile to nothing but sin. The earth will one day be full of the knowledge of the Lord (Isa. 11:9; Hab. 2:14; Matt. 24:14).[22]

77. From the beginning, this congregation as an assembly of believers had [206] a particular organization. Every association of people has an arrangement for its meetings and necessary activities in order to avoid confusion and dissolution and to meet the purpose for which it was founded; so also the congregation of Christ is subject to this general law of human society. God is not a God of confusion but of peace; he has established orders for all his creatures and wants everything to be done decently and with order in the congregation as well (1 Cor. 14:33, 40).[23]

That is why the assembly of the faithful, which is beautiful and exists organically, has never lacked an institution—that is, a peculiar establish-

---

21. The first half of the paragraph is identical to a paragraph in *MD*, 598–99. The remainder of the paragraph is distinct to *Handleiding*.

22. Cf. *MD*, 506–7.

23. This paragraph is identical to a portion of one in *MD*, 507.

ment of gifts and powers, of offices and ministries—by which they could live, grow, propagate, and deepen here on earth, so that it could respond in a word to its multifaceted calling. In the time of the patriarchs, the father was the priest of his family; he carried out circumcision and offered sacrifices (Gen. 17:23; 22:2; 26:1; etc.). The law of Sinai established a special priesthood and cult (*cultus*) and, moreover, regulated the whole life of Israel. Later on, kings and prophets were added to lead the people in the ways of the Lord; and even later, synagogues were established everywhere that Jews lived, where people gathered on the Sabbath to read Scriptures, confess their sins, and in song and prayer call upon God's name (Luke 4:16; Acts 15:21).

Even in the days of the New Testament, Christ gave his congregation on earth a particular structure and government. In the first place, as long as he was on earth, he was personally and physically the teacher and guide of his disciples; and in his resurrection and ascension, he was exalted to be Lord and Christ, Prince and Savior (Acts 2:36; 3:15; 5:31), the head of the congregation (Eph. 1:22), the king of his [207] people (1 Cor. 15:24f.; Heb. 2:7). The government of the congregation, therefore, does not only exist but it is also strictly monarchial in spiritual terms; it has only one master: namely, Christ (Matt. 23:8, 10). Although he remains with his congregation according to his Godhead, majesty, grace, and Spirit (Matt. 28:20), he is physically removed from it for a time by his ascension.

That is why he chose twelve apostles from among the wide circle of his disciples (Luke 6:13), who were personally taught by him and equipped in a special way with the Holy Spirit and with extraordinary powers (Matt. 16:19; 18:18; 28:19; John 20:22) to act as his witnesses (Rev. 1:8, 22; 2:32; etc.), to plant the congregation in the world (Matt. 16:18; 28:19), and to guide and feed it by their word (John 21:15–17; Acts 1:15; 2:38, 42; 4:37; 5:2; 8:13–25; 9:31–32; 1 Pet. 5:2–3). As the congregations expanded, these apostles all received support from evangelists such as Barnabas, Mark, Luke, Timothy, Titus, Silas, etc. (Eph. 4:11; 2 Tim. 4:5), and from prophets, such as Agabus (Acts 11:28; 21:9–10; 1 Cor. 12:28; Eph. 4:11; etc.).[24]

All of these offices—apostles, prophets, and evangelists—have passed away insofar as their bearers have died and by their very nature have not been replaced by any other.[25] They were needed in that extraordinary time when the congregation was to be established on earth. But their work was

24. The previous three paragraphs are unique to *Handleiding*. Cf. *MD*, 510–13.
25. This sentence is unique to *Handleiding*.

not in vain in the Lord. For to begin, they have indeed built the church on the foundation of Jesus Christ (1 Cor. 3:11); and additionally, their testimony lives on in the books of the New Testament, in the Gospels and Letters, in the books of Acts and Revelation, to this day in the church. "This testimony enables [the church] to persevere throughout all times in the apostles teaching, in fellowship, in the breaking of bread [208] and in the prayers" (Acts 2:42).[26] The congregation is built on their confession (Matt. 16:18; Eph. 2:20; Rev. 21:14). The apostolate is and remains the foundation of the church; there is no communion with Christ other than through communion with [the apostles] and with their word (John 17:20; 1 John 1:3).[27]

In addition to these extraordinary ministries, there are also ordinary offices established by Christ in his congregation.[28] At first, the apostles themselves also distributed the gifts of mercy (Acts 4:37; 5:2); but when the congregation became considerably large, they could no longer oversee this work themselves. In response to a dispute that arose in the congregation about daily ministry, they suggested that seven men, full of faith and the Holy Spirit, should be elected to the service of the tables (Acts 6:1–6).[29] It is highly likely that this is where the office of deacon was established; for while the apostles retained for themselves the ministry of the word and of prayer (Acts 6:4), the seven men were charged with the service of tables: that is to say, with the ministry of everything concerning communal meals and the sacrament and the distribution of the offering among the poor. This office of deacon was later extended to other congregations (Phil. 1:1; 1 Tim. 3:8; cf. Rom. 12:8; 1 Cor. 12:28). Like the apostles had in Jerusalem (John 6:3), Paul later established the requirements for it (1 Tim. 3:8f.).

In addition to the office of deacon, the office of elder soon came into being in the congregation as well. There is no mention of its origins, but elders already appear in Acts 11:30, where they receive gifts, and in Acts 15:2f, where they take part with the apostles in the meeting that was convened in Jerusalem for the commissioning of the missionary work. This office was also soon introduced in other congregations (Acts 14:23; 20:28; 1 Cor. 12:28; Eph. 4:11; Phil. 1:1; etc.).[30] In 1 Timothy 3:1f. [209] and Titus

26. This section is nearly identical to a paragraph in *MD*, 513.

27. This section is unique to *Handleiding*.

28. This sentence is unique to *Handleiding*.

29. This portion of the paragraph is pulled from a paragraph in *MD*, 514, which contains the remainder of it.

30. This sentence is unique to *Handleiding*. The remainder of the paragraph is in *MD*, 515.

1:6–9, Paul points out these requirements; in Titus 1:5, he instructs Titus to appoint elders in each congregation. These elders were charged with overseeing the congregation (Acts 20:28; Eph. 4:11 [shepherds]; 1 Pet. 5:2) and were even, within the apostolic age, distinguished between those who ruled and those who worked in the ministry of the word and the teaching of the truth (1 Tim. 5:17; Heb. 13:7; 1 Pet. 4:11; 1 Tim. 3:2 [able to teach]). Perhaps even in the case of Diotrephes who, according to 3 John 9, took the first place in the congregation but abused his power. With regard to the angels or messengers of the seven congregations (Rev. 2:1, 8; etc.), we should think of such as teachers, who work in the word, in distinction from their fellow elders and who therefore took up their own meaningful place in the congregation.

78. This was the simple arrangement made in the apostolic time for the reign of the church of Christ. Not only that but in this entire government there was no question of a governing power (Matt. 20:25–27; 1 Pet. 5:3); all power in the congregation carried and carries a character of serving. Since Christ alone is the head of the congregation (Eph. 1:22), the only Master (Matt. 23:8, 10), and Lord (John 13:13; 1 Cor. 8:6; Phil. 2:11), there can never be a power in the congregation that is beside or against his, but only such power as has been given by him and that remains bound to him.[31]

That was true of the extraordinary offices of apostle, prophet, and evangelist, which were established by Christ in the first time for the foundation of the church in the world; they received their office and their power from Christ and not from the church but were to use this power for the service of the church (Matt. 20:25–27; [210] 1 Pet. 5:3),[32] just as each member is to utilize his gift for the benefit of others (Rom. 12:5f.; 13:8; 1 Cor. 12:12f.; 14:12; etc.). In a stronger sense, this also applies to the ordinary offices; pastors and teachers, elders and deacons also owe their office and authority to Christ (1 Cor. 12:28; Eph. 4:11), but they also have to work for the perfection of the saints, for the building up of the body of Christ (Eph. 4:12).

However, this simple, beautiful ordering of the life of the congregation soon became corrupt and degenerated. First, the so-called episcopate (office of the bishop) came into being. In the New Testament and also in some postapostolic writings, the titles of elder (*presbyter*) and overseer (*episcopus*) still referred to the same persons; the task of overseeing (supervising and

---

31. This paragraph is identical to one in *MD*, 515.

32. This paragraph is identical to a portion of one in *MD*, 515. The remainder of it is a clear abridgement of the same paragraph.

exercising discipline) was a description of the task assigned to the elders or elder assigned to or chosen for this purpose (Acts 20:17, 28; Titus 1:5, 7; 1 Pet. 5:1–2). But in the beginning of the second century, a distinction between the two was already being made in some congregations: the overseer (*episcopus*) was elevated above the elders (*presbyter*) and deacons and was regarded as the bearer of a special office, as the successor of the apostles, as the guardian of pure doctrine (tradition), and as the cornerstone of the congregation.[33]

This led to the hierarchical path being taken: which, on the one hand, deprived the elders and deacons of their independence and reduced the faithful to impoverished laymen; and on the other hand, elevated bishops as priests high above the congregation, gradually elevating from among them the bishop of Rome to be sovereign of the whole church, who, as Peter's successor, carries the keys of the kingdom of heaven, is the vicar of Christ on earth, and is clothed with infallible authority, as the pope, in matters of faith and of life.[34]

[211] This development of the priestly government in the church of Christ found resistance and opposition with every step it took forward. But it was not until the Reformation that such a serious clash took place, and as a result Western Christianity was irrevocably torn in two. Some, like the Anabaptists, fell to a different extreme and considered every office, authority, and power to be in conflict with the congregation of Christ. Others, like the Anglican Church in England, broke with the pope in Rome but kept the episcopal government in place. The Lutheran Church restored the office of preaching but gradually left the government of the church and the care of the poor entirely to the civic government. All kinds of systems of church government came to stand side by side, and to this day there is no less difference of opinion between the many Christian groups about the organization and government of the church than about its confessional difference.[35] Of all these systems, however, the Presbyterian form of church government, as restored by Calvin, most closely resembles that of the apostolic era.[36]

33. The first sentence is distinct to *Handleiding*. The remainder of this section is split between two paragraphs in *MD*, 516.

34. This paragraph is identical to a portion of one in *MD*, 516.

35. This portion of the paragraph is identical to a portion of one in *MD*, 516–17.

36. This is nearly identical to a sentence in *MD*, 518.

19

The Means of Grace

79. [212] Since all power in the church of Christ is of a ministerial nature, all institutions and offices that are established in it find their center (*middelpunt*) in the word of God. That word was already mentioned in [chapter] 4 as Holy Scripture and the source (*kenbron*) of the truth in [chapter] 15 with calling as a means of grace, but it is used here once more in its significance for the church. The church of Christ is not just an assembly of the true believers in Christ, taking them in, gathering them together, and connecting them to each other; [the church] is also the mother of believers, the one who produces and nurtures them. Just like in the natural life every man is born from the intercourse of his parents and is a member of a household, of a family, of a people (*volk*) and of humanity, so also the believer receives from above, from God, this new life only in the fellowship of the covenant of grace that has been established with believers and their seed. Even in the Gentile world, no one comes to faith and no gathering of believers comes about except through the mission that led the church there.

The church of Christ may, therefore, be truly called the mother of believers; it is with all its gifts and ministries the great means by which Christ operates to establish his kingdom of grace on the earth and extend it to the ends of the world. [213] It is the body of Christ, not only because all believers belong to it but also because it is the organ by which the glorified Savior continues and completes his activity as prophet, priest, and king on earth (John 14:12). It is the warring army, the army of salvation that Christ possesses as Sovereign and Leader; and he equips it with spiritual, powerful weapons to destroy all strongholds (2 Cor. 10:4; Eph. 6:13).

All believers are called to this spiritual battle; they are all in active service; each of them has a gift he can use, a talent he can expend, a ministry he has to fulfill. The offices that Christ gave to his congregation do not abolish those gifts, but they assume and supplement them. There are many gifts lacking an office, but there is no office lacking a gift. Christ did not give ministers of the word, elders, and deacons in order that the congregation may leave all their labor to them and sit down in quiet rest. But all believers are called to honor one another (Rom. 12:10), to be taught and admonished (Col. 3:16; Heb. 10:24–25), to bear one another's burdens (Gal. 6:2), to show hospitality (Rom. 12:13; 1 Pet. 4:9), and to be compassionate and merciful (1 Pet. 3:8).[1]

80. All services the church exercises through its gifts and offices derive their content (*inhoud*) from and have their center (*middelpunt*) in the word Christ gave through the apostles. That word is the mark (*kenteeken*) by which the church can be identified in its truth and purity. On account of the rich content (*inhoud*) of that word, it can be administered and applied in many ways—in preaching, in the sacraments, in government and discipline, in confession and conduct—and many others may contain the one mark (*kenteeken*) of this word of which the Belgic Confession of Faith [214] Article 29 mentions three: the pure preaching of the gospel, the pure ministry of the sacraments, and the preservation of ecclesiastical discipline.[2] All of

---

1. The previous three paragraphs are unique to *Handleiding.*

2. The Belgic Confession, Article 29: The Marks of the True Church: "We believe that we ought to discern diligently and very carefully, by the Word of God, what is the true church—for all sects in the world today claim for themselves the name of "the church." We are not speaking here of the company of hypocrites who are mixed among the good in the church and who nonetheless are not part of it, even though they are physically there. But we are speaking of distinguishing the body and fellowship of the true church from all sects that call themselves "the church." The true church can be recognized if it has the following marks: The church engages in the pure preaching of the gospel; it makes use of the pure administration of the sacraments as Christ instituted them; it practices church discipline for correcting faults. In short, it governs itself according to the pure Word of God, rejecting all things contrary to it and holding Jesus Christ as the only Head. By these marks one can be assured of recognizing the true church—and no one ought to be separated from it. As for those who belong to the church, we can recognize them by the distinguishing marks of Christians: namely by faith, and by their fleeing from sin and pursuing righteousness, once they have received the one and only Savior, Jesus Christ. They love the true God and their neighbors, without turning to the right or left, and they crucify the flesh and its works. Though great weakness remains in them, they fight against it by the Spirit all the days of their lives, appealing constantly to the blood, suffering, death, and obedience of the Lord Jesus, in whom they have forgiveness of their sins, through faith in him. As for the false church, it assigns more authority to itself and its ordinances than to the Word of God; it does not want to subject itself to the yoke of Christ; it does not administer the sacraments as Christ commanded in his Word; it rather adds to them or subtracts from them as it pleases; it bases itself on humans, more than on Jesus Christ; it persecutes those who live holy lives according to the word of God and who rebuke it for its faults, greed, and idolatry. These two churches are easy to recognize and thus to distinguish from each other."

these can be traced back to a single mark (*kenteeken*) of the word. As the church agrees or deviates from the word (to a lesser or greater degree), it is true and pure or approaches [becoming] the false church.[3] Indeed, through the word as a means of grace, all true members of the church are regenerated and brought to faith and repentance, purified and sanctified, gathered and confirmed; and from their side, they are called to keep that word (John 8:31; 14:23), to search it (John 5:39), to test the spirits (1 John 4:1), and to avoid all those who do not teach this doctrine (Gal. 1:8; Titus 3:10; 2 John 9). The word of God is indeed, according to the expression of Calvin, "the soul of the church."[4]

This word has not been given exclusively to the church as an institution, to the ministers, but to all believers (John 5:39; Acts 17:11) so that through the patience and consolation of Scripture, they might have hope (Rom. 15:4) and also that they could teach and exhort one another (Rom. 12:7–8; Col. 3:16; Heb. 10:24–25). Rome has misunderstood this, but the Reformation has placed the Bible back into all hands, and with it provided a source of learning and teaching opened for home and school, for science (*wetenschap*), art, society, and state, and for every believer. Furthermore, God has provided an official ministry of that word; he gave and continues to give shepherds and teachers (1 Cor. 12:28; Eph. 4:11; 1 Tim. 5:17; 2 Tim. 2:2), who are to administer that word in public and in houses (Acts 20:20), as milk to the youth, as solid food to the mature members of the community (1 Cor. 3:2; Heb. 5:12; 1 Pet. 2:2), in accordance with the needs of every people (*volk*), of [215] every age, of every church, and of every individual believer (Acts 20:20, 27; 2 Tim. 2:15; 4:2). Yes, the administration of the word includes the preservation, translation, explanation, propagation, defense, and preaching of the word to all creatures; thus the church continues to be built on the foundation of the apostles and prophets (Eph. 2:20) and is what it ought to be: a pillar and buttress of the truth (1 Tim. 3:15).[5]

---

3. The first portion of this paragraph is unique to *Handleiding*. See *MD*, 526–27, for the remainder.

4. John Calvin, *Institutes of the Christian Religion*, ed. John T. McNeill, trans. Ford Lewis Battles (Louisville, KY: Westminster John Knox, 1960), IV.ii.7. "Again, who has without exception dared to call that assembly 'church' where the Lord's Word is openly and with impunity trodden under foot? Where his ministry, the church's chief sinew, indeed its very soul, is destroyed?"

5. Cf. *MD*, 530–31, which is identical to a paragraph in the first edition (see *MD* 1e, 615).

81. This word receives its confirmation in the sacraments that are signs and seals of the covenant of grace and thereby serve to strengthen the faith. In the Old Testament, God instituted circumcision for that (Gen. 17:7) and the Passover (Exod. 12:7f.). Both signs had a spiritual sense, for circumcision was a seal of the righteousness of faith (Rom. 4:11) and of the circumcision of the heart (Deut. 30:6; Rom. 2:28–29); and the Passover, as a sign of the expiation and the sacrificial meal, pointed to Christ (John 1:29, 36; 19:33, 36). Both were, therefore, fulfilled by Christ in his sufferings and death (Col. 2:11; 1 Cor. 5:7), and so in the New Testament, they are replaced by baptism (Matt. 28:19) and the Supper (Matt. 26:17f.).[6]

These two signs are commonly referred to as "sacraments" (mysteries, 1 Cor. 4:1). For Rome, there are five more, although they are without scriptural ground (confession, penance, marriage, priestly ordination, and the last anointing with oil), and more are multiplied with countless ceremonies that do not contain in themselves the grace of God in a localized and material way, but rather are memorials and confirmations of his grace that God, by the Holy Spirit, bestows in the hearts of believers. They have the whole of the covenant of grace with all its benefits; or in other words, Christ himself as its content and these benefits are not shared in any other way [216] than by faith. These are established on behalf of believers and assure them of their share in Christ; they do not precede the word but follow it; they give no special grace that is not communicated by the word and cannot be accepted by faith, but they are built upon the institution of the covenant of grace on the part of God and upon the consent in that covenant from the human side.[7]

Particularly, baptism is a sign and seal of the benefit of forgiveness (Acts 2:38; 22:16) and regeneration (Titus 3:5) is the incorporation into communion with Christ and his congregation (Rom. 6:4). Therefore, baptism is not only given to the adults who are won to Christ through the work of evangelism but also to the children of believers, for they are included with their parents in the covenant of grace (Gen. 17:7; Matt. 18:2–3; 19:14; 21:16; Acts 2:39); they belong to the church (1 Cor. 7:14) and are received into fellowship with the Lord (Eph. 6:1; Col. 3:20).

When these children grow up, when they come to years of discernment to examine for themselves, discern the body and blood of the Lord, and

---

6. This is identical to a paragraph in the first edition (see *MD* 1e, 615). It is absent from the second edition.

7. This is identical to a paragraph in the first edition (see *MD* 1e, 615–16). It is absent from the second edition.

through their own public confession personally consent to the covenant of grace (1 Cor. 11:28), then they are called to proclaim the Lord's death with the whole congregation until he comes and thereby strengthen themselves in fellowship with Christ. For while both baptism and the Lord's Supper have the same covenant of grace as their substance and both give assurance of the benefit of the forgiveness of sins, it is possible to distinguish the Lord's Supper from baptism in that it is a sign and seal, not of their incorporation but of the growth and strengthening in the fellowship of Christ and all of its members (1 Cor. 10:16–17).[8]

82. [217] In order that the word and sacrament might be preserved in their holiness and remain in service for the edification of the saints, Christ bestowed upon his congregation the power, which according to his illustration he himself possessed, that carries the name "the power of the keys" (Matt. 16:19f.; Isa. 22:22; Luke 11:52; Rev. 1:8; 3:7; 9:1; 20:1). This power was first given by Christ to Peter (Matt. 16:19) and then to all the apostles (Matt. 18:18; John 20:20), and then, bound to their word, given to all the congregation in its official organization (Matt. 18:18; 1 Cor. 5:4; 2 Thess. 3:13). It is a power, an essential and comprehensive power—yet again, not in authoritarians or rulers but in servants (Acts 4:29; 20:24; Rom. 1:1) bound to the word and Spirit of Christ (Rom. 10:14–15; 1 Cor. 5:4; Eph. 5:26), and thus, exclusively spiritual and ecclesiastical and not civil (*burgerlijk*), social, or political in nature.[9]

It consists essentially in the church through its office bearers announcing, in the name of the Lord, to the righteous that it is well with them and to the wicked that disaster is upon them (Isa. 3:10–11). It does this generally and publicly through the ministry of the word in every assembly of believers. It does this in a unique and personal manner in the official home visit, which has replaced the Roman confession in the Reformed churches and is based on the apostolic example (Matt. 10:12; John 21:15–17; Acts 20:20; Heb. 13:17). And finally, it also does this in special exhortations that can, in the case of persistent perseverance in sin, lead to banishment from the community (Matt. 18:15–17; Rom. 16:17; 1 Cor. 5:2, 9–13; 2 Cor. 2:5–10; 2 Thess. 3:6, 14; Titus 3:10; 2 John 10; Rev. 2:2).[10]

---

8. The previous two paragraphs are identical to two paragraphs in the first edition (see *MD* 1e, 616–17). It is absent from the second edition.

9. This paragraph is unique to *Handleiding*.

10. This paragraph is nearly identical to a paragraph in the first edition (see *MD* 1e, 617). It is absent from the second edition.

The congregation, therefore, in Christ's name, for the sake of the holiness of the Lord, takes initiative to remove stubborn [218] transgressors from their midst; it handles publicans and sinners with great compassion; it offers all the poor and the sick physical and spiritual provision in their physical and spiritual distress. Christ himself did this (Matt. 11:5), and he commanded his disciples to do it too (Matt. 5:42–45; 6:1–4; 25:34f.; Mark 14:7). They must take care of the needs of the saints (Rom. 12:13), distribute generously (*eenvoudigheid*), show mercy in cheerfulness (Rom. 12:8), visit widows and orphans in their affliction (James 1:27), pray for the sick in the name of the Lord (James 5:14), and generally bear one another's burdens and therefore fulfill the law of Christ (Rom. 12:15; Gal. 6.2).[11]

Faith and love are the strength of the Lord's church, and these both are bound with hope. In the midst of a world that does not know where it is going and often falls into melancholy and despair, the church expresses its joyful expectations: "I believe in the forgiveness of sins, the resurrection of the body, and the life everlasting."[12]

---

11. This paragraph is nearly identical to a paragraph in the first edition (see *MD* 1e, 617). It is absent from the second edition.

12. Heidelberg Catechism, Lord's Day 7, Question 23: "What are these articles?" Answer: "I. I believe in God the Father almighty, Creator of Heaven and earth; II. I believe in Jesus Christ, his only-begotten Son, our Lord; He was conceived by the Holy Spirit, born of the virgin Mary; suffered under Pontius Pilate was crucified, dead, and buried; he descended into hell. On the third day he rose from the dead; He ascended into heaven and sits at the right hand of God the Father almighty; From there he will come to judge the living and the dead. III. I believe in the Holy Spirit; I believe a holy catholic Christian church, the communion of saints; the forgiveness of sins; the resurrection of the body and the life everlasting." This paragraph is nearly identical to a paragraph in the first edition (see *MD* 1e, 617). It is absent from the second edition; cf. 546.

20

The Consummation of the World[1]

83. [219] The end and destiny of things, like their origin and nature, are shrouded in impenetrable darkness to the inquiring mind of man.[2] But he cannot live without hope and extends it to the other side of the grave and to the end of the world. The belief in immortality is common to all people, even among the most ferocious and uncivilized tribes, and is closely associated with religion everywhere. Yes, all people (*volken*) are convinced that man is immortal by nature and, therefore, it is not immortality that must be proven but death that must be explained. Death is felt as unnatural everywhere; it is, according to the faith of many peoples, the work of hostile spirits; there was a time when it did not exist and the portion of mankind was the unhindered life.[3] Many different ideas formed concerning the condition of the souls after death (soul sleep, reincarnation, death cult, apparitions of ghosts, purification process, purgatory, continued development until the dissolution of all things, etc.); all these ideas have returned today to the civilized circles that have turned their backs on Christianity.

Scripture takes a peculiar stance on the question of the immortality of the soul. Philosophy has always sought evidence of the immortality of the soul and has proposed many proofs: such as [220] the *ontological* proof from the idea of immortality; the *metaphysical* proof from the insolubility of the soul; the *anthropological* proof from the peculiarity of man's soul life (*zieleleven*) in contrast to that of plants and animals; the *teleological* proof from the fact that many gifts and powers of the soul do not develop in this life; the *moral* proof from the disharmony in this life between virtue and happiness; between *ethos* and *physis*; the proof of *e consensus gentium* from

1. Both editions of *MD* have this chapter titled as "Het Eeuwige Leven" ("Eternal Life"). See *MD* 1e, 618; cf. *MD*, 546.

2. This sentence is identical to the opening sentence of ch. 24 of the first edition (see *MD* 1e, 618). It is absent from the second edition.

3. The previous two sentences are in *MD*, 547–48. The remainder is unique to *Handleiding*.

the common faith of mankind; and finally, the evidence from the apparition of dead spirits, to which great value is attached to in spiritist circles.[4]

But Scripture never deliberately speaks of the immortality of the soul, nor does it provide any evidence of it. The Old Testament has completely different ideas concerning life and death than those we find elsewhere. In Scripture, death is never equal to annihilation and nonbeing; dying and being dead are the antithesis of the all-embracing, rich, and full life that was originally destined for man in his communion with God here on earth. When man dies, not only his body but also his soul will be affected. The whole human being dies and is then in the state of death according to both [body and soul]: he is no longer a part of the earth but a dweller of the kingdom of the dead (*Sheol*), which is thought to be in the depths of the earth and belongs to the lowest places, which still lie below the waters and the foundations of the mountains (Num. 16:30; Deut. 32:22; Job 26:5; Ps. 63:10).[5]

The dead still exist there, but their existence is no longer worthy of the name of life and is not like being (Job 7:21; 14:10; Ps. 39:14).[6] They no longer know (*weten*), they have no wisdom or knowledge (*wetenschap*), they do not work, and they have no part in what is done under the sun (Job 14:21; Eccl. 9:5–6, 10). [221] It is a land of forgetfulness (Ps. 88:13), of darkness (Job 21:22), and of destruction (Job 26:6; 28:22).

84. On the other hand, life was seen as a fullness of salvation and joy. Life, in its essence, includes a wealth of blessings: fellowship with God in the first place, but also fellowship with his people and fellowship in the land the Lord gave to his people. Life is the full, rich existence of man in the union of his soul and body, in union with God and in harmony with the world; this includes bliss and glory, virtue and happiness, peace and joy. If man had obeyed the commandment of God, he would have enjoyed this rich life and would not have seen death (Gen. 2:17).[7] Yet even though death has come on account of sin, God nevertheless again enters into fellowship with mankind by grace and establishes his covenant with Israel. In principle, it is in this covenant that full communion, which was originally shared by man, is restored; and in that fellowship with God, they are able to overcome not

---

4. This paragraph is unique to *Handleiding.*

5. Cf. *MD*, 550.

6. This sentence is identical to one in *MD*, 550. See *MD*, 550–51, for the remainder of the paragraph.

7. Cf. *MD*, 551, and 551–52 for the remainder of the paragraph.

only all the misery of this earthly life but also the fear of the grave, the terror of death, and the darkness of the kingdom of death.

The wicked may enjoy prosperity for a time, but they perish and come to an end (Ps. 73:18–20); their way leads to death (Prov. 8:36; 11:19). But for the faithful, "the fear of the Lord is a fountain of life" (Prov. 8:35; 14:27). He delivers them many times in this life, but he also has power over the realm of the dead; with his Spirit he is also present there (Ps. 139:7–8), and nothing is hidden from him, no more than in the hearts of the children of men (Job 26:6; 38:17; Prov. 15:11). The Lord kills and makes alive; he can bring one down into the abyss, but he also can bring one up again (Deut. 32:29; 1 Sam. 2:6; [222] 2 Kings 5:7); he can take Enoch and Elijah to himself without death (Gen. 5:24; 2 Kings 2:11) and make the dead return to life (1 Kings 17:22; 2 Kings 4:34; 13:21). He can even destroy death and triumph over it completely by resurrection from the dead (Job 14:13–15; 19:25–27; Hos. 6:2; 13:14; Isa. 25:8; 26:19; Ezek. 37:11–12; Dan. 12:2).[8]

Entirely in agreement with this, the New Testament teaches that death, as a punishment for sin, is a total break with the life here on earth (Rom. 5:12; 6:23; 1 Cor. 15:21, 56; James 1:15); but this death is no destruction (Matt. 10:28; Luke 12:4); a person lives on and receives in the afterlife a reward for his work (Matt. 16:27; Rom. 2:7; 14:12).[9] However, for those who believe in Christ, death has lost its terror. For in fellowship with God, through the Lord Jesus Christ, dying is no longer death. The covenant that God makes by his own grace guarantees complete salvation and eternal life. "God is not a God of the dead but of the living" (Matt. 22:32). Whoever believes in Christ will live even though they die, and whoever lives and believes in him will never die (John 11:25–26), "and will not be judged but has crossed over from death to life" (John 5:24).

Therefore, at death, the souls of believers are immediately taken up into heaven by Christ. They no longer have to bear the punishment for their sins in purgatory (*vagevuur*), for Christ has accomplished everything and acquired everything. According to the parable in Luke 16, poor Lazarus is immediately carried by angels after his death to Abraham's bosom, in order to enjoy eternal bliss in fellowship alongside Abraham. When Jesus died on the cross, he entrusted his own spirit into the hands of his Father; and before this, he promised the murderer that [223] he would be with him in

8. This paragraph is identical to a portion of one in *MD*, 552.

9. The previous section of this paragraph is unique to *Handleiding*. The following section is in *MD*, 559.

paradise today (Luke 23:43, 46). The first Christian martyr, Stephen, during the stoning called upon the Lord Jesus and prayed for him to receive his spirit (Acts 7:59). Paul is certain that having departed, he will be with Christ and will dwell with the Lord (2 Cor. 5:8; Phil. 1:23). According to Revelation 6:8 and 7:9, etc., the souls of the martyrs and of all the blessed are in heaven, before the throne of God and before the Lamb, clothed in long, white garments with palm branches in their hands. For blessed are the dead who die in the Lord from now on; they may rest from their labors that they have done on earth and that follow them (Rev. 14:13; Heb. 4:9). They live and reign with Christ all the time until his return (Rev. 20:4, 6).[10]

85. Scripture teaches us only a little about the intermediate state (*tusschentoestand*), but it is enough. Apart from the soberness with which Scripture always observes this, it can also be explained by the fact that the believers of the Old and New Testaments typically possessed a different circle of thoughts with regard to the future than we do. When we think of the future, we fix our attention almost entirely on our death and on the immediate salvation of our souls in heaven. But for the pious Israelites, their consciousness was of their fellowship with God, which was inseparably connected with fellowship with his people (*volk*) and his land. The covenant was not established by God with a single individual but with the people (*volk*) as such. Therefore, death was not fully conquered until the Lord himself came to dwell among his people in the future, cleansing them of all iniquities, giving them victory over all their enemies, and making them dwell safely in a land of peace and prosperity. That is why the Israelite's vision of faith [224] was seldom focused on the end of his personal life; but as a rule, his gaze stretched much farther to the future, toward his land and people (*volk*), toward the glory of the messianic kingdom that would come with the "day of the Lord" and would bring a treasure of spiritual and material blessings (cf. Pss. 2; 22; 72; Isa. 11; 40f.; Jer. 31; Ezek. 36; etc.).[11]

All these Old Testament promises began to be fulfilled when Christ appeared in the flesh; for in his person and through his work, the kingdom of heaven was founded on earth that had been expected by pious Israelites for centuries; he confirmed in his blood that new and better covenant that the Lord established with his peoples in the last days; and on the day of Pentecost, he sent out the Spirit of grace and prayers into the congregation,

10. Apart from the first sentence, the remainder of the paragraph is identical to one in *MD*, 560.

11. This paragraph is unique to *Handleiding*. Cf. *MD*, 562–63.

who would lead them into all truth and perfect them to the end. What the prophecy of the old covenant summarized in one great image split up as it was fulfilled, one after the other; it was not fulfilled in one moment or day but through a long period of time and from one piece to another. In particular, we are taught by the New Testament that the one coming of the Messiah expected by the prophets has been distinguished and divided into a first and a second coming. According to the prophecy, the Messiah will come to save and to judge, to deliver his people and to judge his enemies. But when this prophecy is fulfilled, it has been revealed that each of these two ends will be accomplished by a unique coming of Christ.

Indeed, Jesus repeatedly said during his sojourn on earth that he had come now to seek and to save that which was lost (Luke 19:10), to serve and to give his soul as a ransom for many, ([225] Matt. 20:28), and not to condemn the world but to redeem it (John 3:17; 12:47; 1 John 4:14). At the same time, he declared with the same clarity and power that through the light he makes shine, he brings about a judgment, a separation in the world (John 3:19; 9:39), and one day will come again to judge all the living and the dead (John 5:22, 27–29). He must now be crucified and killed; but after that, he will be raised up and ascend, as he was before (Matt. 16:21; John 6:62), only to come again at the end to gather all the nations for himself and to repay everyone according to their deeds (Matt. 16:27; 24:30; 25:32; etc.).[12]

Between these two comings, there is therefore a big difference. With the first, Christ appeared in the likeness of sinful flesh, in the form of a servant, to suffer and to die for the sins of his people (Rom. 8:3; Phil. 2:6–8); with the second, he will be seen without sin, in great power and glory, as a king who goes forth conquering so that he may have victory (Matt. 24:30; Heb. 9:28; Rev. 6:2; 19:11).[13]

Both comings belong close together and are, therefore, summarized by one image in Old Testament prophecy: for both together provide sufficient proof first that Christ is the perfect and omnipotent Savior. He has acquired not only the possibility but the reality of salvation and therefore cannot rest until he brings all those whom he bought with his blood and renewed by his Spirit to where he is and makes them witnesses and partakers of his glory (John 14:3; 17:24). As he himself through sufferings entered into glory (Luke 24:26), so he may give eternal life to all those whom the Father has given to him (John 6:39; 10:28) and present his whole congregation

---

12. The previous two paragraph are identical to two paragraphs in *MD*, 555–56.
13. Cf. *MD*, 556.

together without spot or wrinkle, or any such thing to his Father who is in heaven (Eph. 5:27; [226] 1 Cor. 15:23–28; Rev. 21:2). The second coming of Christ is, therefore, not an arbitrary addition that can be detached from his first coming and his work that he accomplished on earth, setting to the side on its own. The first coming belongs necessarily to the second coming: the second coming brings that work to its completion and puts the crown upon it; it is the last and highest stage in his exaltation. The second coming of Christ is the complement of the first.

Because the first and second coming of Christ—both the ideal and the real (in thought and in reality)—belong so closely together, this is why Scripture speaks in such a peculiar way about the duration of time that must elapse between them. A whole series of texts presents the return of Christ as imminent. Jesus himself directly tied the prophecy of the consummation of the age to the destruction of Jerusalem (Matt. 24:29f.). Paul did not consider it impossible that he or his fellow believers might still experience the return of Christ (1 Thess. 4:15; 1 Cor. 15:51). And all the apostles say that the believers of the New Testament live at the end of the ages (1 Cor. 10:11), in the last times (1 Pet. 1:20), in the last hour (1 John 2:18), and have to only suffer trials for a little while (1 Pet. 1:6; 5:10)—for the day is approaching (Heb. 10:25, 37), the future is near (James 5:8), the time is drawing close (Rev. 1:3; 22:10), the judge is at the door (James 5:9), Christ is coming soon (Rev. 3:11; 22:7, 20).[14]

In so doing, however, the Scriptures do not contain any specific doctrine about the intervening period, because elsewhere it expressly testifies that the day and hour of the future are hidden from men and angels and are determined by the Father by his own power (Matt. 24:26; Mark 13:32; Acts 1:7). Just as all the prophecies of the Old Testament concerning the coming of the Messiah, [227] the day of judgment, etc., were fulfilled in the New Testament but at a time and in a way that was in every respect unimaginable and astonishing, so it will be with the return of Christ. All attempts to calculate this time are improper and unfruitful (Acts 1:7), for the day of the Lord comes like a thief in the night, in an hour mankind does not know (Matt. 24:42–44; 25:13; 1 Thess. 5:2, 4; 2 Pet. 3:10; Rev. 3:3; 16:15).[15]

Although that day, according to some statements, can come at any moment, so to speak, other expressions indicate that it may not come for some time. Jesus speaks of the delay of the groom (Matt. 25:5), of a long delay

---

14. The previous two paragraphs are unique to *Handleiding*. Cf. *MD*, 556.

15. This paragraph is identical to a portion of one in *MD*, 557–58.

before the master returned (Matt. 25:19), of a quiet and slow growing of the seed of the kingdom (Mark 4:26–28), of a waiting to gather the wheat until the day of harvest (Matt. 13:30, 40).[16] Even that day cannot come until the gospel has been preached to all nations (Matt. 24:14), the kingdom of God heaven has leavened everything (Matt. 13:33), and the man of sin has appeared first (2 Thess. 2:2f.). When he comes, he will be preceded by all kinds of terrible events in heaven and on earth and sundry signs (Matt. 24:4–29; Rev. 6:19). The Lord has a different measure of time than we do: one day is with him as a thousand years and a thousand years as one day; his apparent slowness (*traagheid*) is longsuffering that does not want any to perish but for all to repent (2 Pet. 3:8–9).

86. While believers in the time of the apostles felt this deep and earnest connection between the first and second coming of Christ, they did not think much of their own personal end at death but kept all [228] their hopes for the reappearance of Christ and the consummation of the kingdom of God. Nevertheless, the New Testament still contains some information that sheds light on the events that occur at the time of death and enables us to avoid and refute all kinds of strange ideas about the intermediate state (*tusschentoestand*).

Some people think that deceased souls, released from all earthly bonds, sink into a deep sleep; others, on the contrary, argue that they maintain a certain physicality, that they continue to live in communion with their earthly environment, and that they can therefore also be questioned and consulted on all kinds of matters; yet others are of the opinion that the dead continue the life they lived on earth in a straight line, beautifully, in a different form, gradually fading away in evil or perfecting themselves in good, or given the opportunity to repent and sanctify themselves. The Roman church teaches that only a few saints can bring their good works on earth to a point where they are immediately taken to heaven upon death, but that the great majority of believers go to purgatory for a shorter or longer period of time (of cleansing and purifying, hence the purifying fire), to be tormented there by tangible fire until the measure of their temporal punishments for sin, which remain unpaid on earth, is filled.

None of these teachings is supported by Scripture. Scripture does, however, frequently present death as a sleep with an obvious and ubiquitous image (Deut. 31:16; Jer. 51:39; Dan. 12:2; John 11:11; 1 Cor. 11:30; etc.). But by doing so, it only indicates that death is a complete break from all ties

16. The remainder of the paragraph is in *MD*, 558.

with this earthly life, in such a way that it is like sleep, a rest, a silence; the dead sleep beautifully; [229] their soul lives on and remains conscious (*bewust*) (Luke 16:23f.; Rev. 6:10; 7:10). Furthermore, Scripture always speaks of the dead as human beings with flesh and blood, because we can never speak of spiritual beings, even God and the angels, except in a human way, in a material form.[Scripture], however, says explicitly elsewhere that the deceased are souls or spirits (Eccl. 12:7; Luke 23:46; Heb. 12:23; Rev. 6:9, etc.), and that they know nothing of any physicality from the earth or that they could form themselves out of some kind of finer material on the other side of the grave—not even in 2 Corinthians 5:1–4 where Paul refers to the building of God or the heavenly dwelling, the heavenly glorification.

Further, the calling upon the dead in Scripture, like all divination and witchcraft, is strictly forbidden (Exod. 22:18; Lev. 19:26; Deut. 18:11; Isa. 8:19; etc.); it also never mentions any invocation or veneration of dead saints. Finally, there is no mention of the gospel being preached in the world of the dead, even if one invokes Matthew 12:32 or 1 Peter 3:18–22; 4:6; and Scripture knows no other place for Rome's doctrine of purgatory than Matthew 5:22, 25 and 1 Corinthians 3:12–15, which do not provide any evidence for this.[17]

87. The biblical account is different from all of these images, such that they regard the time between dying and the day of judgment, in the full sense, as an intermediate state (*tusschentoestand*). Death, as a result of sin, is a total breaking of all earthly bonds, insofar as silence, rest, and sleep are concerned; what man is and does on the other side of the grave is not taken into account on the day of judgment: the judgment is only over what is done by the body, whether it is good or evil (2 Cor. 5:10). That is why [230] the intermediate state (*tusschentoestand*) is often described in this way: as if all the dead, without distinction, were in one and same place, in Sheol or Hades, which is not hell (whereby the Hebrew or Greek word is often wrongly translated into Dutch); it is the realm of the dead, the underworld (Rev. 6:8; 20:13). All who died are nevertheless as if they were dead, as if they were beneath the earth (Phil. 2:10); even Christ was, as long as he was

---

17. Bavinck's viewpoint on Christ's preaching to the dead either changed or is obscured by his condensation. In *RD* IV, 630–31, he argues against the idea of the ongoing practice of preaching to the dead in Hades. He suggests that Scripture is mostly silent and that the texts we do have do not put forth the ongoing practice of preaching to the dead. He utilizes 1 Pet. 3:19 (which he references above) and identifies that ἐκηρυξεν is in the aorist form. He argues in *RD* that this preaching by Christ occurred only once and is unique to Christ.

in the state of death, in Hades, even though it could not hold him (Acts 2:27, 31). All are kept in the realm of the dead until Christ comes back and holds judgment. Even though every man immediately after his death has to wait for judgment (Heb. 9:27), the actual, public decision follows only when, after the resurrection of both his soul and body, he will stand before Christ's judgment seat—not as an individual but in communion with the entire human race.

But this collective in the intermediate state (*tusschentoestand*) does not rule out all difference. There is a judgment that takes place immediately after death (Heb. 9:27), as a result of which [for example] the rich man suffers sorrow in Hades and Lazarus is taken up into Abraham's bosom (Luke 16:22–23). Unbelievers who reject Christ remain under the wrath of God; they have already been judged on earth (John 3:18, 36) and are kept in captivity (1 Pet. 3:19) for the final judgment.

But for believers for whom dying is no longer a death (Matt. 22:32; John 5:24; 11:25–26), they immediately enter paradise (Luke 23:43), into the bosom of Abraham (Luke 16:22), into heaven with Christ (Acts 7:59; 2 Cor. 5:8; Phil. 1:23; Heb. 12:23; Rev. 6:9; 7:9, 14–17). Blessed are the dead who die in the Lord; they rest from their work, and their works follow them (Rev. 14:13; Heb. 4:9). They live and reign with Christ the whole time until his return (Rev. 20:4, 6). [231] Purgatory is not necessary for them, neither as a place of punishment or a mountain of purification, for Christ has accomplished everything for them: not only bearing all the punishment of sin for them but also fulfilling the law and acquiring eternal life for them. They, therefore, receive eternal life immediately on earth through faith; and they fully partake of it in their souls when they put off the body of sin and death (Rom. 7:24) and are received by Christ into his communion (Acts 7:59).

88. This intermediate state (*tusschentoestand*) is, however, for both the righteous and the wicked, liminal and temporary. Even though those who die in the Lord immediately participate in the heavenly bliss, they can enjoy it only in part, according to the soul, as they wait for full adoption, which also includes the redemption of their body (Rom. 8:23), which is the complete victory over sin and death. Moreover, the few cannot be fully blessed without the fellowship to which they belong; the fullness of Christ's love is known through all the saints together (Eph. 3:18); one group of believers cannot reach consummation without the other (Heb. 11:40; Rev. 6:11).

That is why there is room for faith and hope, for longing and prayer among the blessed in heaven as well as for believers upon the earth (Rev. 6:10; 22:17); together, they eagerly await the end of the age. Yes, Christ himself prepares his own coming in heaven and on earth. Just as he prepares a place for his own in the house of the Father (John 14:2–3), so he reigns on earth as king and fills his congregation with the fullness of God (1 Cor. 15:25; Eph. 1:23; 3:19; 4:13). One can say then, according to biblical parlance, that not only will Christ return one day, but that [on account of] his ascension [232] and the outpouring of the Spirit, he is always coming (Matt. 10:23; 16:28; 26:64; John 14:18–24). Just as his kingdom on earth is extended, he comes into the majesty to which he is exalted at the Father's right hand. He came, and he does not come just once, but he is always coming: [as it is written] "who is and who was and who is to come" (Heb. 10:37; Rev. 1:4, 8).

However, it must not be inferred from this that there will be more than one visible return of Christ. The advocates of a millennial kingdom have come to this, because in the New Testament age of the covenant of grace, which has spread chiefly among the Gentiles, they do not see a direct and continuous fulfillment of the Old Testament but a deviation from the path that God took in his covenant with Israel. [Advocates of Chiliasm[18] teach that] all the promises made to Israel in the Old Testament have not been and will not be fulfilled in the congregation of the New Testament, but will ultimately be fulfilled when Christ returns for the first time, conquers the anti-Christian powers, binds Satan, and establishes his earthly kingdom under Israel.

The basic idea of this chiliasm cannot be reconciled with the teaching of Scripture. For humanity does not exist for Israel's sake, but Israel was chosen and set apart for the benefit of the whole human race; the promise made to Abraham was destined to be made through Israel in Christ, just as the actual seed of Abraham (Gal. 3:16) was for the benefit of all people of the earth (Gen. 12:3; Gal. 3:8, 14). Therefore, when this Christ appeared on earth, all the promises of God to his congregation began to be fulfilled. Just as he was in his person the true prophet, priest, and king, and in his perfect sacrifice fulfilled the whole law, so his church is the true seed of Abraham, the true Israel, [233] the true people of God, who inherit the blessing of Abraham (Gal. 3:14).

89. The fulfillment of God's promises, which extends over centuries, falls into two grand parts and times in accordance with the first and second comings of Christ. Whereas until Christ, it was first the natural and then the

---

18. Chiliasm (*chiliasme*) is derived from the ancient Greek word Χίλιοι, which means a "thousand" ("millennial" is from the Latin) and is used to describe the belief of a millennial kingdom. Chiliasm receives attention in *MD*, 563–64 (*chiliasten, chiliastische*).

spiritual (1 Cor. 15:46) through him who is the turning-point (*keerpunt*) of time, the order has been reversed and now the spiritual precedes the natural.

We now live in the age in which Christ has ascended to heaven and, unseen, communicates to his people the spiritual blessings of his mediatory work by the Spirit (2 Cor. 3:17).[19] The kingdom of God does not come now with an external appearance but is within us (Luke 17:20–21); it is not food and drink but righteousness and peace and joy through the Holy Spirit (Rom. 14:17). It is especially the benefits of the forgiveness of sins and rebirth, of conversion and sanctification, which are now applied to believers.

In particular, it is worth mentioning here the benefit of salvation they receive to their soul that is theirs immediately after dying in fellowship with Christ. Although, as those who have died, they belong to the realm of the dead, they do not need to wait for Christ's return in some outer circle or purgatory. Rather, they already receive special grace in advance. The book of Revelation emphasizes this: he who endures under the cross, in tribulation and temptation on earth, and remains faithful, immediately receives the crown of life, is clothed in white robes, eats of the tree of life, and gains power over the Gentiles (Rev. 2:7, 10, 17, 26–27; 3:5, 12, 20, 21). John, therefore, sees those who come out of the great tribulation in heaven walking in white [234] robes; they are made kings and priests to God and serve him day and night in his temple (Rev. 4:4; 5:10; 7:13–14). In [Revelation] chapter 20, this thought returns: the (still bodyless) souls of those beheaded on account of their confession of Christ were not dead like the other dead who did not die in the Lord, but they live, sit upon thrones, and reign with Christ throughout time until his return. They are already blessed and holy, because they participated in this first resurrection (in this life and reign with Christ in heaven); they are already priests of God and of Christ and reign with him; they do not need to fear the second death (in the lake of fire Rev. 20:14) for it has no power over them.

However much this may be, it is not enough. The promises of God include not only spiritual but physical blessings: the image of God and paradise, adoption as children of God and the inheritance of the world, cult

19.This line reads awkwardly according to Bavinck's own Dutch. What Bavinck intends to communicate here is that Christ now works through the Spirit, as Christ has acquired the Spirit, such that we may say, "the Spirit of Christ." Bavinck says essentially this in *MD*, 369, 380, where he states, for example, "This possession of the Holy Spirit by Christ is so complete that the apostle Paul can say in 2 Cor. 3:17 that the Lord [i.e., Christ as the exalted Lord] is the Spirit."

(*cultus*) and culture (*cultuur*), virtue and happiness, holiness and glory—all belong together. The kingdom of God is first and foremost spiritual and internal, but it must also appear in an external form and be visibly established on earth (Acts 1:6–7).

This, however, cannot be achieved through gradual development in the ordinary course of events, or through parliaments or federations of states. Only Christ can accomplish this great work, because at his first advent, he laid the foundations for it in justice and righteousness (*recht en gerechtigheid*). Terrible events are, therefore, waiting at the end of time. In the same way that great disasters were necessary in the beginning to prepare the earth as a dwelling place for man, who was created in the image of God, so there will be no less-shocking scenes at the end of time to fashion the heavens and earth into [235] the kingdom of God. All these future events are drawn for us by Scripture in vivid forms and bright colors; and many times in these expressive images, we do not know what belongs to the scenery and what belongs to the thing itself. But the facts are certain and can be grouped under five headings: return, resurrection, judgment, world renewal, and eternal glory.[20]

90. Nowhere does the New Testament open to the congregation the prospect that, according to the expectation of chiliasm, [the congregation] will again come to power and dominion in this age. On the contrary, a disciple is not above his master and a servant is not above his lord; if they persecuted Jesus, they will do the same to his disciples (John 15:19–20). Persecution awaits them in the world (John 16:33), and only in the next age will they receive eternal life (Mark 10:30). Now they suffer with Christ, and then they will be glorified with him (Rom. 8:17). Even the New Testament repeatedly expresses the expectation that by the end of time ungodliness will increase, and temptation and apostasy will spread (Matt. 24:37f.; Luke 17:26f.; 18:18; etc.). The day of Christ is preceded by a great apostasy, the revelation of the man of sin, the antichrist (2 Thess. 2:4f.), whose coming has been prepared by many false prophets and false Christs (Matt. 7:5; 24:5, 24; 1 John 2:22; 4:3), but who finally appears and concentrates all his power in a world empire (the image from the sea or the abyss; Rev. 11:7; 13:1–10), supported by a false religion (the beast of the earth; Rev. 13:11–18); he has his seat in Babylon (Rev. 17–18), and from there he makes the last attack against Christ and his kingdom.[21]

---

20. The previous sixteen paragraphs are unique to *Handleiding*.

21. This paragraph is within one in *MD*, 564.

However, then Christ sent by the [236] Father (Acts 3:20; 1 Tim. 6:15) appears on the clouds of heaven, which extend under him like a triumphal chariot (Rev. 1:7), with great power and glory (Matt. 24:30) as a King of kings and Lord of Lords, sitting on a white horse with a sharp sword protruding from his mouth, surrounded by his angels and saints (Matt. 25:31; 1 Thess. 3:13; Rev. 19:14), and announced by the voice of an archangel and the trumpet of angels (Matt. 24:31; 1 Cor. 15:52; 1 Thess. 4:16). He only needs to appear and utter his voice to put an end to the power of the beast of the sea and the earth for good (Rev. 19:20) and cast Satan into the abyss (Rev. 20:3, 10).[22]

The appearance of Christ is followed by the resurrection of the dead. Although it is generally attributed to God (1 Cor. 6:14; 2 Cor. 1:9), it is more specifically the work of the Son, to whom the Father gave life in himself (John 5:26), who himself is the resurrection and the life (John 11:25), and who received the power to make all the dead arise out of their graves by the voice of his mouth (John 5:28–29). It is clearly taught here, as elsewhere (Dan. 12:2; Matt. 10:28; Acts 24:15; Rev. 20:12–13), that there will be a resurrection of all people—of the just and the unjust.[23]

But between the two there is a great difference: it is a proof of Christ's power and righteousness, and it is also a demonstration of his mercy and grace. The first exists only in a union of soul and body and is affected in judgment (John 5:29); the second is a resurrection of life, a renewal of soul and body, both in communion and through the Spirit of Christ (John 5:29; Rom. 8:11; Phil. 3:21).[24]

At this resurrection, the unity of persons, both [237] of the body and of the soul, is preserved. We do not understand how this is possible through the immense catastrophe of death.[25] But the resurrection of the dead maintains this unity in a beautiful way: that the body is not a prison of the soul but belongs to the essence of man and must be a temple of the Holy Spirit; that death is a consequence and punishment of sin and must, therefore, be overcome in the body as well as in the soul; and that Christ—the perfect Savior—must redeem the body, no less than the soul, and recreate it in his image. Yet the body the faithful receive at the resurrection does not correspond to their earthly body in external form or shape, in quantity of

---

22. Cf. *MD*, 562.
23. This paragraph is identical to one in *MD*, 565.
24. This paragraph is in *MD*, 565.
25. These two sentences are within a paragraph in *MD*, 565.

material components, but only in essence. It is made up of the same organic germ, from which through all ages and under all metabolic processes the body on earth was formed. It is not a natural body but a spiritual body, elevated beyond sexual life and sensual needs (Matt. 22:30; 1 Cor. 6:13); [it is] immortal, incorruptible, spiritualized, and glorified (1 Cor. 15:42–44), conformed to that of Christ in his exaltation (Phil. 3:21).[26]

91. The resurrection is followed by the judgment. Since God placed enmity from the beginning between the seed of the woman and the serpent, there has been a division of humanity (Gen. 3:15). In the Old Testament, that division was between Seth and Cain, Shem and Japheth, Israel and the nations, and among Israel itself between the children of the promise and the children of the flesh. When Christ came to earth, he confirmed and sharpened this division (Matt. 10:34–36), even though his first coming was not for condemnation but for the salvation of the world (John 3:17). He brought this about through [238] his person and through his testimony concerning judgment—a separation among people (John 3:19–21) that continues to the present day and in the final judgment will reach its conclusion. One of the divisions goes through the history of all peoples (*volken*), generations, families, and persons; indeed, if we had known the mysteries of the hearts of men, we would be much more convinced of this truth than we are now. Yet, world history is not about *the* world. There too much injustice remains unpunished, too much goodness unrewarded, such that our conscience could not be satisfied by the present nature of the times. The head and the heart of mankind, reason and conscience, philosophy and religion, the whole history of the world calls for a final, righteous, and decisive judgment.

We will face such a judgment, according to the testimony of Scripture (Matt. 25:31–46; Rom. 2:5–11; 2 Cor. 5:10; Col. 3:24–25; Rev. 20:12–15). Although God alone is the Lawgiver and Judge of all people (Gen. 18:25; Ps. 50:6; Isa. 33:22; James 4:12), the last judgment is more specifically executed by Christ, whom the Father has commissioned because he is the Son of Man (John 5:22, 27; Acts 10:42; 17:31; Rom. 14:9). Judging the living and the dead is the completion of his work as a mediator, the final event in his exaltation. It will demonstrate that he has done everything the Father gave him to do, that he has put all enemies under his feet, and that he has saved to the uttermost and eternally his entire congregation.

If Christ is the judge, then we also know what he will be like: merciful, gracious, and, simultaneously, rigorously just. For he knows mankind

26. Cf. *MD*, 566.

and knows all that is in him; he knows the hidden recesses of the heart and discovers all malice and deviation; but he [239] also sees the smallest and weakest principle of faith and love that is present there. He does not judge by appearances and does not see the facade of man; but he judges in righteousness and truth. With the law and the gospel as a yardstick, he will judge the works (Matt. 25:35f.), the words (Matt. 12:36), and the thoughts of men (Rom. 2:16; 1 Cor. 4:5), for nothing is hidden and everything is revealed (Matt. 6:4; 10:26). For all those who can say with Peter, "Lord, you know everything; you know that I love you," this judgment is a source of comfort; but for all who did not want this Christ to become king over them, it is a cause of fear and fright.

This judgment establishes a perfect and eternal separation between mankind. Just as there were some among Israel who said, "The Lord does not see; the God of Jacob does not perceive" (Ps. 94:7); "By saying, 'Everyone who does evil is good in the sight of the Lord, and he delights in them.' Or by asking, 'Where is the God of justice?' " (Mal. 2:17). Even today, there are many who embrace the idea that there is no final judgment; that the possibility of conversion might remain open even after this life and after the end of world history; that, therefore, in the long run, all people and even the demons will participate in salvation. Alternatively, some believe that the wicked, who continue to harden themselves, will finally be annihilated forever.

But the conscience and Scripture are equally opposed to these vain illusions. The history of the world ends in an eternal separation (Luke 17:34–36). The righteous go into eternal life, but the unrighteous go into eternal pain (Dan. 12:2; Matt. 25:46; John 5:29). There is a heaven of glory, but also a Gehenna (of Hinnom, of the valley of the Son of [240] Hinnom where idol worship was first performed; see 2 Chron. 28:3; 33:6; 2 Kings 23:10, and later all kinds of impurity was thrown down there), a hell where the worm does not die and the fire is not extinguished (Mark 9:44), where there is weeping and gnashing of teeth (Matt. 8:12), where darkness reigns, and destruction and eternal death (Matt. 7:13; 8:12; 2 Thess. 1:8; Rev. 21.8). It is the place where God's wrath in all its horror will be revealed (Rom. 2:8; 9:22; Heb. 10:31; Rev. 6:16–17).

In this eternal punishment, which affects all the wicked, there will be a great difference of intensity and degree. The Gentiles, who did not know the Mosaic law, sinned against the law that was made known to them by nature through their conscience; they will perish even without the law (Rom. 2:12). It will be more bearable on the day of judgment for the land of Sodom and Gomorrah, Tyre and Sidon, than for Capernaum and Jerusalem (Matt. 10:15; 11:22, 24). Those who knew the will of the Lord and did not do it, will be struck with double blows (Luke 12:47). Even in the case of evil spirits, there is still a distinction according to their wickedness (Matt. 12:45). Therefore, everyone will receive retribution according to his actions (Matt. 16:27; Rom. 2:6; Rev. 22:12). The judgment will be so utterly righteous that no one will be able to criticize it; his own conscience will have to say yes and amen to it. Just as Christ here on earth did not fight with anything other than spiritual weapons, even then on the day of judgment he will justify himself in the consciences of all men by his word and Spirit.

He is, after all, the Faithful and True One who does not wage war except in righteousness; the sharp sword that proceeds out of his mouth is the sword of the word (Rev. 19:11, 15, 21). Therefore, at the end of days, willingly or unwillingly, "at the name of Jesus every knee should bow, in heaven and on earth and under the earth, and every tongue confess that Jesus Christ [241] is Lord, to the glory of God the Father" (Phil. 2:10–11). It is not the punishment of the ungodly in itself that is the ultimate goal but the glory of God that is revealed in the victory of Christ over all his enemies. "Let sinners be consumed from the earth and the wicked be no more! Bless the Lord, O my soul! Praise the Lord" (Ps. 104:35).

92. After the final judgment and the exile of the wicked, the renewal of the world follows. The Holy Scripture speaks of this many times in strong terms and then states that heaven and earth will perish, disappear like smoke, become old as a garment, and afterwards God will create a new heaven and a new earth (Ps. 102:26–27; Isa. 34:3; 51:6; 65:17; 66:22; Matt. 24:35; Heb. 1:11–12; 2 Pet. 3:10–13; 1 John 2:17; Rev. 21:1). Yet it is not possible to imagine a completely new creation. For the present heaven and earth in their current forms are passing away (1 Cor. 7:31) and will be burned and cleansed by fire, just as the old earth was by the water of the flood (2 Pet. 3:6–7, 10). Just as mankind is recreated by Christ—but not destroyed, and then newly created (2 Cor. 5:17)—so the world will be preserved in its essence, even though it will be transformed to such an extent that it can be called a new heaven and a new earth. The whole world is heading toward the great day of its rebirth (Matt. 19:28).

In this new creation, God will establish his kingdom. For Christ has completed the work appointed for him to do as mediator; he has reigned as a king, until he has put all his enemies under his feet and raised up to eternal life all those the Father has given to him. [242] He remains, thereafter and forever, the head of the congregation, giving it his glory and filling it with his fullness (John 17:24; Eph. 1:23). But his work of redemption has come to an end. He has completed the kingdom and is now handing it over to God the Father to be himself subjected as mediator to him to put all things under him, that God may be all in all (1 Cor. 15:24–28).[27]

In this new creation, God will establish his kingdom not only in heaven but also on earth. In accordance with the Old Testament, the New Testament teaches that the faithful will inherit the earth (Matt. 5:5). They expect, according to God's promise, new heavens and a new earth in which righteousness dwells (2 Pet. 3:13; Rev. 21:1). The whole creation, which is now subjugated to futility, will one day be released from its bondage to corruption and will obtain the freedom of the glory of the children of God (Rom. 8:19–22); the plant and animal kingdoms will also share in it (Isa. 11:6f.; 65:21f.). The new Jerusalem, which is now above and indicates the city where God lives with his people, will then descend upon the earth (Rev. 21:2). In this new Jerusalem, there will be no sin, no sickness, and no death; death is swallowed up in victory, and the realm of the dead is cast with [Satan] into the lake of fire; the power, the glory, and the immortal reign in the world of matter too (1 Cor. 15:42f.; Rev. 7:16–17; 21:4), as the revelation and fruit of the eternal, holy, and blessed life that all citizens are partakers in the communion of God (1 Cor. 13:12; 1 John 3:2; Rev. 21:3; 22:1–5).[28]

In this consummated kingdom, diversity will be preserved in unity. There will be little and great (Rev. 22:12), first and last (Matt. 20:16); the distinctions between ethnicities (*geslacht*) and nations will remain; [243] Israel and the nations (*volken*) will not be dissolved into one another, but each will hold their own place and task (Matt. 19:28; 25:32; Acts 3:19–21; Rom. 11:26); the nations (*volken*) that are saved will walk in the light of the new Jerusalem, and the kings of the earth will bring their glory and honor into it (Rev. 21:24; 22:2). Although all share in the same salvation, the same eternal life, and the same fellowship with God, yet there will be all sorts of differences among them in rank and position, in gift and calling, in glory and radiance. There are many dwellings in the Father's house (John 14:2). In proportion to how someone on the earth has been faithful, spent his talents, suffered and labored for Christ, he will receive in the kingdom of God a higher place and a greater honor (Matt. 5:12; 6:1, 6, 18; 25:14f.; 2 Cor. 9:6; Rev. 2–3).

---

27. The previous nine paragraphs are identical to nine paragraphs in *MD*, 566–69.

28. Cf. *MD*, 1e, 644, and *MD*, 569.

This rich diversity will not distract from unity, for all will see God's face and be like him (Matt. 5:8; John 3:2; Rev. 22:4); all will know as they are known (1 Cor. 13:12); and all will be prophets, priests, and kings. God's purposes for creation will then have been reached, for it will proclaim his glory and everywhere behold his virtue. And seeing all that he has made, God will delight in his work and say, "It is all very good!" (1 Cor. 15:24–28).[29]

29. The previous three paragraphs are unique to *Handleiding*.

Subject Index

Scripture Index

Old Testament

Genesis

John

Acts